GABACHO

Drugs Landed Me In Mexican Prison, Theater Saved Me

RICHARD JEWKES
with Brian Whitney

WILDBLUE
PRESS

WildBluePress.com

GABACHO published by:
WILDBLUE PRESS
P.O. Box 102440
Denver, Colorado 80250

WILDBLUE PRESS is registered at the U.S. Patent and Trademark Offices.

ISBN 978-1-948239-29-5   Trade Paperback
ISBN 978-1-948239-28-8   eBook

Cover Photo Credit: Manuel Borbón Montaño - El Imparcial, Hermosillo, Sonora

Interior Formatting by Elijah Toten
www.totencreative.com

GABACHO

CHAPTER 1

DRIVING OVER THE Sonoran Desert is like riding a roller coaster. You feel the rise and fall of the landscape, every twist and turn, every trough and dune, especially when you're going over 100 miles per hour. That's the way it was in 1979, before Mexico completed the super highway from Nogales to Mexico City. Roads followed the terrain.

I looked up from the speedometer to see the moon bouncing along the jagged peaks of the Sierra Madres. Then the road fell out from under me and I nearly lost control as I dropped into a deep wash. "Damn," I said to myself. "Gotta keep my eyes on the road." I looked back to see Jeff sprawled across the backseat with my acoustic guitar nestled between his legs. I shook my head. It was crazy odd that he was able to sleep through all this.

The truck was a mess. Sleeping bags, dirty clothes, and fast food wrappers littered the '79 Ford Bronco. A plastic jug we used to pee in splashed a bit as I hit another dune. The Bronco had two gas tanks and we hoped to drive all the way from Mazatlán to Nogales without stopping. But now I was afraid we might have used too much gas driving at this pace. I didn't want to take any chances until we crossed the US border. You couldn't have pried my hands from that wheel, not even for a pee. Well…maybe a pee or two, but nothing else.

We weren't sure anybody was following us but we weren't sure they weren't either. We had to get across the border as fast as possible. I thought if we could just make it to Nogales before daylight, we'd be able to cross without being searched. Maybe we could even try to cross at Naco, a small town where the guards might be too sleepy to care about us. On the other hand, the guards at a small-town crossing might be so bored they'd have nothing to do but search every single car. We didn't know what to do. It was late, I was hammered, Jeff was zonked, so it was my decision, right or wrong, on how to get us the hell out of Mexico with ten kilos of marijuana sitting in the back of the Bronco.

We'd gone to Mexico hoping to buy cocaine and instead ended up with a cardboard box of shitty, low-grade farmer weed. We needed to make some money for all our effort. We'd spent every cent of our college tuition on what was supposed to be a gritty adventure and we couldn't go back empty-handed. We wouldn't be able to even pay our rent for the next few months unless we could make some money on that box of crummy weed. But then again, it certainly wasn't worth the risk of prison. We hadn't decided what to do at that point. We talked about stopping just before the border to make the final decision. We were just so fucking exhausted.

It was one or two o'clock in the morning and no matter how hard I hit the dunes and troughs, Jeff didn't stir. We hadn't slept the night before and had very little sleep the night before that. It had been seventy-two hours since we'd had any real sleep or anything substantial to eat. I'd been driving twelve hours straight, not counting all the driving the night before when we bought the weed, deep in the jungle along the Sinaloa coast. But I wasn't going to take my hands off the wheel till I crossed the border.

I'd popped a couple of meth tabs to keep awake and smoked some of that dirt-encrusted weed to test it but it just gave me a headache. I hadn't eaten much of anything. I'd been driving so fast and so hard, my hands were shaking and I was starting to see things. I kept my eyes on the road and hoped not to hit a rabbit or something bigger.

Our decision not to throw that box of marijuana out the window would turn out to be one of those life-defining moments: a reckless, hasty, stupid moment that changes everything about your life up until the day you die. We hadn't taken time to hide it because we weren't sure we were going to keep it: the weed didn't get you very high, it didn't taste good, it mostly gave you a headache. We'd spent all the cash we had for tuition and rent for the current quarter at the University of Utah, and even used Jeff's work credit card to buy gas and food.

It all started when we'd concocted a plan to drive way down into Mexico, find some dealers, buy some coke, bring it back, and sell it at school, then pay our tuition and rent for a year with the proceeds. We weren't dealers and we knew absolutely nothing about international drug smuggling. I was a theatre major; Jeff studied chemistry and did plays on the side. That's how we met.

We'd arrived in Mazatlán a few days earlier where we found a fairly cheap hotel on the beach. That was our plan – stay on the beach and find guys selling drugs to Americans. We hung out in a couple of the bars by day and walked the beach at night, looking to score.

We tried over and over to sell the Bronco or trade it for drugs, but no one was interested. We were a couple of pretty white guys who had no connections and didn't speak Spanish, strolling around Mexico looking to buy a shitload of coke. It sounded simple to us, but people wanted nothing to do with us. They thought we were nuts or narcs. There was no way a Mexican drug dealer was going to trade an American car (one that, in their minds, was probably stolen) for drugs. It was a stupid idea. If anything, they'd just kill us and take the damn Bronco.

We started getting anxious and began questioning our whole stupid plan. We had spent every last dime on this adventure and had to get some kind of return. Neither I nor Jeff could speak Spanish beyond ordering a beer or asking, "Where's the *cuarto de baño*?"

Finally, after a couple of days of hanging out, we met a street-level dealer named Antonio. He was a guy about our age who hung around the beach, selling weed to guys like us on vacation. Although he spoke a little English, it was with a very thick accent, and mostly day-to-day phrases about partying and selling weed.

We smoked some dope with him and hung out for a bit before we pitched our idea. "Can we trade our truck for some cocaine?"

He looked at us like we were crazy and said, "No, man. No one is going to want your truck. But I can get you cocaine for a good price."

So this was it! We found our connection. He was a guy like us, no big deal. It was going to work out great. Later that night, he took us deep into the jungle to a small farm two or three hours south of Mazatlán. That's where we met some men who appeared to be cartel guys. They were nothing like Antonio. They were scary. I thought they were going to kill us at one point. Bottom line was we didn't have enough money to buy their coke and so ended up with a big fucking box of shitty farmer weed.

We left Antonio at the farm house and hightailed it back to the hotel, arriving around dusk. We felt lucky to be alive. But we didn't feel safe. We were beginning to get really scared. We went up to our room and paced around, talking a mile a minute. We wanted to crash for a bit. We were so damned tired. I gazed out the window at the beach, mulling over what we should do.

Suddenly, there was a cop car driving below our hotel window. We panicked; we thought the drug dealers might have turned us in. Maybe the reason they didn't kill us was because *they* were narcs! They were working for the DEA or the Mexican *Federales*.

We pretty much lost our minds at that point. We grabbed our stuff, ran down to the Bronco, threw it in the back with the box of weed, jumped in, and took off.

Were we set up? Were they going to catch us at the border? Should we just throw out the weed? Jeff rolled a couple of joints. It was useless. We felt nothing, hardly a twinge. We were fucked. We'd spent our tuition, we had no more money. We needed to pay rent as soon as we got back. There was just nothing about the entire half-wit adventure that worked out.

Jeff was starting to get on my nerves. And I on his. I felt like he blamed me for the whole bloody mess. Maybe it was my fault, I don't know. And to top it off, technically we were driving a stolen vehicle. Even though I was the one who reported it stolen, it was still listed as stolen. Either way, we were screwed.

We were carrying twenty pounds of weed just sitting in the back of the truck in a broken box held together with duct tape. Not even hidden. For a couple of fairly smart guys who'd done pretty well in their lives up to this point, we were about as dumb as one can get. We couldn't make a decision other than to get out of Mexico. We kept saying to each other, should we toss the box out the window? What good would it do us in Utah? Maybe further down in the box the weed was better. If we could just get enough out of it to recoup a thousand dollars, that would be great.

It *had* been all my idea. I was edgy and bored and thought I needed a hardy adventure. Now here we were in the middle of the Sonoran Desert, bouncing up and down, following the desert dunes, carrying twenty pounds of weed that could get us locked away for years in a foreign prison.

I felt a jolt and the truck veered off the road onto the shoulder. I nearly lost control, but I got it back, like I always did, and we drove on. "Shit! I gotta keep my head," I muttered.

I looked up ahead and saw some faint lights way down the highway. I couldn't tell what they were. Maybe an accident... some emergency vehicles?

I eased off the gas a bit, then I saw a sign on the right. It said something like, "*Inspeccion... Federeales. Alto...*" By then the lights were just about on us. "Holy shit!" I shouted.

I was going way too fast to turn around. There was a barricade across the road and nowhere to go. I turned and yelled at Jeff to wake up, and when I turned back around, we were practically on top of the barricades. I was going so goddamned fast! I slammed on the brakes and veered off the side of the road. The car spun all the way around, 360 degrees, throwing dust and gravel in its wake.

When it came to a stop, I was gripping the wheel and could hardly believe we hadn't flipped over. I thought for sure I was going to roll the truck and crash into something. When the dust settled, I opened my eyes and looked around. There were a dozen gun-toting men standing around the truck holding handguns, assault rifles, and shotguns. "What the fuck..." Jeff uttered as he sat up. "Jesus fucking Christ, man. What the hell is this?"

CHAPTER 2

A COUPLE OF months earlier during a late-night poker game at my and Jeff's apartment, fueled by Wild Turkey, weed, and a winning poker hand, I blurted out, "Let's just say to hell with it and start our own theatre group!"

And that's how it started. A wisecrack to a group of would-be actors trying to out-swagger each other. We'd been criticizing the university's theatre department about the kind of plays done there. We wanted to do experimental theatre, maybe even our own stuff. Utah (it's well known) is very conservative, with a ton of Mormon influence, and so went the University of Utah. I was in the musical theatre department and Jeff was a chemistry major who wanted to be an actor. He only took chemistry to please his parents. There was Al, the playwright, and actors Bob and Travis. We were all pretty slammed and boasting to one another about who was the best at this or that when I made the brazen comment about starting our own theatre. And, oh sure, everyone was on board during the poker game. They jumped right in. "Yeah, let's do it, man. Let's just say fuck the U and do our own shit. Plays we write ourselves!"

As we crowed to each other about our amazing talent and capabilities, the talk got bigger and bigger until I blurted out, "I got an idea – let's all go to Mexico and buy some cocaine, come back, and sell it for a huge profit. I'll bet we can get it cheap there."

"Great idea, Jewkes, let's become international drug smugglers and make some quick cash," Bob chimed in. Then everybody started creating scenarios about this amazing adventure and how cool it would be. It was a bunch of actors creating their own dramas.

I recollected how the dealer who sold us the weed we were smoking had told me he'd gone to Mexico once and bought a couple of pounds of marijuana. It was a snap; he just put it in the side panels behind his taillights and crossed the border. According to him, he made a ton of cash from it too. I said, "We could do the same thing with cocaine, which could make us a lot of money." On the reality of that idea, we sobered up a bit and went back to playing poker.

The next day, I called everybody to check in on the plan and they were like, "What …what are you talking about? You outta your mind, Jewkes? Where would we get it? How would we sell it? We're not drug dealers, we're actors. We were screwing around last night, weren't you?"

No one thought I was serious. They thought it was a crazy idea. And nobody wanted to do it. Except Jeff. *I* didn't know if I was really serious when I said it. Do people always believe everything they say? Or do we often say things which then define us? You make a bold statement and then you have to believe it. Because you said it to people, out loud. You have to commit to it and you have to back it up or you're an asshole. Turning a lie into the truth. A guy who talks shit but doesn't back it up with action. I wasn't going to be that guy. I had to follow it up. Or maybe I really wanted to do it and just needed support. Looking back now, I really don't know what I was thinking.

Oddly, Jeff agreed to go. He said, "Okay, let's do it, man. We can at least make enough money to pay rent and tuition." He didn't even question the idea. Merely looked at me and shrugged. Why not? That was it. I had my support. We were going to Mexico to buy drugs.

Neither of us had ever done anything this crazy before. But it was more so for Jeff. I'd had a couple of impetuous moments in high school and even spent a night in jail. But Jeff wasn't at all rash. He typically made appropriate choices. He wanted to be an actor more than anything and loved doing plays. But he'd committed to getting a chemistry degree so he'd have something to fall back on in case he didn't make it as an actor. That was Jeff: he planned ahead, made good decisions. He'd been a high school football star, taking his team to the Wisconsin state championship. He was *that* guy. The guy who went to football practice every summer instead of screwing around with his friends. He was not the guy to go to Mexico and buy drugs. I suppose it made the idea seem plausible to me. If Jeff would do it, it couldn't be all that crazy.

It took us a couple of months to put a plan together, during which time the idea grew bigger and bolder. We decided we needed to buy a pound of cocaine so we'd have enough money to pay rent *and* start a theatre group. But we didn't have near enough money for that. Well, we couldn't let that stop us, so we had to find more money. Finally, I came up with the idea to buy a car, drive it to Mexico, and trade it for drugs.

I bought a Ford Bronco on a low monthly payment plan, then I reported it stolen. We thought it would be the perfect car to drive into Mexico and trade for a pound of cocaine. I mean, hey... doesn't every drug dealer want a super-fast, American-made, four-wheel drive SUV?

I put on license plates from a junk car and stashed the Bronco at a storage lot until we were ready to drive away. It was Christmas break, a week or so before winter quarter. We thought we could make it down and back in time for school. Only a couple of people knew about our adventure. Jeff's girlfriend and my wife knew, of course. They definitely thought we were crazy and tried very hard to talk us out of it. By the time we told them, we'd already stashed the Bronco and were in too deep. There was no turning back. We'd committed to the idea. We had to follow it up with action.

A couple days after Christmas, we got the Bronco out of storage, packed it with food, my acoustic guitar, sleeping bags, and clothes, and took off for Mexico. We had two gas tanks, so we decided to drive straight through to Mazatlán without stopping for hotels or restaurants. We could save money and get there and back fast, before anybody knew we were gone.

On the drive from Salt Lake City to Nogales, we thought seriously about the whole thing. We wondered what everyone would think of us if we turned back now. I was dead certain we would be okay and everything would work out as planned. Jeff, I think, simply followed my lead. He'd never taken a risk like this before. I got suspended in high school and spent a night in jail for disturbing the peace. Jeff was set to graduate with the prospect of a solid career and a beautiful girlfriend who adored him. He had a good plan. He didn't need a crazy adventure.

I was confused and uncertain. I wasn't sure what I wanted. I had been a straight arrow right up until high school. Born and raised a conservative Mormon, I always followed the rules, got straight *A*s in school, and accolades at church. All my teachers loved me. I had the kind of personality and looks people were attracted to. My family and friends thought I was the guy most likely to succeed. I was class president in junior high and a track star. But the summer between junior high and high school, everything changed. That was the year *Sgt. Pepper* came out. The Beatles, whom I loved and followed, made a dramatic change in a couple of years. They went from bubblegum pop to psychedelic introspection. And I went with them. I stopped going to church, started reading Dostoyevsky and Hermann Hesse. It was the late '60s and the culture was changing rapidly.

The summer before high school, I left the Mormon church for good and began making a shift in everything I believed. But you don't just sidle away from the Mormon church. It's like Sunni Islam or Ashkenazi Judaism. If you tell your family you're not going to be a Mormon any longer, it's like saying to them, "I hate you and I never want to see you again for all eternity." That's what they hear. Mormons believe they have a special place in Heaven where only they can go. But if you don't accept the Mormon faith, you won't get in. When I left the Mormon church, everyone in my entire extended family of several hundred people treated me differently. Some with disdain, most with deep sadness. In their minds, I was lost to the darkness forever.

I pretty much sidestepped my family after that. The endless fights and arguments over religion and my 'eternal salvation' left me feeling angry and disillusioned. After high school, I left Salt Lake City and went to Los Angeles for a year or so, where I met a group of actors and film makers. Their style and intellect led me to study theatre upon returning to Salt Lake City. I had little experience in the arts prior to that.

I read Carlos Castaneda and other books on philosophy. I was figuring out that so much of what people had been telling me was wrong. I was sick of doing what my conservative friends and family thought I should do.

I met a girl, thought I loved her, and I was pretty sure she loved me. I dropped out of school for a couple of years, got married, and bought a house. I worked construction, and eventually, I started my own company doing footings and foundations. I was never very good at working for somebody else.

We bought a two-story home in a nice neighborhood. Everybody had a trimmed lawn, bushes down the side, and cute mailboxes with hand-lettered names. It all felt hollow. I was trapped in a life that was just like everyone else's. Go to work, make money, pay your mortgage, and meet for Saturday barbeques. It was the beginning of the end of my marriage and my life in the middle-class, yuppie world of day jobs, strip malls, and Wendy's. I missed the arts. I wanted something more.

I asked my wife for a divorce and moved out. She went back to her home in Albuquerque. I went back to the university and started doing plays again. I thought somehow it would be better than being married. I loved Kathryn; I truly did at first. I wanted to get married. But there was nothing to make me want to stay at it. Going back to school was the only thing I could think of doing that would let me avoid reality for a while. Kate didn't want to split, but she was afraid of what I was becoming. It wasn't easy on either of us.

I was drinking a lot and smoking weed, sleeping with random women. I couldn't find peace. I was restless and unsettled. Although school was different from my business life, it still rang hollow. I had no focus and nothing around me made sense. I didn't even like acting. It just gave me an escape from my mundane life.

If I could have talked with someone, like a mentor or an older person who had similar ideas, things might have turned out differently. I wanted to believe in something, but I couldn't believe in what I had been taught. I needed a massive explosion to break out of the Mormon, conservative, white-bread community where I had been raised.

And that's what put us in the Sonoran Desert, with me driving down the road at 110 miles an hour in the dark of night, Jeff crashed out in the back.

CHAPTER 3

IT WAS HARD to figure out why they didn't kill us the night when we bought the weed from Antonio's contacts. We hadn't taken time to mull over what happened or talk about it much. But that experience is what set us off on such a frantic pace for the border.

When Antonio told us no one would trade drugs for our Bronco but he could get us cocaine for a good price, we thought we should try to at least buy enough to pay rent and get back to the States. We had about five hundred dollars in cash left. We'd paid for our hotel room with Jeff's credit card and only spent our cash on gas, food, and beer.

At this point, it seemed like our only option, so we asked Antonio how much. He asked how much we wanted. I said, "An ounce, maybe more." He lit up, sensing some good business. An ounce or more of cocaine was pretty expensive in the US, so It had to be at least fifteen hundred dollars in Mexico.

Antonio took sip of beer, grinned slightly, and said, "*Fifteen thousand pesos.*" That came out to just about the five hundred dollars we had left. We were psyched! We could buy the coke, go back to Utah, and sell a gram for $150: that was 16 grams at $150 each, which equaled $2,400. That would be a super profit! So we told him we would take it. We had a couple of more beers, and then Antonio took off.

He said he would come by and meet us later that evening and take us to buy the coke.

We were all set. If we could buy cocaine here in Mexico at that price, we could make a fortune back in Salt Lake. We just had to find a way to get it home safely without getting caught. International smuggling at its best!

Around 7 p.m., we went down to the beach to meet Antonio, who was there waiting. He was a bit anxious. I could sense it. He got in the Bronco and we took off.

We drove south on the main highway for a couple of hours. It got dark quickly. No street lights, just little roads through small towns. Antonio was still nervous. We were nervous. What if this was a set up? What could we do? No one knew where we were. Al and the girls had an inkling we were somewhere in Mexico. Our parents certainly didn't know anything.

These guys could steal the truck, take our money, chop us into pieces, and bury us in a field. No one would ever know. Even the license plate on the Bronco was fake.

It was late and pitch-black dark. Antonio directed us to drive off the main road and follow a rugged dirt road going through the jungle. We must have been two or three hours south of Mazatlán. We finally came to a little town. There was no way of knowing where we were or even how big the town was.

Antonio seemed to become even more uptight, which made me really nervous. He had us slow down as he looked for a house. Finally, he tapped my shoulder and told me to stop, then he went through a door in a wall. I guess it was a house, but it was so dark I couldn't tell. We waited, Jeff looked at me, I bit my lip. This was what we wanted – to be international drug smugglers, to have an adventure. To be driving down dark, dangerous streets with the bad guys.

"I don't know," I said. "Maybe we should just get out of here." I was getting paranoid. The situation was out of our control and not what I'd expected. I thought we'd have the upper hand, we'd be the ones calling the shots. Why were we here? What were we doing? This was madness. Suddenly, Antonio reappeared. He jumped in the truck and said, "Okay, let's go."

We both just looked at him. He said, "It's okay, we can go get it now. Let's go back that way." He pointed the way we came in. He seemed settled now, not as distracted or as nervous as before, so we all calmed down and drove back out of the little town.

Just before we reached the main highway, Antonio had us turn off the road again. We were headed further south, down a narrow road into the jungle. "Slow down," he said. There was another dirt road. We took that one. We were driving deeper into the damp, dark forest. It was bumpy and rutted. The air was thick and feted, the sounds of the jungle in our ears making the whole scene even more eerie.

We finally came to what appeared to be a small farmhouse, with a field off to one side in a cleared area of the forest. There was no light. Everything was dark.

Suddenly, it became crystal clear to us both that we were not safe and we had no way to defend ourselves. When we made the original arrangement, we were on a beach in Mazatlán, right near a hotel. It never occurred to us that this was where we could end up. We thought we would make the deal in a noisy bar along the beachfront, not at a remote farmhouse in the middle of the jungle.

Antonio got out of the truck and went inside. He came out a few moments later with four guys. Two guys got in the Bronco with Antonio, and the two others stayed outside the truck, watching. None of them showed guns, but I could tell they were armed.

They were older and tougher than Antonio. They got straight to the point and were matter of fact. They could speak English much better than Antonio, and a guy who appeared to be the leader asked us to show him the money.

I told him we had talked with Antonio about buying an ounce of cocaine. He again asked if we had the money. They were sitting in the back seat while Jeff and I were in the front, turning our heads around to them. We couldn't see their hands. We quickly handed them the five hundred dollars (about fifteen thousand pesos).

He counted it in a snap, looked at us, then at Antonio. Then he glanced at the man standing at my window, who was looking straight at me. We were pretty much surrounded. No one said anything for a moment, which seemed like an eternity.

I sensed they were angry. I could feel the tension. Then the leader asked us if we were playing games. "Is this a joke? Where are your fifty thousand pesos?" he said pointedly.

We looked at Antonio and asked what was going on. I tried to explain. "Antonio said *fifteen* thousand pesos. That's what we brought." Antonio shook his head and said we were wrong, that he had told us the correct amount. He was calm. He knew his ass was on the line. His credibility with these guys was more important than our lives, and he offered no further explanation.

I've thought about that moment many times. How many incidents throughout history were caused by language barriers or cultural differences? Antonio's thick accent sounded like "fifteen" to us, when he was actually saying "fifty." When someone who speaks a different language than you quickly says "fifty thousand pesos," it's easy to understand how it could sound like "fifteen thousand pesos." But that's not a conversation you can have in the middle of jungle, late at night, with four angry drug dealers who were probably cartel guys. We simply didn't have any more money. We had brought one thousand dollars with us. Each of us had five hundred dollars to pay our rent and tuition. We had spent about half of it on gas, beer, and food, and used Jeff's credit card for the hotel. All we had left was five hundred dollars and some change.

It was no use trying to enlist help from Antonio; he didn't want the wrath of the cartel. He was very clear in stating he told us *fifty thousand pesos*.

Fifty thousand pesos was about seventeen hundred dollars, about as much as we would have to pay for an ounce of coke in the US. So sure, these guys were anxious to make the deal. They would love to sell two stupid gabachos cocaine at the US market rate and they'd be the ones to have to carry it across the border. They would make that deal any day.

We tried to explain that we didn't have any more money. We had thought we were going to buy five hundred dollars' worth of cocaine. We said we were fine getting less cocaine for our fifteen thousand pesos. We just wanted to go. The cocaine and the James Bond fantasy – all of that was secondary now. We just wanted to get the fuck out of there.

They were angry. Very angry. They began to talk to each other in Spanish rapidly. It seemed like we were going to get shot, or worse. Finally, Antonio suggested we buy some weed. We didn't want any weed and started to tell him so, but the cartel guys made it clear that we were going to buy weed from them. That was the end of it. The leader said, "You must buy some *mota* from us for five hundred dollars, this is your only choice." And when he said "only choice," he made it very clear: we were not leaving without that deal.

Jeff and I knew we were about to be killed. There was no reason for them not to kill us. They had our money, they could take our car. I really don't know why they didn't kill us. We said buying some weed would be fine. More than fine, actually. Thanks so much for the weed!

Jeff didn't want to take it He was concerned about getting it across the border. "Just give them our money," he said, "and let's go." But that wasn't an option. They wanted us to buy something, to have drugs in our possession. We needed to be part of this deal somehow. I looked at Antonio and he confirmed my fears. We had to make a transaction with these guys and that was it. I said, "Okay."

They sent one of the guys away. During those few minutes, it was so tense you could cut the air with a butter knife. No one spoke. We were scared. They weren't sure who we were, but they could sense we didn't know shit about dealing drugs. I really think that's why they didn't kill us. We were just too pathetic to kill.

Soon, the man came back with a big box of weed. Later, we discovered it was ten kilos (about twenty pounds) of absolutely terrible dirt weed. We put the box in the back of the truck and left. Antonio stayed with the men. We took off as fast as we could.

After a few wrong turns, we found our way back to the main highway, keeping an eye in the rearview mirror the entire time. Once on the highway, we drove as fast as we could in the dark of night. All we wanted to do was get back to the hotel and then think of a plan. We were exhausted and shaken, but glad to be alive.

CHAPTER 4

THE MEXICAN FEDERAL Police rarely, if ever, dress in uniform. When you think FBI, you picture guys in suits. In Mexico, the national police are guys in jeans and t-shirts.

There was a tap on my window. I heard Jeff say "Fuck, man" under his breath.

The man outside my window had hard eyes, a big belly, and a handgun strapped to his waist. A man near him held a machine gun pointed toward the ground. I quickly rolled down the window.

He pointed the flashlight in my eyes and said, "*De donde vienen?*" I just stuttered, trying to grasp what was happening. Then he said, "From where you come?"

I felt like I was going to throw up. I made myself say the word "Mazatlán." I tried to say it in a way that sounded like all of this was completely normal. Sure, two white guys driving down the road at 115 miles an hour in the middle of the night and coming to a screeching halt right in front of a police road block? Happens all the time.

"For what?" snapped the man. He was shining the flashlight through the truck, moving it back and forth slowly. He shined it into Jeff's face, who blocked the bright light with his hands. The truck was a mess. Even before we spun off the road, there were clothes and trash and empty food wrappers everywhere.

"Uh....*vacacion*...*estudientes*...Christmas vacation." I was trying to be calm, but I didn't think I was pulling it off. He looked at Jeff. "Do you have drugs?"

Jeff stammered, "No," then made a pitiful attempt of explaining we were just a couple of innocent students tearing down the road in the middle of nowhere.

The man with the machine gun moved closer to my window as the fat man moved around to the passenger side. He got in and sat in the seat.

"*Estudientes?*" He picked up the empty pill bottle on the dash, looked at me, and barked, "*Estudientes, de que?*" He shuffled through the debris on the floor and console, opened the glove compartment, and picked up my alligator hide case.

He opened it. I knew what was in there: a pack of rolling papers, small mirror, razor blade, and a tiny spoon.

He then began speaking English. "What is this?" he snapped. I stupidly tried to explain it was something for school, but he cut me off. "This is a story for children!" He drew a big .45 from his holster and motioned for Jeff to get out. "Now you get the big search."

A man looking in Jeff's window opened the door, training a revolver on Jeff as he stepped from the truck. The man motioned for Jeff to put his hands up. The big fat man, *El Jefe*, told me to drive the truck a few yards toward a small adobe hut where there were some large lights affixed.

"Nothing funny, *gabacho*." He put his .45 near my face as he said this. I tried a different tactic and said it must have been left in the truck from long ago, but again he barked, "This is a story for children!"

My mind was spinning. I kept thinking, *there must be something I can say, something that will make sense so we can get away.* The alternative was simply too overwhelming to think about.

I carefully started the motor and put the Bronco into gear. My hands were shaking. I hadn't been to the bathroom in hours. We hadn't slept for two days, our eyes were bloodshot, and a couple days' growth of beard made us look pretty ragged. I looked over at Jefe. His .45 was right next to my face. I kept thinking ".45" though I didn't really know; the hole at the end of the gun was so big. I could barely imagine the size of the bullet that would come out the end.

I was trying to be calm. I was trying to cooperate. I couldn't help thinking how if I was really, really nice, they'd let us go. I mean, we were just fucking around; we had nothing valuable. We weren't really criminals.

I turned the wheel toward where he pointed. "*Calmate, gabacho.* Very slow," said Jefe, waving his gun back and forth. I started moving the Bronco as slowly as it would go for a few yards towards the hut underneath the big bright lights.

I stopped and turned the ignition off. There was a moment when I couldn't decide if I should take the car keys. Habit always kicks in so you do the things you always do, no matter the situation. I've always made it a habit to take my car keys. There is a little voice that says to me, "Take the car keys." And I always do. But I hesitated, my hand still on the keys. The man outside whipped the door open as Jefe said, "*Vamanos!*"

I got out of the car and stood back a bit while the Jefe came around to me. The man with the machine gun kept it trained on me. We were in Mexico surrounded by police, with drugs in the car. We were just a couple of college students from Salt Lake City, Utah. The scene did not make sense. If I saw it in a movie, I'd think it didn't fit. It's not right. It's out of place.

The big man came around to me, holding the alligator case. He looked me up and down, noticing something in my shirt pocket. He pulled out a small bag of weed, then held it up to his compadres. "*Estudientes!*"

Back in Mazatlán, Jeff and I had taken a small bit of the weed out of the box. Jeff rolled a couple of joints on the way and we smoked it. It was how we knew the weed was no good. It didn't get you high. But we never made the decision to chuck it out the window. That twenty pounds of marijuana represented our tuition for the semester. It was all we had. Maybe we could find some idiot to buy it back home. Somehow, we just couldn't make the decision to rid ourselves of it. That indecision was going to haunt us for years.

Jefe held the baggie of weed up to my face. He said, with a big grin, "This is a story for children, *gabacho*. Now give me the coke!"

The coke, I thought. *Shit, they're looking for cocaine. Of course! They don't care about weed. They're looking for hard drugs.*

"We don't have coke," I said, latching on to some small bit of hope for a moment. I was starting to see a way out of this. He didn't care about marijuana, just cocaine. Jeff was standing on the other side of the truck with his hands on his head. There were about a dozen Federal Police standing around the Bronco, inside the doorway of the hut, and in the general area of the roadblock.

I came to learn later that these roadblocks are called *aduanas*, and they are set up randomly for this very reason. They are partially funded by the DEA to catch drug dealers and petty smugglers before they get to the US. The Americans even help fund the building of many of the prisons in the northern part of Mexico.

"Here, let me show you." I started quickly toward the back of the truck. I was thinking, *I'll just give them the weed and we'll be off. That's all they want. If we don't have any cocaine, weed isn't a big deal. They won't care about weed. Everybody gets high. I mean, they probably smoke weed.*

I never dreamed of going to jail. I thought they just wanted the drugs and we'd go. I'd just hand them the dope they'd find anyway as it was just sitting in the back, not even covered up. Then they'd let us go for being such good guys and we'd be on our way.

I took a couple of steps toward the back of the truck, and several men moved immediately to stop me. The fat man grabbed my arm. "*Alto!* You, stop."

"I'm just… let me just get it for you, it's right there in the back," I said as I backed toward the rear of the Bronco. "No *problemas*, no *quiero problemas*," I said over and over as I slowly backed toward the rear of the truck with my hands up.

Jeff said, "What are you doing?" Two men held him roughly.

"I'm just going to give it to them. They'll find it anyway," I said, trying to pretend like everything was going to be okay. I turned to Jefe. "*Si*, we have *mota*, right here. I'll give it to you."

I was trying desperately to make friends with these guys. Maybe they were not really police. Maybe they were cartel guys getting back the drugs they sell. Maybe they were local police and this was what they did for a little side money. No reason we all can't be cool about this.

Jefe moved right with me, his big gun sticking in the back of my head. I slowly opened the tailgate, reaching inside, and pulled out a big box. We'd poked a little hole in the top corner to pull out the test weed. The rest remained intact.

I handed the box to Jefe. "Here," I said hopefully. "We don't want any problems."

He holstered his gun, took the box from me, and held it up high. "*Ay cabron … mira la mota!*"

He looked at me, his eyes narrowed. "*Son estudientes, de veras, gabacho?*" He slowly pulled back the corners of his mouth into a great big grin. "This is a story for children!" He turned to the other men, and they laughed hard and loud.

Jeff just stared at me and shook his head. It was not quite the result I was expecting. They didn't seem to be happy enough to let us go. It seemed more like they had achieved some kind of success. It was not the happiness a little extra money brings, but the happiness that success brings.

Jefe barked orders at the other guards, who grabbed me and Jeff and took us into the little adobe hut with the broken windows. The other guards descended on the truck. As two of them handcuffed us to the broken windows, I watched as tools came flying out of pickups, and pieces of my truck started coming off so fast I could hardly believe my eyes.

There were jagged bits of broken glass sticking up from the windowpane dividers where the glass had been broken out. They reached one arm around the front, then handcuffed our hands together above the broken glass. That way we couldn't move. We had to keep our wrists up above the jagged edges.

But I hardly noticed this danger. They were taking everything out of the truck. My tapes, our clothing, my guitar, our sleeping bags: everything was thrown into a pile. Others searched through the pile of personal items as it was all strewn across the gravel. The Jefe lifted a box of cassette tapes. "*Confiscado!*" he shouted triumphantly, then walked away with them.

Tools, a spare tire, fenders, engine pieces, bumpers, door panels, seats – everything you could imagine was coming off the truck and thrown into the pile. I felt sick. I couldn't bear to see everything so discombobulated. I thought, *how will I ever get it all back together? And what about my tapes? And our clothes? They're going to get dirty lying there in that pile of crap. They're not keeping the nuts and bolts and screws in order. Everything is a mess. I'll never get it together again!*

This was the breaking point for me, the point that brought up that raw, gut-wrenching feeling that makes you want to vomit. I tried to swallow, but couldn't get any saliva worked up. My eyes were dry. My mouth felt like sand and dried leaves.

Suddenly, my lower abdomen was exploding. "Scared shitless." That really happens. You see it in movies, when someone says "I soiled myself" after a terrible fright. It sounds so simple, hardly worth talking about. But that's not exactly what occurs. It's not that simple. And it's not just a little soiled underwear.

There was an agonizing pain in the pit of my stomach, down through my bowels it traveled, grinding away like acid eating through my internal organs. And there was nothing I could do. I had lost all control. I had no way to stop it.

"I've got to go to the bathroom! *Por favor, cuarto de baño. Por favor,*" I said to the guards standing nearby. I begged and begged, but they just looked at me and said nothing.

I called out to the Jefe, "*Por favor, señor.* I gotta go to the bathroom. Please. I can't hold it."

My bowels were ready to explode, my head pounding. I couldn't feel my legs. It was like they'd gone numb. I didn't care about anything at that moment other than relief. I had lost all sense of propriety and personal concern. I had no sense of shame or embarrassment.

I didn't care about anything but relieving myself. I begged and pleaded. By then, I'm sure I was crying. I didn't care. I *had* to go to the bathroom right now!

Finally, the Jefe barked some orders at the guards near me and motioned away from the hut.

The guards laughed and talked to each other in Spanish. It didn't faze me. I didn't care what they were saying or what they intended. I needed to go outside and drop my pants very fast. It was all I could focus on.

They pushed me outside the hut. I could see out of the corner of my eye that a bus had pulled into the *aduana*. It was a big bus, and looked to me like it was filled with tourists. The door opened and people exited. I walked further, but the two guards stopped me. I was just in front of the passengers now, maybe ten yards away. Some were trying not to look at me. Others seemed scared and confused. I was only slightly aware of them. It wasn't until later I even recalled what had happened.

The two guards were laughing even harder. They told me to go to the bathroom. "*Vamos,*" they said. "*Vamonos, gabacho!*" Each man put a gun to my head, hemmed in on both sides by the steel barrels. The passengers were standing there staring at me. The bus driver opened the luggage storage space under the bus. They were being told to open their luggage. Bags opened and guards rifled through them. People kept looking back at me.

I didn't know what to do. My hands were cuffed behind me. The guards shoved their guns into my head harder I tried to drag down my pants from behind. Slowly, pulling with all my strength, I got them down.

Then I bent down and let go.

It was a terrible sound.

Some passengers were looking away, others were giggling, and some seemed frightened. All the while, the two guards were shouting and laughing at me, with their guns held tightly to my skull.

"*Corre, gabacho, corre!*" they said over and over, laughing and slapping themselves, gun barrels butting against my head.

It was finally over. My guts had exploded and I was relieved, momentarily.

There was nothing I could do but slowly, arduously get my pants back up without cleaning myself. I had to drag the belt around my jeans up from behind. I pulled and pulled, and slowly got the pants up higher and higher. My penis got caught on the unbuttoned fly.

Everyone was really laughing now. They were saying all sorts of things. The passengers were trying not to laugh, but many couldn't help it —there was a young American man in handcuffs with shit dripping from his jeans and his cock stuck behind his belt, poking out from the unbuttoned fly. I am sure it was not anything these people would soon forget.

I finally got my pants back up and over my penis. The guards were laughing so hard they could barely move. They just gave me a little poke in the direction of the hut, pushing me back inside, stumbling over themselves with laughter. Jeff looked at me with a deep, forlorn look on his face.

But it was over. The huge wrenching feeling in my abdomen was gone, the passengers, the guards, even my truck – those feelings were now past me. I just didn't give a damn. I could breathe again. That was all I cared about. Whatever was going to happen would happen.

Jeff stared at me, then took a deep breath. "Now the adventure begins," he said with a look of horror yet unbelievable calm.

It was in that moment I finally began to understand: this is really happening. The humiliation and powerlessness was real. The drugs were real. The police were real. We were caught trying to transport illegal drugs from Mexico into America. Jeff was right: now the adventure begins.

They found nothing more in the Bronco. They gathered up everything lying around, including my guitar, and tossed it all into the back of a couple pickups.

Two guards walked Jeff and me over to the Jefe and a man standing with him. We learned later the Jefe was the captain and the other man was the lieutenant. We still had our hands cuffed behind our backs. They pushed us inside a late-model Pontiac Grand Prix. It was a big, low, heavy Detroit automobile, long and fat. The kind of car Americans used to love to drive across country and around town. A gas hog is what they're called now. But in Mexico, it was still a status symbol.

The Jefe got in the driver's seat, the lieutenant got in the passenger side. The lieutenant turned around to us and leveled a big handgun at our faces. He stayed in that position for the entire hour-long ride into town.

The Jefe pulled out a cassette tape and popped it into the dash, revved the engine, and pulled onto the highway going the same direction we were before we spun off the road.

Back on the same highway as before, only now looking out the front window of this big old sedan and a large handgun trained on our faces. Then I heard the slow rumbling of an electric piano and the far-away cry of a guitar. *I think I know this music*, I thought. I was expecting some *Norteño* music with an accordion and the yodel of a Mexican singer. Then the horns came in. They built to the kind of crescendo that carries you away into the ether. Then I realized, oh my God, it's "Also Sprach Zarathustra" by Deodato, the rock version of the music from *2001: A Space Odyssey*; it was a piece of music celebrating Nietzsche. It was blaring out of the great wide dash of that Grand Prix and slamming us right in the face.

We picked up speed, going faster and faster, so I glanced at the speedometer: it was bouncing around 100 mph.

The man with the gun bounced up and down with every rolling dune, and his gun went with him. His hand never left the trigger. Jeff and I watched that gun going up and down, over and over, across the vast Sonoran Desert.

CHAPTER 5

THERE IS A moment, sometimes, when realization or even epiphany strikes. When you know your life has changed forever. Maybe you cheated on your wife and got caught, so your marriage is over. Maybe you lost all your money gambling, and had to sell your home. Maybe you became addicted to pills after an injury, and lost everything you ever loved. There is a moment when it all becomes real, and you say to yourself, "My god, this is really happening." Whatever run you were on, whatever high you were chasing, it's over. Now there's a payment to be made, a piece of your life will be sucked away. And there's no way out of it.

We were in a concrete cell. Two Mexican men were sitting on the bare floor with their backs to the wall. It was cold and dark. No chairs or benches, nothing to sit on. Some newspapers scattered around the floor were a pathetic buffer from cold concrete. We didn't say anything and neither did they. We made no eye contact. All of us were trying to ignore the groans, screams, and shouts we heard outside the cell. I didn't know who was making them, but they were loud and they were close.

It was early morning. The Jefe and the lieutenant had taken us here a few hours ago, right before dawn. They said nothing, did nothing, just put us in the cell, slammed the door, and walked away without answering any of our requests to make a phone call or talk to someone in charge.

There was a toilet at one end with a sink nearby. Everything was filthy. I cleaned myself off a bit using some of the newspaper on the floor. Jeff paced, trying to look outside but the angle of the cell door didn't reveal much. The only thing we knew was we were in some kind of compound, with an office along one end and a large wall around everything.

Later, we learned that we were at the compound of the Mexican Federal Police for Drug Enforcement; they are known as the *Federales* in Mexico. The Mexican Feds have a lot of latitude. They're almost like an arm of the military, but they don't wear uniforms, and they have been known to get away with extreme coercion — or what we in America would call torture. It's hard to tell these guys from the drug dealers. They look an awful lot alike, and sometimes their tactics are very similar.

But at that moment, we didn't have that information — or any information, for that matter. We were sitting there in a cold, dark, concrete jail cell, open to the elements, with a couple other young Mexican guys, who seemed as scared as we, listening to the blood-curdling screams from outside our view.

A middle-aged woman came to the cell door and blurted out something in Spanish. She was short and fat and of undistinguishable age, though her long, messy hair was streaked with gray. The other two guys looked at her and shook their heads. She looked at us and repeated what she said to them, glaring at us with an incomprehensible disdain. What the hell did she want from us? She barked at us again. Jeff and I looked at each other and shrugged.

I glanced over at the two Mexican men. The older of the two made an eating motion with his hand. Jeff and I looked at each other again nodding happily; we were very hungry. We hadn't really eaten much the day before, and the night's events had taken a toll. So this was the cook. She was going to bring us some food. Everything suddenly started to feel less crazy, like somebody was in charge.

I looked back at the woman and nodded to her with a smile. She continued her dagger-like stare, then mumbled something and waddled off. Jeff came over to me and said, "Well, they're going to feed us at least."

"This must be some kind of police organization," I replied. We weren't sure who the guys were who captured us and brought us here. There was no fingerprinting, no mug shots taken, no paperwork filled out. It was like we had been arrested by a secret organization operating outside the regular justice system. It added a degree of fright even beyond the expected.

A moment later, the yelling outside stopped, and two *Federales* brought a man to the cell. He was Mexican. A nice-looking guy, he appeared to be about thirty but he'd been badly beaten. They opened the cell door. He stumbled in, then leaned against the wall and slowly slid to the floor. Even as he did so, he maintained some level of dignity. It was apparent that neither we nor the *Federales* were to know he was affected by his ordeal. Evidently, he did not break. There was a triumphant look on his face, even though it was sore and bleeding.

One of the *Federales* called to me and Jeff, and made a motion for us to come closer. He was the man who drove us back in the Grand Prix and held a gun in our faces for an hour. Pleasant face, spoke English well, dressed in a chambray shirt and blue jeans. My heart was beating so hard I could hear it. It didn't make any sense, we gave them the marijuana. I thought, *why would they want to torture us?*

When we got close to the bars, he spoke to us in English. He was calm, easy going, like he was just chatting with us after lunch together. It was not the manner one would expect from a guy who just spent a couple hours torturing another human being.

"Hey, guys," he said with a smile, "where did you buy the marijuana?" Beneath the smile, there was a deep sense of menace. He had selected that moment to ask us these questions – right after we'd seen the effects of his work.

I stammered a little as Jeff told him we got it in Mazatlán. I mentioned we drove to a farm, way south in the jungle. He asked who the people were, what were their names? I told him I didn't remember. Jeff said we didn't know the guys, just some people we met at the beach.

"Did you buy the drugs from Antonio?" he asked politely. I told him I was not sure; it was dark. He looked at me for a moment that lasted too long for comfort. Then he nodded and walked toward the office.

Jeff looked concerned. "How did they know about Antonio, you think?"

"I don't know," I said. "But they didn't ask about my truck." Jeff ignored me and walked over to the man who had just entered the cell and asked him if he was okay.

The man looked up. "Goddamn sons of bitches," he said through his teeth.

Jeff asked, "Do they do this to everyone?"

"If you don't tell them what they want," said one of the other men sitting nearby.

I was worried about my Bronco. It had the wrong license plate, registered to a completely different vehicle. If they did a check on it, they'd see it was the wrong plate, and then I'd be looking at two crimes instead of only the drug possession. Being charged with another crime, at that point, would have been too much to deal with and I was freaking out.

Jeff turned to the guy in the corner who made the comment about telling them what they wanted to know. The man looked at Jeff for a moment and then began to speak. He explained to us, in broken English, that drug possession in Mexico is often a seven-year sentence. He said the system was so messed up that it took too much time to prosecute people, so they tried to get as many confessions as possible in order to avoid going to trial. It saved doing real investigations and kept the prisons full so the Americans would give more money to stop the drug trade. It made the *Federales* look like they were doing good work, and the Americans felt like they were getting their money's worth. It was a vicious cycle.

He went on, saying that often if you don't confess, they let you go; so if you can stand a few days of beatings, then you save yourself a lot of time in prison. I didn't know if this was good news or bad news. "But it is very hard not to talk," he added.

"They use a cattle prod, *y a los juevos tambien*!" He grabbed hold of his balls as he said this.

We all looked at the beaten man sitting on the floor. He wasn't so tough now. What happened to him was starting to show. He shivered, blood dripped from the corner of his mouth and from his nose. He looked like he was going to pass out, then fell over sideways and lay down, shaking.

There was a clanging on the cell bars and we turned and saw the little fat woman banging on the bars to the door. She had two plates of food, which she put down on the ground outside the door. She shouted something to us and held out her hand. Her disdain for us was baffling. You'd think we shot her only child.

We looked to the man in the corner for help who told us that we had to pay for our food, and she wanted sixty-five pesos. Jeff looked at me and lifted his hands in a gesture of *what the hell?* I looked over at the fat woman, who had her hand sticking through the bars. She snapped her fingers a couple times.

We didn't get to keep our things and they took my wallet. But they did give me the money I had in it, which seemed odd to me at the time. I reached into my pocket and pulled out some pesos, enough to cover the food. As I moved to give it to her, she reached in and grabbed it out of my hand quickly, then turned and walked off in a huff.

Jeff dragged the plates under the cell door and we gobbled up the food. It was just scrambled eggs and refried beans and I could tell she put water in both, but it tasted amazing.

I looked at Jeff. "So that's why they took everything except for our money. We have to buy our own food." They put you in jail and make you use your own money to buy food. What else? Do we have to build our own beds? There was nothing in the cell – no chairs and no beds. It was just a cold, dirty, concrete bunker.

"Shit, man," Jeff said, putting down the plate. "This is not looking good."

The guy on the floor had his balls and mouth ripped apart by a cattle prod and his nose burned from mineral water being forced into his nostrils. We had no idea what was going on, who these people were, and what they intended to do with us. Jeff too was slowly but surely starting to freak out a bit. He told me he wasn't sure he would make it if we were sent to prison. He didn't know how he would handle it.

"I can do almost anything for a year, I think," I told him. "But if they find out about the truck and we spend time for that in the States, I think I'll lose my mind."

The two guys who arrested us came and got one of the other men. A few minutes passed until we heard the same sounds as before. There were thuds and slaps at first, then came the sound of liquid spraying around. Finally, we heard the sounds of electric sparks and the screams of the victim.

The *Federales* would use torture on anyone if they wanted a quick confession. Apparently, they didn't want that from us. They would hit their victims a few times in the back, legs, and arms to debilitate them. They'd beat their feet and then hogtie the person and lay them on a table. One of the Feds would sit or push down on the person's mid-section while the other one shook a bottle of mineral water and forced it into the nostrils of the victim. The mineral water burned going in, and they pushed down on the person's mid-section to force out any water that got into the lungs. That way the person wouldn't die. The water burned again coming back out, and the guards would hold their hand over the person's mouth or tape it shut.

Finally, they used a cattle prod, designed to be applied to the hard, thick hide of a cow. It was meant to give a penetrating shock through their thick hides and force a cow to move quickly. But when applied to human skin, especially genitalia and the soft tissue of your mouth, it's devastating. It tears holes in the tissue and leaves permanent scars. They stripped the guys of their clothing right at the outset so there was the added humiliation of being naked while all this happened.

They did this throughout the day to the remaining two inmates, making sure we heard every sound and saw the results. During that day, Jeff and I tried to engage in conversation to keep our minds off the noise and on our own sanity. We talked about philosophy, the differences between the US and Mexico, and all kinds of other things. Then suddenly the unfairness of the whole situation smacked us hard.

We were there because of marijuana – a substance that, by some standards, is less dangerous to humans than alcohol. Today, marijuana is becoming legal across nations. Yet at that time, it was considered dangerous and was illegal in both Mexico and in most of America. You could go to jail for years just for having it on your person, not to mention trying to distribute it.

Jeff was angry about this and blamed both the US and Mexico for such an absurd situation. He didn't feel we'd done anything illegal, so we should be let go immediately. He wanted to contact the American Consulate and start proceedings to get us out of there.

It's a conversation we would have many times. Unlike Jeff, I recognized that we had, in fact, committed a crime. We knew marijuana was illegal. We came here, bought the weed, and carried it north to America with the intent of crossing the border and selling it in the States. That's a crime. Whether it should be or not was irrelevant.

"That's not an excuse," I said to Jeff. "We did the crime. We have to take some responsibility. I don't know, maybe if we apologize, they'll let us go. Or maybe we need to claim that we're addicts and that's our yearly supply. I know one thing, whining about being arrested for having a huge box of weed in our possession isn't going to help."

Jeff disagreed. "The justice system is broken. They torture guys in Mexico, with the support of US drug enforcement agencies, to help perpetuate a system by which none of the really bad guys get caught and a bunch of common people go to jail for smoking weed. That's the crime." His voice rose as he spoke.

Our differing views on personal responsibility began to drive a wedge between us. In that moment it was apparent to us both that we didn't feel the same way about the situation and why we were there.

These questions kept popping up in our conversations: were we responsible for the mess in which we found ourselves? Was it up to us to figure out a solution? Should we have to pay for our mistakes? Should we feel angry about it or just do the time?

Jeff thought it wasn't our fault, but I thought we had some culpability. Maybe it was because I felt more responsible since it was my idea. Nevertheless, for the first time, our unified front was starting to crumble.

CHAPTER 6

LATER THAT DAY, the little fat woman came back to take our food order. We paid another sixty-five pesos for some more watered-down beans and eggs in a tortilla. As we ate in silence, they brought in the second of the two men who'd been in the cell when we arrived. Now there were three men who were beaten and sore, although one seemed like he had been beaten less severely than the others. I suppose he gave them what they wanted. He was the youngest of the three and looked to be high school age, maybe seventeen or eighteen.

Jeff was sitting on the floor, leaning against the wall with his arms wrapped around his knees. Now and then, he gave his right knee a hard rub with his hand. Jeff played quarterback in high school back in Wisconsin. He was pretty good, according to his brother, got a full a scholarship to the university. But he blew out his knee the last couple weeks of the season and ended his potential college career. We played a round of sandlot ball a few weeks earlier, and he, his brother, and some guys from the chemistry department thrashed my team from the theatre department.

The younger man spoke to Jeff, saying something in Spanish. Jeff didn't know any Spanish at all so he looked at me for help. "I don't understand what he's saying, but it seems important to him."

I took two years of Spanish in junior high, and while I didn't remember much of what I learned then, I could recall a few words. I turned to the younger guy, who stood and spoke to me in a hushed voice. Jeff came nearer.

The young kid seemed anxious and scared. It was apparent he wanted to tell us something. He held his hand up to his head, miming a phone. He pointed at himself, then at us. Then he said, in very broken English, "I call, for you." He kept nodding. Jeff and I were confused. I looked at Jeff. "So… he wants to make a phone call for us? What does that mean?"

After a few minutes, the first man – the older guy who was being tortured when we arrived and was in the most distress – said to us, "He will call your home." He seemed to be the only one who could speak English, at least a little.

We looked back at the younger guy. He was nodding. *"No sabian, no sabian, sus padres, no sabian nada de ustedes,"* he kept saying.

The guy on the floor said, in several bits of broken English, how no one would know where we were. The only way to get out of here would be to get some money from America. Our families could buy us out if they could get money down here quickly. But it would have to be soon, before we got to the prison.

Prison? To hell with that. I looked at Jeff, and he looked at me. "We got to get out of here," Jeff said. "We can't go to prison. We're Americans." Then the man on the floor told us to give the young guy a phone number in the US and he'd call someone for us.

I looked at Jeff. "But he doesn't speak English. How can he call anyone?"

Then I thought about my ex-wife's mother. She lived in Albuquerque and spoke Spanish. So I told them he could call a woman in Nuevo Mexico, Albuquerque. They knew of it. These guys had been across the border before. Tucson, Albuquerque, Phoenix – those places they knew.

Her name was Sarah Jonns. We didn't have anything to write with or any paper. So we took a scrap of newspaper and scratched her name on it with some old, burnt matches lying on the floor.

Jeff and I looked at each other. He shook his head. "This is crazy. This can't be our only hope. Some kid who doesn't even speak English trying to call Kate's mother in the US and tell her we're in jail somewhere in Mexico. And he's somehow going to keep that little scrap of newspaper for the number?"

But all three guys were certain it was the only way out. Otherwise we would be in prison for a long time. The young kid carefully folded the piece of paper and put it in his pocket. It seemed completely nuts to me, but I was in favor of anything that offered hope at that point.

A few minutes later, one of the guards came to the cell and motioned for the young guy who had our paper to come with him. He quickly walked to the door and left with the guard. We watched him cross the courtyard and go inside an office area. He didn't come back.

The wind howled through the cell all night long, with no blankets, no beds, and no heat. It might have been the Sonoran Desert, but it was January. It wasn't cold like January in Utah, but the desert was terribly cold at night. I was trying to hold on, but I wasn't sure how long I could take it. We huddled in the corner farthest from the cell doors, sitting close together.

In the morning, the little fat woman came to the cell again. This time, I only had twenty-five pesos left. She came to the door and I showed her what I had. She scoffed at me, took the money, and waddled off. I thought, *Well, at least we'll get one plate to share.*

She returned with two plates of food, the same as the day before. Jeff and I were stunned. She would bring the food even if we didn't pay? We realized she was probably paid by the *Federales* to feed inmates, and took money from them on the side. She was scamming us. *Was everybody a crook?*

The guy on the floor said, "Because you're Americans, she will feed you." That's one of the things that popped up time and time again – how Americans are treated differently.

Later that day, two guards came to our cell; the same guards who came to get the others and took them away for the beatings. They motioned for us to come, but we just stood there, unable to move. I didn't know if I could take it. I'd been in a couple of fistfights in school, but I never got hit very hard. I wasn't sure what I'd do if they tortured us.

But why would they torture us? We gave them the weed. We didn't have anything else. They tore my truck apart looking for cocaine. But still, they motioned for us to come, and then shouted at us, "*Vamos, gabachos!*'

Jeff and I shuffled to the cell door and walked away with them. But they didn't take us around the other side where they took the others. They walked us toward the door where they took the young guy the day before.

We walked into an office and saw several secretaries, then went through a door into another office where we saw a heavy-set, grey-haired man sitting behind a desk shuffling through some papers. He was dressed in a cheap-looking suit and didn't look up when we entered. He looked to be about fifty. Nearby was a woman who looked to be in her thirties, dressed in a tailored jacket and skirt. She had light brown hair and light skin and didn't look Mexican. She seemed very business-like, sitting calmly, paying little attention to us.

By the atmosphere in the room, it seemed we were in some kind of formal meeting. The Jefe was standing in the corner. The lieutenant remained inside while the other guard left. Curiously, they didn't handcuff us. They told us to sit in a couple of chairs in front of the desk.

The man behind the desk nodded to the woman, who was sitting on a couch. She introduced herself as Gloria and said she was with the American Consulate. She conversed with the man at the desk in Spanish. She didn't smile or give us any other indication of how she felt.

Still, we were relieved for a minute, thinking she would get us out of there. *At last*, we thought, *we'll be going home. This will be over. It was just a stupid mistake. Why would they want to imprison a couple of idiots with a box of shitty weed?*

This feeling didn't last long. Gloria began speaking to us in a business-like tone, quite matter-of-fact. She explained her responsibilities, then gave us a list of attorneys. She went through a synopsis of the Mexican judicial system, explaining it as though we were in court. She told us she would notify our families and relay any messages from us we wished.

Jeff and I were dumbfounded. What the hell was going on? We began a flurry of questions, both of us talking at once. She raised her hand, stopping us with a frown that conveyed slight anger. She stared at us for a moment, then pointed to the man behind the desk. "This is the *ministerio público*. He is in charge of your case. Please listen to him and do not speak."

He began to speak, and as he talked, the other guard entered the room carrying the box of marijuana from our truck. The *ministerio público* (district attorney) told us that he was charging us with possession and transportation of illegal drugs, and we had around six kilos of marijuana. I glanced at Jeff, wondering what happened to the other four kilos.

He pulled out a yellow notepad that was found in our truck. On it was a bunch of scribbled notes, figures, and dollar amounts, along with a phone number and a name. He asked whose notepad it was. I told him it was mine. He paused for a moment before he asked whose number was written on the paper. "Perhaps it is the phone number of your drug dealer?" he asked. I said nothing. Jeff didn't speak either.

Gloria spoke to us in a way that made it clear she was annoyed. She told us these proceedings were informal and we would not be charged with any crime until we had a lawyer. What we said there meant nothing, according to her. Once we were in the prison, there was nothing she could do to help us. Anything we said could only help us, and they might treat us better if we cooperated. She inflected the last phrase with a tone I took to mean she realized they used torture on people.

Jeff looked at her and said, "So if we cooperate, they might let us go?"

I thought to myself, *This is all we have to do? Tell them what happened, rat out Antonio, and we can leave?*

Gloria stared at us with a look of disbelief. She took a moment, as though trying to gather her words, and then spoke slowly and sternly. "You have been arrested for possession of drugs in a foreign country, and you are subject to the laws of that country. In Mexico, there is no bail. You will be taken to the prison in a few days, and there you will wait for the judicial process to run its course. If you plead not guilty, it could take up to four years before the trial would be over. Even pleading guilty and not having a trial could take a year to eighteen months. After you receive a sentence, you can apply for a transfer to the States and possibly serve out your sentence there." She looked at us coldly while that settled in.

Good fucking hell! Years, months – my head was reeling. It was just some shitty farmer weed! This was a bloody nightmare.

Jeff felt the same. He looked at the *ministerio publico* and blurted out quickly, "That name on the notepad next to the number is the guy we bought the marijuana from. He ripped us off. The weed was shitty, and he overcharged us. It doesn't even get you high!"

They all just stared at us. No one was even remotely moved by Jeff's comment.

The two guards came to our sides and motioned for us to get up, then took us back to our cell. The lieutenant still had the yellow notepad from our truck. He showed it to me again. Pointing to Antonio's name, he asked me if there were any other names I could remember. I shook my head . He looked at me for a moment, as if trying to assess if I was telling the truth. I did everything I could to look sincere. Then they left.

Jeff and I paced and discussed our options. "I don't know if we should plead guilty," said Jeff. "I think we have a better chance doing something else."

I didn't agree. "Look, man, we got caught and we had drugs. That's it. We fucked up and now we have to pay for it. We will go to the prison, we'll work on acting and music, and we'll stay in good shape. We will get our sentence as soon as possible and then get transferred. We have no choice. We came down here for an adventure, and this is it."

Jeff just stared at me. I threw up my hands in exasperation. "Jeff, we handed them the box of weed. We are screwed. What the hell do you think we can do to get out of this?"

He looked at me for a long time and then said, "*You* handed it to them."

At that moment, Gloria came to our cell door. She had a small Spanish-English dictionary and a notepad. Through the cell bars, Gloria handed us the notepad and the dictionary. "Write down the name of a family member you would like me to call. Each of you, please." As Jeff and I each wrote down the names, she looked at us with a little more compassion. There was some kindness in her voice as she spoke again. "Have you been treated well?" We just stared at her for a moment. We looked over at the guards standing a few yards away.

"I ask this question as a representative of the US government. I will make a report. But realize there is nothing I can do to help you or intervene. Try to be helpful and learn to get along within the system, and you should be fine. But this is not America. If you've been mistreated, I can file a complaint, but while you are here with the *Federales*, there is little I can do. I suggest you try to help them as much as you can, and things should go okay for you. Good luck."

She turned and walked away. I looked at Jeff. He wasn't the same as when we started this adventure. There was something different about him. I couldn't tell what was happening, but it didn't seem good to me.

EL CENTRO DE REDEAPTACIÓN SOCIAL HERMOSILLO

PRISON ONE

CHAPTER 7

EARLY THE NEXT morning, the same two guards woke Jeff and me. They rapped on the bars and called for us to come over. We were still reeling from the information we had gotten the day before, and were barely able to hobble over to the cell door.

It didn't seem possible we would have to go to prison for a couple years or more. It wasn't real. We were going to classes at the University of Utah only a few days ago. I had been cast as Silvio in Goldoni's *The Servant of Two Masters* and had to be back soon for our first rehearsal – the meet and greet and read through.

I couldn't go to prison. We were just screwing around. I mean, what were we going to do with the weed? We weren't drug dealers; we didn't know how to find enough people to sell drugs to. Shit, man, we didn't even smoke weed very much. The whole thing was stupid. It was just an adventure, for fuck's sake. We weren't real criminals.

The guards put handcuffs on us and escorted us in another direction – not toward the office and not toward the backyard where they'd tortured the other guys. We came to the driveway where we had arrived the first night. There was a van with its back door open. They put us in the back and we headed out. They didn't say a word, even though we asked several times what was happening.

It was one of the first lessons we learned about prison, at least Mexican prison: none of the authorities ever told us anything. We didn't have a clue of what the hell was going to happen next. They'd just come and get us and take us someplace, and we'd find out where that place was once we got there.

I always thought, *what's the big secret?* We're not spies, for hell's sake. What were we going to do, call our middle-aged, Mormon Utah families and tell them to break us out of prison? Like my mom and dad would be waiting behind a road block in the middle of downtown Hermosillo with machine guns and grenades to come get their boy out of jail.

The guards drove us to the outskirts of Hermosillo to the Sonora state prison. It was a large complex about the size of a dozen football fields. There were seven cellblocks, *pabellones*, which were two stories high, and each of them contained forty-eight cells.

Inside the prison was a soccer field, a running track, a baseball diamond, a large gymnasium connected to an auditorium, a small store with a café, a soda stand, a cinderblock plant, and several vegetable gardens. There was also a walled-in playground area with tables and fire pits used for weekend visits. Each Sunday, and sometimes Saturdays, families and friends were allowed into the prison to see the inmates. The visitors had to acquiesce to a body search, and even a strip search if prison officials thought there was a need for it. This was the way Mexico managed visitation; the visitors were searched, not the inmates.

After entering the main gate, there was a parking area where the administrative offices were located, along with auto, carpentry, and upholstery shops *(los talleres)*. People came in from the outside to manage these shops using cheap inmate labor. There were about 850 inmates and forty to fifty guards.

A large, twenty-five-foot concrete wall surrounded the compound, with armed guards patrolling the top. At points along the wall were gun towers. Inside the wall were two fifteen-foot chain-link fences about ten feet apart, with barbed wire rolled along the top.

The prison was like a large, isolated town. The guards made few appearances inside. The inmates ran the place and those in charge paid fees to the administration for food, concessions, and other perks. The prison food was barely adequate, and few other essentials were furnished. Some inmates were allowed conjugal visits in addition to the normal weekend visits from family and friends.

It was quite different from American prisons. The quality of life for inmates inside a Mexican prison depends entirely on how the warden decides to manage it, and also, of course, how involved the inmates' families are. Your family can bring food, supplies, clothing, etc.

Jeff and I knew none of this as we climbed out of the van that brought us to the prison. All we saw were the very high walls surrounding what we imaged to be hell. One of the *Federales* unlocked our handcuffs while the other dumped our sleeping bags and clothes on the ground.

Prison guards escorted us inside and led us to an office where they took our fingerprints and mug shots. Then we met with a man (whom we later learned was an inmate who did office work) who assigned us to a cell.

We didn't understand anything that was going on. We moved where they pushed us, and sat, often impatiently, waiting while they took nearly the entire day to process us into the *Centro de Readaptación Social Hermosillo Sonora*.

It was impossible to believe we were there to stay. It was still incomprehensible what was happening.

Later that afternoon, we were escorted to a double-gated room known as the *sala de guardia* (living room of the guards). We were, by then, carrying all the personal belongings we were allowed to keep, including our sleeping bags, clothing, my guitar, and a few personal grooming odds and ends.

Another guard let us through to the inmate part of the prison. He made a joke I did not understand, but he seemed to be poking fun at our obvious fright. We were scared out of our wits.

We hadn't eaten or slept well in several days. Our ordeal began with confronting the cartel guys in the jungle and wondering if we were going to survive. After came the arrest and the days with the *Federales*, the torture we witnessed, and the way they refused to give us information about what was happening. But there, at least, we were in a holding cell in a sort of county jail kind of place. At the time, we had the thought if minds could be changed, we might get out somehow. Those thoughts were now gone.

We were dumped into this giant prison compound with no explanation of what we were supposed to do or where we were supposed to go, other than a cellblock and cell number written on a scrap of paper. All our fears about Mexican prisons had to come to a head. We assumed we would be fighting for our very survival day after day. We would be raped and beaten. We could be killed. They simply opened the big steel gates and we walked in.

After the gate clanged shut behind us, Jeff and I looked at each other for support. He said, "Okay, this is it. Back to back, we start fighting right now and don't stop until we show them we're not going to take any bullshit, or we will end up getting killed in the first couple of weeks."

We either had to fight as hard as we could, like a couple of crazed honey badgers, or just sit there and wait to be beaten, raped, and killed. We decided we'd go out with a bang. That was our vow to each other in the moment. We didn't know it then, but it was pretty much the last time we actually felt like a team, like two good friends facing a horrible situation together.

We could hear the guards behind us laughing and joking on the other side of the steel gate. But we didn't take our eyes of the yard in front of us. There we stood, back to back, waiting for an onslaught that didn't come. We were both trembling a bit, ready for anything, trying to assess the situation and our new home. But there was hardly anyone in sight.

A few inmates were hanging around in open areas of the compound. They were milling around lazily, talking. All of a sudden, two men approached. They were walking along the sidewalk, coming from the direction of what appeared to be cellblocks. One was about 6'2". He had an afro and dark glasses, and was carrying a bat. The other was short, with long, straight hair down to the middle of his back, and was carrying a big shiny box. A strange screeching noise got louder and louder as they approached.

Jeff looked at me. "Well, it looks like we are going to have to prove ourselves here and now; that guy's got a bat."

I grabbed my guitar by the neck like a club and said, "Shit, man, I was hoping I was going to get to hang onto this baby for a while, but we can't let these guys take us without a fight. If we do, we're going to be everyone's bitch the whole time we are here."

The two men turned the corner toward us. The taller one was wearing gym shorts and a basketball jersey that said *Celtics*. In addition to the bat, he was carrying a baseball. The other man looked like he had come straight out of the '60s. He was carrying a ghetto blaster and the screeching sound was "Purple Haze" by Jimi Hendrix.

They walked up to us casually and looked us up and down for a moment. The short one nodded at us and said, "Hey, man, you guys want to smoke a joint?"

I thought I had to be dreaming.

"You can put the guitar down now," he said with a little bit of a laugh. "We just got done playing baseball, so that's why Martín has a bat. It's okay. *Calmado*, take it easy."

Jeff and I looked at each other, then back at the steel gate. The guards were on the other side and we could see them through the window. They weren't the least bit interested in either us or the two guys standing there asking us if we wanted to go get high. They hadn't been laughing at us, they were into their own conversation. Through our own paranoia, we had misinterpreted the entire situation.

Martín, the tall one, finally said, "*Vamanos, gabachos*." Then he turned and started walking off toward what appeared to be a big gymnasium. The short one gestured at us as if to say "Don't worry" and followed Martín. Jeff and I followed them like two lost puppies.

The shorter one, Thomas, was the only other gabacho in the prison. He had been there two and a half years because he had run out of money for his lawyer. Martín was Mexican, although he was one of those guys who lived on the border and watched a lot of American television shows, so he knew and followed a lot of American culture. He had fairly light skin, medium brown hair, and always dressed in some kind of sports attire.

Martín was a cool guy but, as we later discovered, he liked to get his way. If he didn't get his way, he wouldn't join in. Everyone in the prison knew Martín; he wasn't one of the power brokers who ran the place, but he knew how to get things done and worked every angle to help his situation. Both he and Thomas were there for possessing a little bit of weed.

Thomas explained that the *comandante* had asked them to meet us so they could show us around the prison and help us find our cell. He took us to his cell first. It was a dark and dirty concrete room with three slabs of concrete stacked like bunk beds and a small bathroom with a sink and a toilet. Cockroaches were everywhere, as were flies.

The cells were meant to house three inmates, although most of them held only two. The inmates took care of cleaning and security, and were allowed to decorate however they wanted. Each cell was an indicator of how much money the occupant had – the more money, the larger the lock. Thomas had no lock at all.

We met a bunch of other guys as we checked out our new home: a guy named Ramon; a seventeen-year-old named Chabita; a guy named Diego, who always had a guitar with him; and Arturo, who was with the Mexican mafia and was Martín's cellmate.

A bit heavy, dark-haired, and on the short side, Arturo was connected to one of the drug cartels. He was doing time for the organization in order to appease the authorities. He was a round, jolly guy who made jokes all the time and mostly hung around and watched TV. He was in his forties, with a young wife and small children who came to visit him every weekend. He had enough money inside to eat well every day, and his family was being taken care of on the outside. He had few concerns. No one would touch him. Because of this, Martín was equally well protected from theft and trouble.

After meeting this crew, Martín took us into a cell on the second floor and then into a bathroom. Once there, we went up through a hole in the ceiling and out onto the roof. We got high while listening to a Neil Young tape and watching the sunset. Between us, Jeff and I hadn't said ten words since we arrived.

As we sat on top of the cellblock looking out over our new home, I was practically falling into some kind of trance. I had been reading Carlos Castaneda recently and found myself thinking about the ideas in those books a lot. Could I learn to fly up over these walls, like Don Juan and the other sorcerers?

We smoked some really good weed and got super stoned. It seemed so ironic. There we were in a Mexican prison for attempting to transport marijuana into the United States. Now, instead of having to fight our way through a bunch of crazed, bloodthirsty inmates, we were sitting atop a cellblock getting stoned in front of the very guards who put us in prison. They sat in the gun towers watching us but clearly didn't give a shit. And there were no guards anywhere inside the prison.

That night, almost everything I saw and experienced was contradictory; in fact, almost bizarre. It was like a Salvador Dali painting or a Castanedan "separate reality," nothing made sense according to the template I had in my mind. It was several days before I came to grips with it all and stopped watching from the sidelines and started engaging.

CHAPTER 8

THE *COMANDANTE* HAD assigned Thomas and Martín to help settle us in a cellblock. Thomas had just lost a roommate, so they decided to have us bunk with him. He was the only other English-speaker in the prison, and since we spoke hardly any Spanish, it seemed like a sensible choice. It left me with the impression the warden, or *comandante* as they called him, was someone we could get along with. Maybe he was a good guy.

There were three bunks in every cell. The bunks were just slabs of concrete coming out from the cinderblock walls that made an area where you could place a blanket or a foam pad. The entire cellblock was built out of cinderblocks and concrete. Each cell had a single bathroom, which consisted of a small toilet with no seat and a very small sink with only cold water. There was a single light switch and one bulb in the center of the ceiling. There were steel bars across the front of the cell, which had sliding doors and a latch where you could place a padlock. It looked very much like a typical prison cell you might see in a movie, perhaps a little bit bigger, since each cell had to accommodate three inmates.

The cells were not locked or managed by the guards. The inmates locked their own cells and pretty much oversaw the cellblocks. In tougher times, this proved to be a disastrous situation for many inmates. Not two years prior, a very different *comandante*, who allowed hard drugs and alcohol inside, ran the prison. Many of the previous inmates were of a vicious caliber, hardened criminals bent on intimidation and brutality. That was before the state of Sonora restored the old prison near the downtown Hermosillo and transferred about a hundred of the worst inmates there.

The current *comandante* was installed at that time and he stopped the flow of heroin, speed, and alcohol, and only allowed marijuana inside. This, it seemed, was the way prisons were handled in Mexico. From state to state, prisons and the inmates' experiences varied greatly. A change in *comandante* could bring about enormous changes in the character and livability of a prison. The state governor usually appointed the *comandante*, so corruption often influenced how a prison was run.

As it turned out, we hit the prison in Hermosillo at one of its good times, though it didn't seem that way to us. It was still prison in a foreign country, with very different laws, culture, and language. We were the foreigners, the outsiders, the illegal aliens, so to speak. For the first time in my life, I got a taste of what it was like to be different: to be an African-American in Utah, or a Mexican in Montana, or a Muslim anywhere in the US – to belong to a different religion or to have a physical deformity.

I was the singularity in a sea of sameness. This was both distressing and enlightening, at least for me, and an important realization that curved my perspective. Jeff and I had never been outsiders or outcasts. We had each grown up in neighborhoods where we were part of the status quo. Part of the culture, members of the dominant religion. Our physical appearance set us apart; not because we were unusual or lacking in attributes, but because we were good-looking, light-skinned, bushy-haired boys, always sitting with the "in" crowd. We were guys who were chosen first to play sandlot football; the guys who, in fact, usually did the choosing.

But now we were the outcasts, the strangers, the bad guys, even, to some, and it made us targets to many of the inmates. We were "rich" Americans, responsible for this prison in the first place. Our government had built it and was pushing the Mexican government to catch drug dealers and slow the drug trade from Latin America. Or at least it was what they believed.

For many people in Mexico, especially northern Mexico, the US had been more of an imperialist neighbor than friendly neighbor, beginning way back with the Mexican-American War campaign. Most of the inmates believed America had stolen Texas, New Mexico, Arizona, and California from Mexico, and that was why the US was rich and Mexico was poor. Unable to speak Spanish very well, I couldn't discuss the complexities of the two economies and had to suffer their complaints. And to some extent, I did agree with their characterizations of American imperialism.

"If only Mexico had those states back," inmate Guero Rivera said to me, "then Mexico would be the rich country and America would be the poor country!"

"*Yeeeguuaaaa!*" I heard a voice yelling. It echoed in my head and woke me up from a bad dream. I laid there for a moment thinking about it. *Jesus!* I thought I was in prison and couldn't get out. It was so frightening. Then I rose up out of my bunk and looked around. *Shit! It wasn't a dream.* I *was* in prison. It was the first night we'd slept in anything resembling a bed. I remembered we'd gotten our sleeping bags, which made the concrete slab a bit nicer. But it was still like sleeping on a hard slab of cement.

I heard that voice again. "*Yegua!*" Guys were racing down the hallway outside our cell. I could hear tin plates banging and lots of yelling. Thomas was already up and moving around the cell, gathering plates. He said, "Get up, guys, it's time for breakfast."

Then he emphasized that we had to hurry; we needed to get food, and if we didn't get there soon, all the bread would be gone and that was the best part. After breakfast, we were going to meet with the *comandante*. I jumped down from the bed and looked around for my clothes. I would have liked to have splashed some water on my face and maybe tidied up a bit, but Thomas grabbed a bowl and spoon for each of us and started down the hallway.

We scrambled down the hall after him and into the common area on the first floor of the cellblock. There was a big rolling soup tureen, and a couple of inmates were dishing out a mushy-looking liquid. A big steel bowl next to the mush was filled with *bolillos*, a type of Mexican bread baked into a round clump, about the size of half a cantaloupe. It turned out *yegua* is what they called the food. Three times a day, inmates from the kitchen rolled a large soup tureen to each of the *pabellones,* and served rice-water mush and bread for breakfast, soup and tortillas for lunch, and beans and tortillas for dinner. That was it. No vegetables, no meat, no salad. Just bowls of soup, mush, and beans with tortillas or bread.

It was starting to look like the kind of prison food I'd seen in the movies. Mush with bread. Somehow we'd have to find some better food or we'd be pretty gaunt by the time we got out.

We headed back to our cell to eat. Some guys hung around the common area or sat outside on the stoop. Most went back to their cells. While walking back, I asked Thomas, "What does it mean, *yegua*?"

"It's slang," Thomas said. "It means old grey mare."

"Because it tastes like horse meat?" Jeff asked.

"Nah, it's because of the way the guys hover around, drooling over it like a bunch of vultures," I added to his sarcastic comment. Jeff and I had a short laugh together for the first time in several days.

Thomas remained steadfast. He could've chosen to scare us with stories of the nastiness and cruelty of Mexican prison, but instead he chose to be kind. He told us it was not such a bad place, really, and we would eventually get used to it. He said he had been in jail in the States and it was much worse there.

Thomas was small, thin, and unbelievably easy to get along with. He didn't rile anyone. He was polite and friendly to a fault. Not once did I ever see him get mad or even use foul language. He was the quintessential hippie – only a decade or so too late. Everything to him was about peace and love. He was a good guy; you wouldn't want him on your side in a fight, or in a game of football, he was just too nice. But he was the guy to know if you ended up in a disgusting prison.

"You guys can make this a much better place by trying to fit in. Maybe even find something to do to help occupy your time," he said with the kindly smile he used when he was not sure how he was going to be received.

I joked sarcastically, "Oh yeah, maybe we should start a school for the performing arts."

"Hey, man, we had *Jesus Christ Superstar* come here a while back," Thomas replied quickly. "And it was far out, man. Like with costumes and actors and everything!"

"Really?" I looked at him, quite surprised. It was hard for me to imagine a production of *Jesus Christ Superstar* in Mexico done correctly, let alone one that would come to a prison to perform. But then, what did Thomas know about theatre? "Where from, a local college or something?"

"No, man, from Mexico City. A real professional show, touring all over the country." Thomas was actually proud, as though this was his country, his roots. He was partly Hispanic but had lived all his life in the U.S. "It was amazing. Families came from the outside and all the inmates went to see it. The auditorium was packed!"

"Auditorium?" I asked. I wondered what kind of auditorium a prison would have.

"Yeah," said Thomas, again with that odd sense of pride. "We've got an auditorium and a gymnasium, basketball court, boxing ring, soccer field, tennis court, and even a running track."

Although he and Martín had shown us those areas yesterday, we were so dazed and confused, it had all seemed surreal. Neither Jeff nor I could assimilate what we were seeing at the time. But his enthusiasm was beginning to infect me and my mind was running through crazy ideas. *Maybe we could start a theatre group or something. What if we had to be here a long time? I would need something to do.* I mentioned the idea out loud and Thomas was pumped. He began telling me about all the guys who would want to join the group, getting more and more excited. Jeff wasn't paying attention to either of us. He was gazing off toward the barbed-wire fence and the high walls, lost in thought.

We both tried to get his attention a couple of times but he didn't sway from his steady gaze. Then finally he blurted out, "Has anyone ever escaped from this prison? You know, got away and didn't get caught?"

Thomas looked at him curiously for a moment. I thought to myself, *Jeff's going down a bad road.* We had only been there a day or two and he was already talking about escape?

"Not while I've been here," said Thomas. "A few guys bought their way out though, but not any of the *gabachos.* I think a cartel guy and a couple of rich kids. That's it."

Jeff looked at me for a response to his query. I had to look away; I didn't want to think about this. He was nutty. There was a twenty-five-foot concrete wall with gun towers. Inside that were two chain-link fences, maybe electric, but at least with razor ribbon rolled heavily across the tops. We didn't speak the language, we didn't know the territory, and we didn't have any money.

"Well, there's gotta be a way out," Jeff said with increasing intensity. His eyes looked strange, his voice sounded tense. "There's always a way. Has to be. Nothing is set. There's always a way around any obstacle, you can count on that."

Thomas reacted to this with a kind of edgy timidity. He wasn't sure what to make of Jeff. Jeff was one of those guys who hugged everybody. He always seemed pleasant and was very emotional. He was unabashed about crying or showing any emotion to anyone. He had shown Thomas his super friendly side. But this – this was another side of Jeff that Thomas hadn't seen; even I hadn't seen him like this. Jeff was determined and focused, but not in a good way – in a scary way.

We spent that day organizing our belongings. We found a couple of raggedy foam pads so we could build up our beds a bit. Thomas took us around the prison and introduced us to a lot of the guys. They all seemed like a bunch of college kids, guys like us, just living their lives and trying to make the best of it. Not criminals, not convicts, just a bunch of guys. Then again, that is what we were, until we bought that weed.

In general, people were there for drug possession and trafficking. We hardly met anyone who committed a serious or violent crime. Of course, there were 850 inmates in the prison and we only met the ones in *pabellones seis* and *siete*. Evidently, these cellblocks were the cool cellblocks. Guys in these two *pabellones* were younger. They were in for drugs and still liked to get high. Some had money from the outside, and their cells were filled with nicer stuff and their lives were much better.

Pabellones uno through *tres* were mostly older guys there for more serious crimes, like assault and robbery. *Pabellon quatro* had a mix of inmates. *Pabellon cinco* was the gay/trans cellblock; everyone there was a transvestite, transgender, or gay. Many dressed in women's clothing and acted like females. A lot of the inmates would visit *pabellon cinco* for sexual favors.

We headed back to our cellblock at lunch and then again at dinner for the *yegua*. If this was all I had to eat for a couple of years, it was going to be tough on my body. The next morning, Arturo and Martín came by our cell. Martín rapped on the bars and said they were on their way to eat breakfast at the restaurant and asked we want to go with them? We didn't have much money left, so we decided to save it.

For those who didn't want to eat *yegua*, there were several options. One was a restaurant run by a couple of inmates who had the concession. The food there was costly. Martín and Arturo ate there often. We stepped out into the hallway to talk with Martín for a moment, and he asked if we were interested in playing basketball. There was a team from another prison coming to play against us. I nodded, Jeff only shrugged. He gave us the time of the game and told us to be at the gym early so we could warm up and go over the game plan.

After they walked away, Thomas said, "They never ask me to play basketball. I guess I am always too loaded."

After breakfast, Thomas took us to meet the *comandante*. He had a pretty secretary who assisted him and she took us into his office where we sat down in front of his desk. Thomas waited outside in her office.

The *comandante* didn't look up until after she walked out. He was a short, stout man with a long handlebar mustache. It was hard to tell his actual height though, since he was wearing an enormous cowboy hat and thick-soled cowboy boots. If he had a pair of pistols, I would have sworn he was Yosemite Sam on vacation in Acapulco. There was a door on the other side of the office that evidently went to the outside.

Gloria from the Consulate was there as well. I began to think this meant something good was going to happen. They'd changed their minds and were going to let us go. But Gloria told us she had informed our families of our situation and as soon as we got a chance, we should call them. Also, the sooner we hired a lawyer and got sentenced, the sooner we could apply for a transfer to the States.

The *comandante* explained all of the dos and don'ts of the prison and the Mexican legal system. Visits were Saturday and Sunday mornings. To use the phone, we had to put in a request and wait our turn. We would be allowed conjugal visits after the first time we had visitors if our wives were approved. He asked if we were married and we both nodded.

He got up, came around, and sat on the front of his desk. I noticed his chair had a couple of extra cushions to boost him up. The *comandante* gave me the okay to call my wife.

I could go ahead and do it now and wouldn't have to wait to put in a request. Jeff wasn't interested in calling anyone.

Jeff and I never did mention we weren't really married. Well, I was technically married but had filed for divorce. I figured since I was in prison, I would most certainly be divorced soon. Jeff had a girlfriend.

Later we learned many couples in Mexican prisons aren't married, at least legally. They live together and call each other husband and wife. It's just a term. So a lot of guys in the prison had conjugal visits, even though they were supposed to be with legal wives only. The prison didn't want to be associated with prostitution, so everybody called the women who came to visit them their "wife."

The *comandante* told me to go into the next room with his secretary and make the call. When I got Kate on the phone, I heard all the things I expected. She was very worried and concerned. Even though we'd split and I had filed for divorce, she was still a friend. I could tell she wanted to talk about our relationship, but I was standing there with people in the office, including Thomas. Jeff and the *comandante* were on the other side of the door. I could hear them, so I was sure they could hear me.

I couldn't get into it with her. For some odd reason, I didn't want to sound weak and mushy. I suppose I was holding on to some kind of dignity: I had made this choice, I was going to see it through, and I didn't want people – including Kate – to feel sorry for me. And I didn't want the prison staff to think I was some kind of baby. So I kept it cool.

I told her not to worry, that it wasn't like *Midnight Express*. I did, however, mention I needed money for a lawyer. She told me she and my parents were planning to drive down to Hermosillo the following week. I told her about the weekend visits and to plan on that. I would need some of my things, and I asked if maybe she could sell all the stuff in my apartment and bring me what I needed. She sounded sad and a little angry. She really expected more from me. She wanted to hear me say I loved her, that I had changed my mind, that I missed her and needed her. Before I hung up, I said, "Oh, can you also bring all of my plays? I may end up starting a theatre group."

I knew she was taken aback. She expected me to sound frightened and perhaps defeated. They were all back at home scared out of their wits about our desperate situation, and here I was, excited about starting a theatre group in a foreign prison. It was an uncomfortable call and I must have seemed, to her, a bit incoherent. But I didn't know how to make her feel okay, and she didn't know how to tell me what she needed from me. That was likely one of the reasons we were getting divorced in the first place.

When I went back in the *comandante's* office, there was another man talking to Jeff. He was dressed in a light grey suit and tie. His name was Pedro Villareal and he was an acquaintance of the *comandante*. He had a skin disorder that kept all the pigment in certain areas of his face. I found out later the inmates called him "Pinto" because his face looked a bit like a pinto bean. Pedro seemed quite nice and was trying to help us. He gave his card to Jeff, who seemed completely uninterested, almost rude. I was starting to get mad at Jeff. After a moment, Pedro shook my hand and left, accompanied by Gloria.

The *comandante* explained how Pedro was honest, but he was not the kind of lawyer who would get people out "quicker." This he said looking mostly at Jeff. That was fine by me. I wanted to get sentenced, then get on the transfer list. It seemed like the only option. Jeff, on the other hand, wanted something quite different. He wanted a lawyer who would find some way to get him out now. Evidently, he had told the *comandante* that while I was making my call.

"If you're looking for an attorney who can make big things happen, you should know that they are expensive," said the *comandante*. It was difficult to understand him, but he knew enough English to communicate simple concepts.

"I totally understand," I said, then I turned to Jeff. "You better go in there and make a phone call or you won't be able to afford any kind of lawyer."

Jeff stared at me for a moment, then got up, thanked the *comandante*, and left. Before I left, I mentioned to the *comandante* I would like to start giving English lessons as soon as I learned a bit more Spanish. The *comandante* thought it was a good idea and told me he would like some lessons himself. We shook hands, and he told me to take care of my friend, he didn't look too good. I shook my head and left.

On the way back to the *sala de guardia*, I saw Jeff talking to a man at the holding tank area, which was a very large cell where they put the inmates coming and going into the prison, or those who had committed an offense while inside and had to be removed from the main population. It was dirty and there was no place to sleep.

The guy was a tall Caucasian with a lean, sallow face and hardened, dark eyes. "Holy fuck, man, it is great to talk to Americans," he said as he spat on the floor. "These fucking spics are crazy!" I saw Jeff smile for the first time that day. Not his pleasant smile, but one with an underlying darkness.

The guy's name was Wells. He was arrested outside a warehouse with 250 pounds of high-grade Columbian marijuana. He scoffed and spat again. "They can't prove shit. Oh they tried. They stuffed my head in a toilet and beat the shit out of me for a couple of days, but I didn't give them a fart!"

Jeff laughed and asked if he knew anything about the US transfer. "I ain't gonna do that, man, I won't be here long enough. My people will get me out of here in a couple of days. Shit, I got warrants over there longer'n my dick! And don't ask me to show you." He laughed at that one until he coughed. "Ya transfer to the States and the record goes with you, and that is what they fucking want, man. So the feds can keep track of who's running dope."

I was trying to pull Jeff away as one of the guards called to us to come back to the *sala de guardia*. As we left, Wells asked, "You got any warrants or records?" Jeff shook his head as we turned and began walking toward the guard who was motioning for us to get going.

Wells hollered after us, "Well, get your folks to bring you some money, get a good lawyer, and you'll be out of here like a cheap fuck." Though I don't think Jeff heard him, he spat again and mumbled, "Dumb fucking kids."

As we went back into the inmate side of the prison, I said to Jeff, "I didn't like that guy's vibe at all. He's got the wrong advice for us."

Jeff disagreed. "He knows what is up, he's been around. I think we have other options here we don't know about. I want to talk to him more. I've got some ideas about what to do. It's not just the transfer."

"Jeff, seriously, man. Call Arlene and your mom, and have them come down here. We will find an honest, inexpensive lawyer to work our case. We can do some plays, play some music, and write our stories. Then we can go home."

Jeff looked at me scornfully. "I can't talk to my girlfriend in front of these people."

"Well, you have to do something, man!"

"I don't have to do anything. And I'm not ready to just give up and stay in this shitty fucking place." He had something on his mind and I didn't like it.

I was the one who got us into this mess. I wanted the adventure. It was my idea to go to Mexico, drive my truck after reporting it stolen, and trade it for drugs. I mean, come on! What is that if not a great, big, stupid fucking fantasy. And yet here I was, ready to go with the flow. Follow the rules. Make my decisions according to appropriate suggestions. This was life now. There was no way to change it. We needed to live in the moment and do it the best way we could.

Jeff wanted to keep fighting, buy his way out, or dig a hole under the wall, I didn't know. Anything but stay here and follow a normal routine. Now he was the one living a fantasy. How did we flip flop like that?

As we walked through the main gate, Martín came running up to us carrying a basketball and an extra jersey. "We need an extra player! *La Pinta Vieja*. Which one of you wants to play?" He was mostly speaking to me.

Quickly and enthusiastically I said, "I want to play!" I was going to start joining in and making the best of things whether Jeff did or not. If playing basketball was a thing to occupy my time, then that's what I was going to do.

Martín tossed me the jersey like he was expecting me to say yes, then nudged me toward the gym with his hand on my shoulder. "*Es la pinta vieja, Gabacho, la pinta vieja! Duro, muy duro!*" I trotted along eagerly, trying to comprehend what he was saying as Jeff stood there with his hands in his pockets and watched us go.

I couldn't understand Martín's comments. I thought basketball must be something the prison allowed to keep the inmates occupied. Everybody played to have fun, not too serious. I wasn't much of a ball player, but I was taller than most of the other guys, so I figured I could hold up my end.

When we got to the gym, I couldn't see anything unusual about the other team. They were a bit smaller than us perhaps, but that was it. I looked around and it seemed the entire prison population had come out to watch the game, even some of the guards. That seemed odd. But I thought, *Maybe that's what they do.* They all come out to watch a dumb basketball game because there's not much else to do. It is prison after all.

When the game started, though, it was clear it was taken seriously. These guys played like gladiators, not basketball players. I was pushed and shoved around like we were on a football field. It was violent and aggressive. Everyone, including my team, was playing for real. *Shit, these guys are playing to win!*

It took me a few minutes to get my bearings. It'd been so long since I played basketball, I was having trouble managing the ball. The spectators were excited, cheering loudly whenever a shot was made by our team.

There were two players on the other team who were especially aggressive. One was short and stocky with long, mangy brown hair and a thin goatee. The other was a bit taller, with a thin, wiry body. He had straight black hair and appeared to be Native Mexican, one of the indigenous tribes of Sonora. In Mexico, they refer to them as *Indios*, and they tend to be Aztec or Olmec. Whatever he was, they both seemed to hate me. Somehow, I ended up being the object of their aggression. They clearly wanted to hurt me.

I got bashed around, pushed from behind, even tripped. It was another of those situations I couldn't seem to grasp. It was so surreal. They didn't know me; I had never played before. I had no history with them or anyone they knew, and yet there was a distinct hatred and an unmistakable assault directed at me.

So then I started getting more aggressive. In fact, I was getting pretty mad. The game was becoming more of a fight than anything. The inmates watching the game were shouting and cheering feverishly. Someone got a bloody nose. Another guy had a cut lip. This wasn't basketball anymore. It was an all-out battle!

Martín shot and missed, and I jumped for a rebound. As I went up, the short, mangy guy pushed me from behind while I was in the air. Not an accident or a body block, but a deliberate push in the back with both hands as hard as he could. I slammed into a wall beyond the basket. He grabbed the loose ball and took off down the court. Now I was really pissed. I jumped up as fast as lightning, though the wind had been knocked out of me and my head was bleeding. I ran down the court after him, yelling every obscenity I could think of, trying to get in a few in Spanish.

The short guy threw down the ball and came running right up to me, a couple of inches from my face, then growled like an animal, flailing his arms about my head. I was so stunned and surprised that I stopped for a moment staring at him, still confused by the surrealism of it all. *What the fuck? People don't growl, animals do.* Martín ran up behind me and quickly pulled me away, saying, "*Calmete, Gabacho, calmete.*"

The ref gave the ball to the other team and we played on. As the game continued, no one said anything and none of the guards acting as referees called any fouls. In fact, not one foul was called during the entire game. I didn't understand why the refs weren't doing their job. No one seemed to care that the game was way out of hand. Not even Martín.

Then Martín and the guy with the long black hair, the Native Mexican-looking guy, both went up for a rebound, fighting for the ball. The guy pushed Martín to the floor, completely forgetting about the ball. Martín kicked his legs out from under him and he fell. Both he and the Native Mexican were kicking at each other while on the floor. This brought the mangy-haired, growling guy into the fray. He jumped on Martín, pummeling him with his fists.

It all happened so fast I didn't have time to think about it, but I was so mad by then, I jumped on the short guy and ripped him away from Martín and threw him to the floor. I was ready to tear it up, I was so angry. By then I had absolutely no concern for my life or any repercussions I might receive for fighting.

As the mangy-haired, growling guy jumped up toward me with venom in his eyes, the refs blew the whistle and the other players began intervening. They pulled the fighting players apart and separated us. I got pulled away by someone and held by a couple of guys, as did the short, mangy-haired growler.

Guards quickly stepped in to make sure we all stopped fighting. The refs called the game a tie, and everyone on both teams accepted it except me. We were ahead, and I was still mad about the fight, and even madder they didn't call the game for us. But I was the only one who wanted the game called in our favor. Martín came up and grabbed me by the shoulder, pulling me aside, saying again, *"Calmete,*

Gabacho, calmete." He was laughing a little, as though I was acting like a spoiled child.

The inmates who'd been watching the game were yelling and laughing and calling out names of their friends on both teams. They were having a great time. I guess this was what they had come for. They knew it was going to be a fight. They wanted to see the blood fly.

I was confused and frustrated. What had happened? I didn't know. Everyone started moving out of the gym. What had seemed to me like a big fight was now over and no one was the least bit upset. I walked outside, where I ran into Thomas and a couple of his friends. They were laughing and talking about the game.

Everyone acted like their team had won. It was as though I was walking out of the stadium on college game day. They were all happy and shouting and laughing. People were looking at me and giving me some kind of thumbs up sign.

I walked up to Thomas, a bit bewildered. "What the hell was that?"

Thomas was smiling. "Do you know who that team was? Those guys you fought with? Did you know who they were?"

"Fuck no, I didn't know shit." I was just trying to play a game of basketball.

"That was the team from the old prison. Those guys, all of them, used to be here. When things were crazy and violent. Guys got killed over little things. We used to have to carry bats to protect ourselves, me and Martín. The two guys you fought with are two of the biggest murderers in Hermosillo, ever! The little guy is called *El Mato Venado*, the deer killer."

He went on. "A *mato venado* is a huge white spider that lives here in the desert. It can kill a baby deer with its bite. You'll find them here in the prison sometimes. They are really dangerous, man. *El Mato Venado*, the short guy. He is so small and so fiery, but he's killed at least twelve or thirteen people. He even killed guys here in prison. He and that other guy with long, straight hair fought all the guys in *pabellon siete* one day. Just the two of them, fighting all the rest with chains and knives and rocks." He explained how this was the incident which made the officials move those guys to the old prison, and now when they came to play basketball, everyone watched. Everyone was waiting to see blood.

"You know, man, you are famous now!" Thomas said. "You are one of the only guys to fight with *El Mato Venado* and live, so I don't think you're going to have problems in the prison now. These guys saw you take him on and now they think you are one bad fucking dude!"

CHAPTER 9

ON THE WAY back to my cell, I noticed many of the inmates watching me. Some made congratulatory gestures. None of inmates were aware I didn't know how dangerous the guys I fought with were. All they saw was me, an American, risking my safety, maybe my life, to come to the aid of Martín, for nothing more than a basketball game. My street cred had gone through the roof.

When I got to my cell, Jeff was in his bed, reading. Thomas was close behind me, looking very excited. Thomas was elated, in fact. It seemed all of the inmates were now referring to me as *El Gabacho*.

"What exactly does that mean?" I asked.

Thomas laughed. "Well, for Mexicans, a *gabacho* is a fat American who wears plaid shorts and has a camera hanging around his neck. But the way they're saying it is altogether different. It's like, cool. You should be a-okay with everyone around here from now on. I've seen Americans here in the past, and they didn't do so well. But I think you are going to have it better."

Jeff was ignoring the conversation. He glanced up from his book once or twice, and only when he'd thought I wasn't looking.

Martín came quickly into the cell, full of big energy. That was normal for him. I'd begun to find out Martín went everywhere quickly. Like many high-strung people, Martín was also quick tempered. He had a low attention span too. He couldn't stay focused very long on anything. In fact, the only thing he could do for longer than a New York minute was watch *Las Chivas*, his favorite soccer team from Guadalajara, play.

He slapped my shoulder. "*Ese, Gabacho! Estas Fuerte, no?* Come to dinner, okay? You guys come too." He took a moment to look around at each of us, grinned and nodded his head, then ran back out as quickly as he had come in.

As I cleaned out some cuts on my knees and forehead, I thought to myself how much I needed to learn the language, and fast. There was going to be little we could do to pass the time if we didn't learn to speak Spanish. Communication is everything. And language is its main ingredient.

I thought back to when my wife and I had gone to Mexico on our honeymoon. Kate spoke Spanish pretty well because she and her family had lived there for several years when she was a girl. Her father was an artist who painted Western-style art – horses and cowboys and lots of wildlife. That was how he made a living Kate's entire life. When he started out, he didn't have a lot of income from it, so he moved his wife and three children to Mexico while he developed his art career. They could live there much cheaper, and he wouldn't have to give up his dream of being a painter. Kate went to school in a small town where they only spoke Spanish, so she learned quickly. I thought to myself, as I applied a piece of duct tape to a particularly large cut on my leg, that if she could do it at five years old, why couldn't I learn the damn language myself? I certainly had enough time to do so.

The idea became my single-minded purpose. I didn't focus on anything else for weeks. I was going to lay it out there. I was going to make a fool of myself and try to speak whenever I could, then let people correct me if I did it wrong. If I didn't learn to speak Spanish and learn it quickly, I could see myself just lying in bed all day, masturbating like so many guys did.

Some inmates fell into a malaise. Nothing could get them moving. That was not going to happen to me, but I could see it beginning to happen to Jeff. I didn't know what to do. I was sure I couldn't help him and myself at the same time. He would have to do his own thing and live with it.

I picked up the little English/Spanish dictionary Gloria gave us and put it in my back pocket as we hustled off to Martín's cell for dinner.

Over the next few weeks, I watched TV in Martín and Arturo's cell with the little dictionary in my hand. As the actors spoke, I sounded out the words and used the book to try and make sense of what they were saying.

Their cell had cream-colored walls. A curtain divided the sleeping area and kitchen. Martín was sautéing strips of beef with tomatoes, onions, and chilies. *Una bandera* he called it. You could buy a kilo bag from one of the inmates who tended a garden inside the prison. It contained some small tomatoes, a couple of onions, and a number of serrano or jalapeño chilies. Just like the Mexican flag: red, white, and green. Therefore, *una bandera*: Spanish for flag.

This was a common meal inside the prison for those who had a little money. A couple of the inmates kept refrigerators and others made tortillas. Two or three had gardens. The growing season is longer in the Sonoran Desert, and you could buy a bag of vegetables just about any time, along with beef, chicken, pork, and tortillas. Most guys had a small hot plate in their cells and could fry some beef with the *bandera* and serve it with fresh, hot tortillas and Coca-Cola. Yeah, guys even had sodas for sale. Just about anything was for sale inside the prison. Even sex, if you were willing to have it with another man.

After dinner, we watched a popular Mexican variety/comedy show. More and more inmates arrived as the night went on. Martín and Arturo split one bunk, and the other two were packed with guys like sardines. There were guys sitting in the kitchen area, on the floor, anywhere they could find space.

I couldn't believe how many people could fit into a single cell. There must have been twenty-five to thirty of us in there in no time at all. I couldn't tell if it was a normal evening or if Martín had let everyone show up to meet the new guys. Later, I learned Martín liked to befriend Americans. He fancied the American lifestyle: listened to American music, watched American sports, and kept an American wardrobe. He was our guy, and he wanted all the other inmates to know.

Jeff came along with us, seemingly in a better mood. Of course, everyone was feeling good because we smoked a lot of weed. A couple inmates had brought some great stuff and it was one reason Martín allowed them all to join us. He loved to get high, and since he didn't have a lot of money himself, he would find the people who did, including Arturo. Soon we began talking and joking so Martín turned the sound down on the TV. Jeff and I couldn't really follow a lot of what was being said, so Thomas interpreted. We were beginning to meet a lot of new guys, some of whom would turn out to be friends.

Samuel and Godoy were among the inmates there that night. Samuel had played on the basketball team with us that day, but I hadn't known who he was. It was unusual for them to make that kind of appearance, I learned later. For some reason, this particular night was different. Guys who didn't usually hang out with Martín were all gathered in his cell for this moment.

Samuel and Godoy were known as "the terrorists" but that wasn't really accurate. The state government had used those words to describe them when they were prosecuted and the inmates continued to think of them in that way.

In reality, Samuel and Godoy had been student activists who were convicted of killing a policeman. Their side of the story was quite different. They had been involved in a Mexican student revolt, the Tlatelolco Massacre of 1968, where three hundred protesters were killed in the Plaza de las Tres Culturas in Mexico City.

That event, and others during that time, were considered part of the Mexican Dirty War, when the government used its forces to suppress political opposition. The massacre occurred ten days before the opening of the 1968 Summer Olympics in Mexico City. Arising from a reaction to the government's violent repression, the student movement in Mexico City quickly grew to include large segments of students across the country who were dissatisfied with the regime of the PRI (Mexico's ruling political party for fifty years prior). The students were united by a desire for a stronger democracy, but their understandings of what democracy meant varied widely.

Throughout Mexico, students began to fight with government forces in an attempt to bring down the repressive regime of the president at that time, Gustavo Díaz Ordaz. However, many of the regular citizens did not support the movement because they felt it was based on socialist ideas.

Samuel and Godoy were part of a group of students from the University of Hermosillo who became tagged as terrorists.

They hid in the hills outside Hermosillo and fought with military units. One night, they went into town to rob a bank for money to support their cause. A policeman was killed in the attempt. It was never actually proved who shot the policeman, but he was well known in town and beloved by the people.

Both men – along with Samuel's wife, Grace, and several others – were convicted of murder and terrorism and sentenced to thirty years. The main prison population didn't consider them heroes; they were viewed as socialists and radicals. They'd roomed together from the start of their incarceration and had kept pretty much to themselves. But after seven or eight years, they were finally becoming integrated into the prison population. Samuel played on Martín's basketball team. Martín didn't particularly like Samuel, but Martín was nothing if not practical. He wanted to win at any cost, in whatever he did. Martín actually preferred the PRI party and its more conservative politics, and he was a big fan of Ronald Reagan. But he could overlook anything – even a committed socialist – if it brought him some kind of success or triumph.

Martín turned off the television as Diego started playing guitar. People kept passing around joints. Diego was very good and played Brazilian-style jazz. I put down my dictionary for the night and simply tried to follow the conversations. Diego suddenly gave his guitar to Jeff, who fumbled with it for a minute, then handed it to me, saying I was the guitar player.

I really wanted to play something amazing and impress them with my artistic abilities. If I were going to start any kind of arts group, I may as well begin it here. They were staring at me, waiting, so I hammered out some fast blues licks so they could see I played well. They perked up. "Maybe this *gabacho* is an artist," I could imagine them thinking. But I couldn't think of a song to play. I had spent so many years studying theatre, I couldn't remember any of the rock songs I had known. What was I going to do? Play a tune from Stephen Sondheim's *Sweeney Todd*? That wouldn't cut it with this crowd. These guys wouldn't know anything about theatre. I leaned over to Thomas, who was sitting nearby, and told him, in English (so no one could understand), I couldn't remember any rock songs. All I knew was a bunch of theatre stuff, and I didn't think they'd dig it. All of a sudden, he blurted out, "How about something from *Jesus Christ Superstar*?"

They all went crazy. The minute Thomas said those words, the guys were chanting and singing phrases from the show. "*Jesu Christo Superestrella*," they shouted, over and over.

It was another amazing coincidence. I'd gotten into a fight with *El Mato Venada* that day and accidentally made myself look like some kind of super tough guy. And now this … *Jesus Christ Superstar*. I didn't believe in guardian angels or anything like that, but if they did exist, they were with me now.

Jesus Christ Superstar was the reason I had gone into theatre. I played in rock bands all through my high school and post-high school years. I moved to Los Angeles to make it in the big city, maybe find a great band to play with. I did play in a band for a bit, but with no success. Then I became friends with some gay guys. They took me under their wing and showed me some things about life I had not known growing up Mormon in conservative Utah. While I wasn't interested in having sex with them, I did like learning about food, wine, and the arts.

They taught me to cook and showed me the difference between single malt and blended whiskey. I learned the stuff you shake out of the green can is not real Parmesan cheese and you can find shops off Melrose Ave for cool clothes at a great price. They played showtunes and taught me a lot about film, theatre, and performing arts.

When *Jesus Christ Superstar* came out, I fell in love. For me, it was amazing. It had the elements I couldn't find in radio pop music. There was a great story driven by a fantastic score. It was an idea I'd never considered in rock and roll.

Soon after, out came *Tommy* by The Who, and suddenly I began to be attracted to a new kind of music. Big, edgy rock music, staged in a grand setting with a story supported by the music.

After a year, I went back to Utah, checked into the university, and signed up for theatre classes, but I continued playing in rock bands in order to bring the two genres together.

I tried telling my counselors and teachers what I wanted to do, but they thought I was loony. Rock music didn't mix with musical theatre; they were two different genres. But if that was my goal, then I'd first have to learn the trade – the craft of musical theatre. In order to go forward with my dream, I had to learn to sing, dance, and act. Then I could try my hand at creating rock musicals if I was so inclined.

During my six years in school, I had learned a lot of theatre material. One of my favorites was a particular song from *Jesus Christ Superstar*, "In the Garden of Gethsemane." It was sung by Ian Gillan of Deep Purple on the original cast album. I had never gotten a chance to do the show. I did play Judas in *Godspell*, but that was musical comedy, not big rock on stage. Ian Gillan had turned me into a guy who wanted to sing great big rock songs on a stage with sets and cool lighting and special effects. I had learned and worked on the song for that reason. I had it down cold. I could do all the high notes, the screams, and the hard rock vocals, just like Ian on the original album. But I had never sung it for anyone but myself.

That all crossed my mind in the short moment while everyone was staring at me.

"Yeah, I know one song from the show," I said. "How about 'In the Garden of Gethsemane'?"

There were whoops and hollers; everyone was so excited to hear that tune. I couldn't believe it. They all knew the song. They'd just seen a performance from the touring group from Mexico City. On top of that, there's the Catholicism, crucifixion, and atonement, all of which were important elements in their lives.

There I was, sitting down, not warmed up. I wasn't sure if I could remember all the chords. I could sing it all right, but I had usually sung along with the record and had not accompanied myself.

I started doubting my ability to do it. I didn't want to screw up. I really wanted to make an impression. It's difficult to perform a song like that. Not your typical "sing around the campfire" kind of number. You really have to belt it out, scream and everything. There were twenty-five guys in a tiny room about the size of a large bathroom. I was sitting next to people, inches from my face. And they were so ready for me to play and sing.

If I'm ever going to sing this song for the perfect audience, this is it, I thought. Where would it mean more? Where would it have a bigger impact? I just fought *El Mato Venado* and made a lot of new friends. *If I'm going to make this time in prison work for me and not fall into depression and self-pity, I need to start right fucking now!*

I began the guitar intro. They completely shut up. No one uttered a sound.

And then I started. "I ... only want to say ... if there is a way ... take this cup away from me ... for I don't want to taste its poison..."

And that was it. It was one of the only times in my entire life when a song, a piece of art, actually made sense. Mirrored the situation. Had a deep impact on me as well as on those listening.

I felt Andrew Lloyd Webber and Tim Rice had written this song for me and this moment. I didn't know how it sounded. I didn't know if I was singing on key. I had no sense of the performance. I was completely lost in the words and the music and the moment.

It's was one huge whirling mass of human emotion, no separation between artist and art.

That was the only time it ever happened for me. There, in the Sonoran Desert, in prison in Hermosillo, in front of those inmates. Everyone listened to the entire song. Then a loud cheer went up when I finished. I didn't really think it was for me. It was for the moment and for the song.

We had all experienced some kind of pain in our own "Gardens of Gethsemane." Most of the guys in the room had been tortured. Jeff and I had been through a lot too. And we were going to have to face even more.

There was pleading, begging, and penitence. We wanted absolution. Forgiveness. *Please, don't make us have to live through this pain.*

"Take this cup away from me. I don't want to taste its poison." Yet, like *Jesu Christo*, I knew full well there was no other way.

CHAPTER 10

I FELL IN love with falling in love. That's the best way to describe why I got married. I relished the courting, the first few dates, and getting to know someone intimately. I was tired of one-night stands and the random sex we had in college. As a musical theatre student, I spent all my time in the dance and theatre departments where there was an imbalance of straight females to straight males; I would say at least four to one. And with so many late night rehearsals, no one had a chance to go out to bars and parties. Needless to say, there was a lot of interdepartmental sex, and for me, it got boring. I longed for a committed relationship, something substantial.

But as it turned out, I wasn't so good at maintaining a long-term relationship and working to satisfy my partner while keeping my own needs in play. Once I fell in love, I lost focus, just like with my career path. I wanted do it all over again with someone new. Not for the sex, but for the courtship. It was the adventure and the newness with which I fell in love.

Kate, on the other hand, was amazing. She did everything right; she loved to cook and entertain, she was charming and beautiful, she was smart and talented, graduated magna cum laude – the whole package. She was also a fine actress who worked hard to make a living in Salt Lake City, which is no small feat. But her career kept us apart a lot of nights.

I didn't pursue a degree, I kept changing my focus; from dance to acting to directing to music. I couldn't stay on a single path, so after Kate graduated, I dropped out of college and we got married. I worked construction while she did plays around town as a semi-professional actor.

She was a good partner, but she didn't know how to help me, and I wasn't a very good husband. We floundered, then finally separated for a few months. While she was away visiting family for a few weeks, I met a girl, we had sex, and I thought I was in love again. It started all over. Kate came back and I asked for a divorce. She was having difficulties with me as well and didn't contest it. We sold our house, I moved into an apartment, and she went back home to think it over and reflect on what had happened to us.

It was shortly after that I got the bright idea to go to Mexico, buy cocaine, and become an international drug smuggler. I wanted to put everything on the line, to experience something daring and unfamiliar. So there I was, falling in love with another kind of newness.

Kate had a choice to make when she found out I was in prison. She could step in and help me, or leave me to my own stupidity and selfishness. What would be in it for her? Would I want to get back together? Did she even want to? If she helped me and I changed, would that be the beginning of a better marriage and a healthy relationship, or were we too far gone to start over? In the end, I think it was more a matter of choosing to do the responsible thing and helping the man she had married. How could she give up now in this moment of crisis? That's who she was.

A couple of weeks after Jeff and I landed in prison, Kate, my parents, and my youngest sister made the 1700-mile journey from Salt Lake City to Hermosillo in my parents' rickety old motor home. They were bringing cash for our lawyer and badly needed supplies for us. And, of course, they were worried sick over the situation and in what shape they expected to find me. Everyone envisioned the movie *Midnight Express,* with filthy cells and cruel guards so they were pretty shaken and distraught on the entire drive down.

No one came to see Jeff as he hadn't called to let his family know his circumstances. I urged him to take action, get involved, make a call, do something, but he refused. He and I were fractured; like a marriage that breaks apart after facing a terrible crisis, we couldn't keep it together. We all deal with catastrophe or disaster differently, and Jeff and I couldn't have been farther apart. It was driving a wedge between us that was not likely to help our situation. And that's what troubled me the most.

The visiting area was crowded and the noise deafening. There were at least three hundred people gathered in an area the size of a couple of tennis courts. Children played on the swing-sets and slides off to one side, and a covered patio with tables, benches, and barbeque pits served the inmates and their families. That day, there was going to be a presentation in the auditorium with a mariachi band, so later, the visitors would be allowed into the prison.

Martín was there with his mother and wife, along with his son, younger brother, and sister. I had met them the weekend prior and so I was sitting and talking with them. Jeff didn't have visitors and wasn't allowed to enter the visiting area.

My family and Kate spent the night in my parents' motor home, then got up early to start the process of entering the prison. They waited outside in the hot sun for a couple of hours, then it took another two hours to go through the first-time visitor paperwork, and finally, the humiliation of a full strip-search. The prison officials were much more thorough with the families of Americans because they supposed large amounts of cash or weapons might be smuggled in. Reason being the typical American inmate was an actual drug smuggler with friends and associates who often tried to help them get out.

Martín tapped me on the shoulder and pointed to the entrance with his typical sly grin. He knew immediately who they were. There stood a heavy-set, blond-haired man in blue slacks and a pinstriped shirt. He stuck out like a marshmallow in a vat of chocolate chips. I ran over to him and gave him a hug. It was the first time I had hugged my father since I was a child. A few minutes later, Kate, my mother, and my sister Maria came through the gate. My mother and sister were crying, Kate was frantic, but collected. After the hours-long ordeal and the demeaning disrobing, they were all four extremely upset.

My parents were straight-laced Mormons who lived in a small town in rural Utah. They had never known anyone who'd been in prison and never, in their wildest nightmares, had imagined visiting one of their own, their flesh and blood, in a Mexican prison. For the first time in my life, I felt preeminently grateful to them. In a matter of a few moments, the experience erased years of conflict and arguments over religion and politics. We hugged and kissed and hugged again.

We all sat down with Martín's family, and I took special care introducing his mother. She was very astute, and an indelibly strong woman who raised her four children alone because she and her husband divorced early. Both Martín and his mother were very kind to my family and made them feel at ease and more comfortable. Martín's wife was also helpful, and Martín's son, about five years old, was cute as button. He ran around and played, completely fearless, engaging with anyone and everyone. That was, no doubt, the thing that calmed my family the most, seeing a little boy happily playing.

They couldn't stop hugging me and wanted to wrap me up in their arms and sneak me out, but that was not to be. I began to get annoyed. I never enjoyed a lot of drama and emotion over sad or scary things. My mother was almost always crying about something, and my father was almost always mad about something. They hardly ever laughed and were not the kind of people you would describe as easygoing. So I went the opposite direction in my life, rarely taking anything seriously.

Case in point: going to Mexico to buy drugs seemed like a fun thing to do. No problem. It would be a snap.

At last my folks began to calm down, they could see the prison wasn't as bad as they had anticipated, especially with the support of Martín's family. The gates opened and we all went inside the main body of the prison, which, unfortunately, reinvigorated their fears. They were now completely inside a Mexican prison, with all the inmates, the razor ribbon, and the twenty-five-foot concrete walls. I could sense my dad was concerned they might never get out again. It's rather disconcerting to walk inside a prison for the first time, especially for non-inmates. There's always a sense of impending doom, as though a prison riot or some other chaos could bring everything crashing down.

I began showing them around the prison, doing so in a cavalier way: talking too much, making the occasional joke. I knew I was being nonchalant, maybe even a bit insensitive, but I didn't know what else to do. I needed to make them feel like everything was going to be all right or they might never have left Hermosillo, and I couldn't have that. So I made the prison seem like a big, happy college campus.

We went into the gym, and I regaled them with the story of the basketball game (leaving out the part about *El Mato Venado*). Then we went into the auditorium and I mentioned how *Jesus Christ Superstar* had been performed there and how I was planning to start a theatre group.

This all seemed crazy to them, I could tell. They hadn't really accepted the fact I would be here for quite a while, perhaps a couple of years, and here I was, planning my life in prison as a theatre director. They'd expected a living hell, and most certainly, the prison had been very much like that a few months prior. But now it was different. It was still a foreign prison: we were facing difficult laws, and had no idea when we'd get out, and there were some rather dangerous people around. But our lives were not as terrible as they had expected and I wanted them to see that.

At last we wandered into the café. I was hoping they might eat something since they hadn't eaten well for a couple of days. But they were afraid to eat the food and kept looking around nervously, anticipating something terrible, as though the guards would put on handcuffs and lock them up too. I ordered a couple of quesadillas and some sodas to try and quell their fears.

We sat down and a few moments later, Jeff came in and joined us. Kate handed him a letter from his girlfriend. She had told Arlene about our plight and Arlene had called Jeff's mother. His mom was going to wire money to him so he could help pay the lawyer and have living expenses. I had given Kate Pedro's name and contact number to give to Jeff's mother. All this had happened behind his back and I could tell Jeff was not happy about it. But evidently, he didn't want to make a scene in front of my parents, so he said nothing, not even "thank you."

Everyone was uncomfortable for a long moment, then the *comandante* came in, saw us sitting there, and came over to introduce himself. I was relieved; it broke the uneasiness hanging over the group. The *comandante*, always the consummate PR spokesperson, was friendly, jovial, and charming. He made Kate and my family feel better about leaving. He clearly tried to make a good impression and even joked around a bit before sitting down to lunch at a nearby table. Meeting the *comandante* was the moment my parents finally began to settle into the fact that yes, their son was in a Mexican prison and would be there for some time. But he might be okay.

A couple of guards entered the café and announced the visit was over and all the guests had to leave. I was actually glad to see them go. It was difficult holding my emotions at bay. I never liked being the center of attention, and weepy, sentimental feelings of concern. I would rather have people ignore me than gush over me or wrap me in some kind of schmaltzy endearment.

But I did want to see Kate alone for a moment, so as my family got up to leave (my dad was never one to question authority and jumped up the moment they said it was time to exit), I walked over to the *comandante* and asked if I could see my wife in a conjugal visit. He said that conjugal visits had to be planned in advance and it would have to be the next time she came, but he would allow us to visit a bit longer in his office.

My parents and sister hugged me goodbye. My mom was crying, but they all seemed more lighthearted than when they first entered the visiting area like frightened sheep headed for slaughter. I walked them through the *sala de guardia*, then Kate and I were escorted to a little room off the *comandante's* office. It was a small room with a desk and chairs, used by attorneys to meet with their inmate clients. Just outside the room were prison staff and a couple of guards, but none spoke English, so Kate and I could converse freely.

Once inside the room, I immediately launched into all the plans and big ideas I had for my prison life. I was going to move up very fast. I was confident and powerful, not the meek and grateful man she had half-expected to see. I was as cocky and arrogant as the guy she was divorcing.

"Rick," she said with some exasperation, "don't you think you're being a little crazy? How do you plan to get all the supplies and other things you would need for a theatre group? That's so ambitious."

Kate always called me *Rick*, the name I used in high school. I didn't go by *Richard* until after I moved out of my parents' home to go to college. I hadn't used the name before because it was my dad's name; he was Richard and I was nothing like him. He was a religious conservative who'd been a member of the John Burch society. That's what Richard meant to me. But on my first day at the University of Utah, the instructor called my name as it was written on her roll and I accepted the moniker from then on.

Why Kate called me by my high school name, I don't know. She never gave me a reason. She met me after I went by Richard, but upon hearing a few of my old high school friends call me Rick, she started calling me by that name and dropped Richard. Does the pet name your significant other calls you have something to do with the way they see you? Does it impact your relationship? Would things have been different between us if she had thought of me as Richard?

"Rick, why not just settle in for a while and see what's going to happen with your case? Try to …" She trailed off as she saw my reaction.

Kate had driven twenty long hours in a motor home with my parents, taking turns driving with my father. She was tired, scared, and confused about the entire situation, especially our personal situation. Were we now a couple again? Was she working to help her husband or a friend?

I wasn't sharp with her, I didn't need to be. I simply said, "This is a great opportunity. I can make something happen here. I'm going to be in prison for a year or two, maybe more. That's the deal. There's nothing I can do to alter that outcome. I can't just sit here and do nothing for two years. I'll be too far behind when I get back. I need to keep up, keep moving, do everything I can to get better and better. I'm going to form a theatre group, maybe even get noticed in the news. I need a few things from my apartment. All you have to do is the next time you come down, just bring everything from my apartment. Load it up and bring it all here. I'll make do with whatever you can get."

If she had fallen out of love with me, I couldn't tell from the way she acted that day. I suppose I assumed everything had changed after hearing about me being in prison. She listened quietly and then told me she would do her best to help me. I never doubted she would. At some point, I could tell she'd made a decision to get involved with me again. Maybe she thought we would reunite and get married all over again. Our divorce papers had been submitted and, though the divorce was not official yet, it soon would be.

She gave up trying to convince me. She always gave up arguing with me. Most people did. I was stubborn and refused to give up on an argument. I often didn't know if I even really wanted to do the thing I was pursuing. But if someone told me *no* or tried to talk me out of a thing, I was even more committed, more focused on doing that thing. In fact, it was the force that drove me the most: not the goal I had in mind, but whatever someone didn't want me to do. That was the thing I would often choose.

Then she dropped this bomb. "Jeff's brother has moved into your apartment, along with a couple of his friends. Someone had to pay the rent, and he offered to do it, so we let him have it. Your brother and your Aunt Grace are holding onto your car and piano, but all your plants are dead, and Jeff's bother has taken most everything else. We got out some of your kitchen supplies and a few of your books. But the rest is gone, I'm afraid."

"What the hell? What do you mean, gone?"

She finally became irritated with my complete lack of understanding of the situation and let me have it. "Rick, you took off to Mexico and got caught trying to smuggle drugs into the US. Everyone said you were crazy. Al Brown called me after you left and said how he was afraid you and Jeff were going to get caught. When we got the call from the Consulate, we had almost expected it. Who was going to pay your rent? Pay the utilities? You can't expect everyone to just drop everything in their lives to support you and your adventures! You're being pretty selfish, don't you think? We've driven all this way to come and help you, bring you some comfort, and see if you're all right. And all you talk about is starting a theatre group. You didn't say thanks to your mom and dad, and you've barely showed any kindness at all toward me! You need to get real about this!"

She was right. I had gotten myself in here and it was totally my fault. Not hers. Not my parents'. I was still mad though. I didn't say any more about it, but I couldn't believe my apartment and all my personal things were gone. My brother was driving my car, my aunt had taken my piano into her home, and the rest was gone. My furniture, my house plants, my giant water bed – all my stuff was gone or confiscated by either the *Federales* or Jeff's brother.

I felt terrible. Somehow I had expected that I would be here for a couple of years, then all my stuff would be waiting for me when I got home. Kate was right. Who was going to keep it? She and I had separated and were getting a divorce. She had her own life now and my parents had theirs. And Jeff's brother had mine!

I was devastated. She could see that and didn't say any more. There was no need for her to humiliate me. Kate was too kind, she always cared for other people and how they felt. I was arrogant and cocky and thought everyone should roll over and help me get my life going here in prison. Like they should see how important it was to me and drop everything and give me a hand. Is it ever alright to be selfish, especially when you have something important to do?

Kate set me straight. This was on me; I had to face it the best I could. She could bring me some plays and some kitchen supplies, maybe a few clothes, and that was it. If I were going to start a theatre group or a music band, I would have to use what I could find inside the prison. I would have to work with what I had at hand.

I didn't want to say that to her but I should have. I should have acknowledged she was right and given her credit for what she had done already. But I didn't. I just let it lay there, the really important things left unsaid.

CHAPTER 11

AFTER KATE LEFT, I went back and gathered some clothes and supplies she and my folks had brought me. I stacked it all on a cart and started towing it back to my cell. Occasionally, the guards let us use their four-wheeled carts for transporting our personal goods inside.

As soon as I saw my cell, I realized something was amiss. I rushed inside, looking everywhere, then noticed my brand-new Nike sneakers were gone – the ones I had played basketball in the day before. They were the best sneakers one could buy, light years ahead of any other shoe out there. And they were expensive, especially for a college student. I felt like they helped me run, jump, and play any sport so much better. It had been suggested I placed too much emphasis on the sneakers because I worshipped them, like some kid from the projects. I needed those Nikes more than I needed food. But more than that, realizing someone had gotten in my cell and stolen them pissed me off.

"What the fucking hell!" I shouted. "How could this happen?"

I shook the bars. I kicked the bed and slammed my hands down on the table, sending a bowl of fruit rolling across the floor. It was the realization I was vulnerable that hurt the most, that I was not in control of my personal space. I was in prison. That fact was creeping up on my peace of mind. Like a virus attacking the back of your throat and bringing a cold with it. There's nothing you can do. You know it's coming; you can feel it. There's no preventative measure you can take. You're going to have a stuffy nose, headache, and a nasty cough. It's inevitable; you're going to get sick.

What else could they do to me? What else could I lose? I sang for these inmates, I opened up to them, I was kind, and they fucking stole my sneakers! I put my dick on the chopping block with *El Mato Venado*. Could they not see I was one of them?! "For Crissake!" I screamed one more time.

Right in the middle of my meltdown, Jeff came waddling down the corridor, a towel wrapped around his waist, holding a bottle of shampoo.

I said to him, with no attempt at civility, "God damn it, you left the door unlocked and someone stole my Nikes!" Jeff offered nothing in the way of an apology and mumbled maybe Thomas left it open.

"Shit, man, I need those sneakers. I can't play ball without those sneakers."

"I know how great the shoes are," he said cynically. "I bought them for you. Remember?" He was nonplussed.

Yeah, that's right, I remembered. Jeff had given me the shoes for Christmas barely a couple of weeks ago. God, it seemed like another lifetime. He had come home a few days before Christmas with a shoebox, opened it, and told me to try them on. He already had a pair and was always talking about how great they were. I put the shoes on, and he said, "They're yours. Early Christmas present, man." Then he smiled.

Jeff was better at that than me, he bought presents for people. His girlfriend, his brother, even me.

Jeff looked at me and said, "Listen, Richard, this isn't a good time for you to be giving me a hard time. I'm too upset about you pushing me into a deal with Pedro. I don't know that I want him for a lawyer. Why did you bring that up in front of everyone? I'm working on finding a lawyer who can get us out of here. And if not us, then just me." It was almost a threat.

I stared at him for a moment, incredulous, then I backed off a little. "What are you thinking? Man, we need to get going on our case right now so we can get the hell out of here. There's no time to mess around, Jeff. The sooner we get sentenced, the sooner we can apply for transfer and go home. That's what everyone has told us."

Jeff sneered. "Not everyone. And I am not going to be here long enough to go through all that shit anyway. I talked to some guys who know a few ways out of here. There's a sewer system big enough for a man to crawl through."

I'm sure my eyes rolled up and around. "Jesus, Jeff, I don't know who you're talking to, but no one has gotten out of this prison, ever. Martín has been here for years. Samuel and Godoy even longer. No one has escaped."

"You think Martín knows everything," he said with accusing eyes. "A lot of people don't hold him in such high esteem as you do. You ought to hear what some of the other guys say about him. He'll turn on you, he's not the loyal friend you think he is." I could sense some hurt under his anger.

I shook my head and looked away for a moment. Was he jealous of Martín? I couldn't understand what was going on with Jeff. He was starting to scare me. *Escape through the sewer? What the fuck was that about?* I started thinking that I might have to stay away from Jeff. He could become dangerous and mess up everything – my theatre group, my life here, maybe even getting on the transfer.

"I don't *think* anything about Martín," I said defensively. "I'm not making him out to be anything more than what *I see* he is. He's just a guy who knows the system and he can help us in here." I was getting tired of arguing with Jeff. "An escape attempt is just plain crazy. I don't even want to hear about it," I said, starting to flail about the room. "You can't escape from here, and if you try, it could ruin everything. You might never get a transfer. I don't want anything to do with this, man. I want to learn the language and the customs of these people. I want to start a theatre group, maybe a band. You can do whatever you want. But leave me out of it."

Jeff looked at me blankly. "Fine with me, man." He dropped his towel and sat on the bed naked. I hated that. I didn't want to look at some guy's junk. I thought, *geez, could you put some fucking clothes on?* I walked out of the cell and headed down the hall.

I didn't know what to do about all this shit. Jeff was getting weird, changing into someone I didn't recognize. But then I'm sure he felt the same way about me. It was like getting a divorce; you know it's partly your fault, but all you can think of is how many things the other person does wrong and you're not going to change unless they do.

I decided to go see if Martín could help me get my shoes back. He might know how to find the person who took them. Martín lived in *pabellon siete*, and we were in *pabellon seis*. I went out the main door and crossed the yard to Martín's *pabellon*. He was coming out at the same time. I anxiously told him about my Nikes and asked how I could get them back.

He was smiling the entire time I was telling him about the shoes. Then he shook his head and laughed. "Your shoes are gone, *Gabacho. Olvidalos. Ya estan afuera. Rapido.* You're in the *carcel, Gabacho!*" He grinned at my inability to accept the fact prison was prison. You don't get back the things you lose.

Most of the inmates had no money and no one was helping them from the outside. They were getting by as best they could, eating *yegua* daily, and hoping somebody would get them stoned now and then. A pair of Nike sneakers like mine would buy a guy a couple of months' worth of weed. They were stolen while we were at the visit, that's how they know you're not going to be around. Whoever took them gave them to a visitor to take outside and sell. That's how it went. Guys would reach into your cell with a long stick or broom handle and steal anything they could hook onto, then give it to an accomplice to sell on the outside. The only way to prevent it from happening was to leave your *socio* (cellmate) in the cell during the visit or make sure everything was out of reach or locked down. Or, as Martín had done, put some kind of material over the front of your cell bars so they couldn't see inside.

"Forget about your shoes. Get your family to send you a new pair. *Esta en la carcel, Gabacho. No olvidalo,*" Martín emphasized his point shaking his finger at my face.

I walked off burning mad. *Yeah, that's right*, I thought, *I'm in prison, and I can never forget it.* I'll watch my own back. Take care of number one. I need to find some allies who can help me and forget about trying to help Jeff. He's fucking nuts!

Ramon Caro Curiel had the cell right next to Martín in *pabellon siete*, which was the preferred cellblock. It was on the far end of the cellblocks and on one side, you could look out over the soccer field toward the walls. It wasn't a view of the majestic Wasatch Mountains from my apartment in Salt Lake City, but it was a view, nonetheless, and a welcome respite from the ever-present claustrophobia of prison. Martín told me to talk to Ramon and ask if he wanted a new *socio*. He was sure Ramon would want to live with me because Ramon had no family and no money and had always lived with someone who could help him. He was kind, polite, and because of his situation, was willing to do favors for a *gabacho* like me. It would be like having a personal valet.

Ramon was in his cell, lying on his bunk, reading. I stood inside the doorway looking around for a moment. Breaking away from Jeff would be a bit cruel, I thought. Jeff wasn't talking to his family yet. He didn't have much money or food. All he did was stay in his cell all day and masturbate, re-reading his girlfriend's letters that Kate had brought to him.

Like Martín said, Ramon was eager to have me move in with him. Many of the cells had three inmates, but in *pabellon siete,* most had only two, and some even had only one guy. Odds were I could live with Ramon and not have to put up with another guy because the cells were pretty small, and three guys in one cell was awfully crowded.

I went back to my cell to find Jeff still there. I brought up the idea of the two of us splitting up by explaining I didn't want to get involved with his escape plans, nor be implicated in an escape attempt. I made the idea seem less personal and more about my concerns for a potential theatre group. We could split up the food my family had brought me, and I would give him some of the money sent to me by one of my cousins. He didn't want the money and said he was going to contact his mom and get some things going with her. I didn't really believe he had actually decided to do that until I started the conversation about splitting. But I used that notion to justify to myself that going ahead with spitting up was in Jeff's best interest. It would force him to contact his family and start working toward a rational solution to getting out of there.

We argued some more over Pedro, the attorney, and his plan for us to pursue the prisoner exchange program. I told him I was going to go forward with that plan and he could join me if he changed his mind; I wouldn't say anything to Pedro yet. But I urged him again to talk to his family and see what they wanted to do. He needed to make some decisions soon and couldn't just let his case linger while counting on some ludicrous, pie-in-the-sky escape plan.

I tried one last time. "Jesus, man, we're not prisoners of war. We committed a crime. And to some degree, it's our responsibility to accept our punishment."

Jeff was bowled over at that comment. "You know as well as me that marijuana should be legal. And we're not major drug dealers, just regular guys who wanted to smoke dope. The US drug laws are all fucked up, Mexico's laws are all fucked up, so I'm going to get the fuck out of here any way I can. It's my right and my duty to try and escape!"

He was on the edge of losing it. I had never seen this side of him, almost seemed like he was going insane. I suppose that should have been a sign for me to reach out and help him because I was somehow able to make sense of this whole situation. I could see a way for us to live as pleasantly as possible while here. But he just couldn't see anything like that. Everything looked bleak to him. He felt trapped and scared.

I stopped arguing with him. It's not that I didn't agree with him; I did. I thought it was absurd to put people in prison for marijuana. I knew someday the laws would be changed... and they were. And all the people who had their lives ruined or drastically altered for smoking weed would be vindicated if not forgiven by the law. But that was another matter. We were here now. We broke the existing law and had to make the best of it. Escape was not an option.

I sat down at the little table and calmly started pulling out the cans of food we had. I would hold up a can and see if he wanted that one. Occasionally, he would nod or shrug, and I separated us that way; not saying a word, just dividing up the food and sundry items into two separate piles. That's what we were reduced to: two piles of stuff.

It made me think of splitting up our wedding photos when Kate and I separated. I had the sick feeling we were cutting up our photos with an old, rusty pair of scissors – each photo cut in half with me and my family on one side and hers on the other. It's hard to breakup with someone close, even when it's your idea. But even then I persevered and divided our marriage that way. If I came to the realization there was no other way to do something, I could make a cold, clean decision and move forward without remorse, shame, or compassion.

That's the way I split up with Jeff. I knew he was going downhill and I thought he might not make it. But I had done everything I could think of to change his mind and couldn't convince him. So in that moment I made the decision that he should go his way, and I would go mine. I had to survive this the best way I could, and it didn't look like it was going to include Jeff.

I packed up my clothes and bedding, picked up my guitar, and left. It was weird, at the very least. Jeff and I had been roommates for months. He and I had taken off for Mexico to do something crazy, exotic, different, new, and not anything like Utah. We'd done it together, and like many things, we shared a certain camaraderie, a kinship, a similar philosophy.

We both disliked living under the Mormon influence. The church maintains tight control of the culture and day-to-day life of Utah and we were both tired of it.

I think, in an odd way, the trip was an act of rebellion, a way of saying, "Hey, fuck you. We're not Mormons and we don't want you people controlling our lives." Albeit it was an unbelievably stupid thing to do, certainly not a worthy statement of rebellion. What would this do to change our lives in Utah? Nothing. Nothing at all. The only people who were going to be affected by my actions were my parents, and all it would do was prove they were right; that I had misbehaved and ended up in Mexican prison, and was now relying on their help, love, and support. It was not a statement of rebellion at all, but an affirmation of the fact their philosophy was better than mine.

I could never ever let them see it. I could never let them or anyone else see I had failed, that I was wrong. I had to let everyone see I was fine. I was doing well. I was going to make a great life in prison, come hell or high water. And I couldn't let Jeff, or his potential demise, get in the way of that purpose.

My determination toward that goal began that day I split up with Jeff. I couldn't let him see I was hurting too, that I was scared, that I was unsure of what to do. Instead of commiserating and empathizing with him, I made him feel like he was on his own and couldn't turn to me for help. I'm sure that left him feeling weak and alone. But it had to be that way, and he would either sink or swim. My determination had to be unflappable, it had to be solid; everyone had to believe I was doing just fucking great.

I dragged my stuff over to *pabellon siete* and moved in with Ramon. He took the bunk above and let me have the lower bunk, the preferred bunk. He deferred to me then and every time thereafter. I never asked him, he just did it. That was the beginning of my new relationship, my new *socio*. Another guy who held me in some high esteem, who wanted my approval, who wanted to make me happy.

When I went to LA to become a rock musician, I left a great band with some guys I really liked to go to LA and find something bigger, better. I had met a guy at a drunken party of high school friends who was (and I knew it at the time) gay. Although he had not come out to anyone, including his family, all the kids in his high school knew he was gay. He was flirting with me and so some of my friends pulled me aside to warn me that he was hitting on me and to stay away from him.

I never understand the fear people had, even back then, about gay association. How does associating with or interacting with a gay person make you gay? By the time I reached high school, I was already beginning to think that people were born homosexual. It was not a choice. But hardly anyone I knew in 1979 felt the same way. In my conservative religious environment, I was taught homosexuality was a sin, it was sodomy, and you would burn for it. So as my thinking about religion evolved, my entire philosophy of life changed as well.

I brushed off my friend's warnings about Scott and met him the next day for lunch. He was heading to LA to get into acting, comedy, producing, anything in show business. He asked me If I wanted to go with him and another friend who was a straight female. He had contacts in LA and told me he could get me into the business as a model and do what I wanted from there. I said *sure, let's go*. I could tell he was attracted to me, but it was not the first time it had happened and I was unfazed by those kinds of flirty come-ons. All my straight, redneck, and hippie friends, of course, thought I had "turned gay." But I didn't give a shit what people thought of me one way or the other. Scott's plan was something new, something far away from the life I had been living.

After a couple of weeks, Scott eventually gave up on trying to convince me to have sex with him and we moved into a house in Encino with some guys he knew. Half the guys were gay and everybody was hustling for something. It was 1979, and the crazy disco scene was just beginning: cocaine, 'ludes, and party-party.

There was another guy who hung around with us named Stevie. He was the lighting guy for the Whiskey a Go Go and had connections with people in the music business.

One night at a big party at our house with a number of would-be models and a lot of cocaine, Stevie made a direct pass at me. I was so fucking horny that night. I had been watching the cool, sexy girls dancing all night, but couldn't seem to make advances with any of them. They thought I was some kind of country bumpkin from nowhere. Then around four in the morning, Stevie saw me walking down the hallway to the bathroom and pushed me into the coat room. He threw me down on the bed and started rubbing my body. He was headed for my crotch when I pushed him away.

I thought about it for a moment. Sure, I could let him go down on me. What the hell, a mouth is a mouth. Girls, guys, what did it really matter? I really wanted to get off and was dying to have sex with someone. But then it struck me: when he was finished, I wouldn't want to do anything to him, and I would more than likely be a bit pissed at him for pushing me into it. It would possibly even ruin our friendship.

So I told him, "Hey, Stevie, I could let you do this, because I really don't care whether you're gay or not. I'm not homophobic, but I'm not gay either, so once you're finished, I'm not going to want to do anything to you. And I might even be a bit annoyed that I let you do it to me. So I think it's best if you and I just go to our respective bedrooms and jerk off. I'll think about the hot girls who were here tonight and you can think about me. But no good is going to come for either one of us by me letting you suck me off just so I can have an orgasm." He was a dejected and a little embarrassed, but comparatively unscathed by the experience and we remained good friends.

That was the closest I ever came to a gay encounter, even in prison. It just wasn't in me. It was as I had always believed: you're born with your sexual identity, it's not a choice you make. I was drawn to the gay culture at that time. They were cool people, they ate well and dressed well, and knew what kind of Scotch to order. I was starved for that. Growing up in a lower middle-class, religious, conservative household in Utah, I never had an opportunity to experience the things I did while living in LA.

There were a number of occasions in my life where some guy, a straight guy, a gay guy, wanted something from me that I couldn't or wouldn't give. Some kind of verification or confirmation or validation, I didn't really understand what was often going on.

It was odd, my relationship with other men. I was never the slap-your-ass-in-the-locker-room kind of guy, and I wasn't the mushy sort of huggy guy either. I basically didn't really care much for other males, at least the way I saw other men carry on. There was a shared camaraderie I didn't understand, a "band of brothers" mentality I never tapped into.

Jeff, Ramon, Stevie, all wanted something from me I couldn't give, though I let them do things for me just the same. But in prison, there were 850 other brothers, all of us in the same boat. You needed allies, comrades, and friends. I had to think differently now. Work a little harder at being close to men.

Over the ensuing days, I began to make a home of my prison cell. I painted the entire cell white with red and gray trim. My grandma had made some red and white gingham curtains for my apartment in Salt Lake for Christmas one year. I had asked Kate to bring them with my other stuff. I used them to curtain off the bathroom and my bed. I built a table from scrap wood I found in the prison dump. I glued little blocks of wood to the cement walls and put nails in each of them so I could hang pots, hot pads, and other kitchen paraphernalia. I filled in all the cracks in the walls and floor with plaster so the cockroaches couldn't get in.

Then, finally, as a result of my shoes being stolen, I used papier-mâché to cover the entire front of my cell in a thick wall of hardened paper. I used newspaper dipped in a mixture of flour, water, and salt, then wrapped the bars of my cell in strips of the papier-mâché. I covered both sides of the bars to form a solid wall, then painted the hardened paper. It created a completely enclosed room. No one had ever done that before. It made it very difficult to steal anything from my cell. A potential thief would have to break through the papier-mâché in order to see in, and breaking through would take too long and they would fail. It worked perfectly. No one ever stole anything from me after that.

Almost everything I used to create my showcase cell I found in the junkyard or some other place inside the prison. Newspaper was free, of course. I got flour from the kitchen and found some old paint in the shops. Occasionally, I traded inmates for something I really needed and couldn't find for free. The heat was the worst thing. In the Sonoran Desert, temperatures can reach 120° Fahrenheit in the summer months. Everyone had a fan. Martín had a cooler. I bought an old fan and cut a square of papier-mâché from my bars and installed the fan so I could circulate air.

I was meticulous in creating the perfect environment. Martín and Arturo would come by while I was working, pop their heads in and laugh at me, saying, "Too much work, *Gabacho. Estas loco!*"

I eventually made my cell the showcase of the prison. Even the guards came inside to see the *gabacho*'s "house." One day the *comandante* came by and I made him tea and cake. The cooking I learned in LA was paying off here in Mexican prison and I became adept at making stellar meals from the barest of ingredients. I had a hot plate, a toaster oven, and a spice rack. I had to tap into the electricity from a nearby cell so I could get enough power to run my TV, radio, coffee maker, tape recorder, and extra lighting. Some of the items were brought to me by my family or Kate and some stuff I found in the prison junkyard and repaired. I don't think my family fully understood what was going on, but they brought the items, and I made a home of my prison cell. I was told later that when I left the prison, Ramon sold the cell to the highest bidder; he made pretty good money on that sale, so in the end, everything he did for me for that year was worth it to him.

CHAPTER 12

A FEW DAYS after I moved in with Ramon, I hosted the first meeting of the new theatre group. The day following my performance of *Jesus Christ Superstar*, I was approached by a couple of the guys, Godoy and Chabita, who also wanted to form a theatre group. Their idea was to do shows for visitors, even charge a few pesos and use the money to buy scripts, costumes, and other necessities. This made me want it even more, discovering there were guys in the prison who had an interest in theatre. They just needed a director, someone who knew how to produce shows on a stage.

Upon returning to Salt Lake City, Kate assembled a box of things she had pulled from my apartment and shipped it to the prison via the mail. It contained some kitchen items plus everything in my play library: Shakespeare, Neil Simon, David Mamet, Arthur Miller, etc.

I had cleaned up my cell early, even more than usual, and neatly arranged all the kitchen paraphernalia Kate had sent: a wooden rack filled with spices and condiments, shelves for my cookware, and a small table where I arranged some refreshments.

Attending the first meeting were Chabita, Samuel, Godoy, Soto, Luiz, Diego, Thomas, and Ramon. They became the core group. I handed out some of the plays as I served cake and coffee on matching cups and plates. They made jokes about how I had decorated my cell, made coffee, baked a cake, and chided me about putting in this kind of effort in prison. I was beginning to learn enough Spanish so I could joke around with them.

"Hey, I'm just getting started. Wait till you see what I do with the bathroom. Sure, it takes a lot of work to create something worthwhile, something admirable," I said, hinting at the work ahead in the theatre group. I wanted to make an impression and demonstrate the importance of presentation and organization. I knew that trying to produce plays, especially in a Mexican prison, would be extremely challenging and a lot of hard work. Guys would get discouraged and want to quit; I'd seen it before in community theatre.

But they seemed undaunted. Godoy wanted to do experimental theatre. His idea was to create a theatre company that explored plays like *Waiting for Godot*. Some of the others wanted to do *Jesus Christ Superstar* and other musicals they had heard about or seen on TV. For me, the really good news was they were excited, and that meant I could push them hard. I was amazed at how many of the playwrights they knew. They handed around my scripts and began chatting about what would be good to showcase their abilities. There was always an underlying desire to impress the other inmates and their families. Most the guys did not have families who came to visit, and as such, did not live particularly well in the prison. So the theatre group was more than just a diversion or a desire to do something artsy, it was a way to elevate themselves in the eyes of the prison community.

As we talked, I told them about my past theatre work and handed around my portfolio. I showed them a photo of me doing a play by Arthur Miller titled *Incident at Vichy*. "This is a play about the Germans arresting and interrogating people in France during World War II who looked like they might be Jews," I said, trying to push them away from experimental theatre. "This would be a good play for us here in the prison." I emphasized the fact we had all experienced being arrested and most had suffered a brutal interrogation, so we could identify with the emotion of the characters in *Vichy*.

Ramon pointed out it would have to be in Spanish, and Samuel said he had some experience translating English to Spanish. He also mentioned that his wife, who was on the outside, spoke English and Spanish fluently and came to see him each week. She was from the US and had been arrested with Samuel ten years ago, but recently had gotten released through the efforts of Amnesty International. The other inmates didn't seem to excited about *Incident at Vichy*, so I let it go for the time being.

Soto and Chabita wanted to know what we could do for Mother's Day. In Mexico, *La Dia De La Madre* is a big deal as mothers are celebrated more passionately in Latin America than almost anywhere. On the day, there would be more people visiting than any other weekend. Families were allowed inside the prison and could enjoy picnics with their inmate relatives. Sometimes, a program was presented on Mother's Day, but was usually not done well. The auditorium had terrible acoustics, and no one could hear anything performed on the stage. So people tended to walk in and out of the performance for curiosity's sake and perhaps a slight diversion.

After some discussion, we decided to present a variety program for Mother's Day. A few bands could play, there might be a speech by one of the administrative staff, we could do a short play or some scenes from various plays, and maybe someone would read a Mother's Day poem. We settled on a tentative list of performances for the program: a couple of scenes from various plays, three poetry readings, and four musical numbers. The musical numbers were easy because there were several guys who had already indicated they wanted to perform, and Chabita and Luis had Mother's Day poems they wanted to do. So it was up to me to find some plays which would work.

I had been watching TV during the daytime to learn Spanish and had seen reruns of *The Odd Couple* (*La Pareja Dispareja*) with Jack Klugman and Tony Randall. I noticed my copy of the play sitting on the table and picked it up. "What about something funny, like this?" I handed the script to Godoy. He looked at me like I insulted his intelligence, then handed the play to Samuel.

"That's too commercial," Godoy said, shaking his head.

I had directed non-actors previously in community theatre productions and knew this was going to be very, very hard. These guys weren't actors, they had no training and no experience. I didn't speak the language well enough to elicit a performance from anyone, let alone prison inmates. We didn't have translations of any plays, and, evidently, the auditorium was terrible. More than likely, the inmates' families would be more interested in talking to and engaging with them than watching a bunch of non-actors do a boring, esoteric theatrical piece like *Waiting For Godot*. We needed to do something funny or the whole program would fall flat and the group would disintegrate. These guys needed a success to keep them motivated enough to do all the hard work it would take. Failure wasn't an option.

Suddenly it hit me and I blurted out, "What if we do a scene from *The Odd Couple*, but rewrite it to be about two guys here in prison sharing a cell together? We would use the basic script from the play, but change it to be more like prison dialogue, and change the location and setting."

At last, this notion caught their attention. Even Godoy liked the idea because it was a more on the experimental side. Then I slammed it home. "In fact, we should do it with Godoy and Samuel as the Odd Couple. They've been here for a long time; people certainly know them. They also know they are *socios* and have been living in a cell together. There must have been a lot of times when you both wanted to kill each other, no?"

They nodded. "More than you know," said Godoy.

"You two are the quintessential Odd Couple," I said. "We'll write the scene as though it takes place in *El Centro De Readaptación Social Hermosillo*, here, in this prison. You should play Jack, Samuel, and you, Godoy, should play the Tony Randall part. Everyone will go crazy for it!"

They all thought it was a great idea, even Godoy. In fact, he *wanted* to play the Tony Randall character because, as he stated emphatically, it would be more of a stretch for him to play an effeminate man!

In the meantime, while we worked on a translation of *The Odd Couple*, we decided to participate in a play titled *The Padre Contra Todo*, which was directed by a theatre instructor from Mexico City. He had been responsible for the touring production of *Jesus Christ Superstar* and worked in theatre in Mexico City. Somehow, he had received a grant or other funds to take plays into the prisons of Mexico. I never quite understood why he did it. He seemed sincere and worked hard to make the plays a success, but it felt like there was an ulterior motive. He was, in my estimation, gay, and tended to flirt with some of the inmates, but that couldn't have been the only reason he was doing it. I couldn't get my head around it and decided to help him as best as I could. But it highlighted for me the fact there was some interest in using theatre or other arts for prison inmates.

The Padre Contra Todo is a very traditional and often done play in Mexico, especially in grade schools. It is about a Catholic priest who tries to help the poor and powerless. There is an undertone of it being subversive, but the main character never criticizes the government or the wealthy and powerful. Most Mexican citizens recognize political corruption and dishonest politicians as a fact of life, and in private will often blame the government and the wealthy for Mexico's problems. But the play only distinguishes between good guys and bad guys without pointing a finger at any single group, so it's popular with rich, poor, liberals, conservatives, and everybody in between. People are able to identify with the good guys no matter who they are, so the play is presented often.

Rehearsals were to last about three weeks, and then we would perform it at a Sunday visit. We all agreed to put in a sincere and concerted effort because, we believed, it would help us launch our own theatre group.

The director cast me in the part of the padre, since the character was written to be non-ethnic, as though the padre was representative of Caucasian priests from Europe. The other characters in the play were notably native and mixed race. I was confused and thought it odd at first since I had just arrived and could barely speak Spanish, but the character of the padre didn't speak very much. In fact, he only came in at the end to wrap up the story. Later, after we presented the performance, I saw the director had a purpose in casting me; an American portraying the title character of a traditional Mexican play inside prison would bring additional attention to the production and, therefore, the press. It was my first lesson in marketing.

We had accomplished a lot during the first meeting of the group. I was pleasantly surprised; you might even say ecstatic. The idea of a theatre group and producing plays inside prison looked very promising. We finished off the coffee, and everyone took back an assignment. They left walking down the corridor, talking and joking, more excited than I had seen them at any other time. Samuel stayed, and we worked late into the night going through *The Odd Couple* (*La Pareja Dispareja),* making notes about which scene to do.

The next morning I hopped out of bed with a brand new attitude and walked down to the main plaza to touch base with everyone. As I passed some of the guys from the theatre group, I could feel a new camaraderie among us. Like we had a secret. They were pumped. Godoy was carrying the copy of *the Incident at Vichy* I had given to him to read. That was promising. Then I saw Jeff coming out of the café with a couple of guys I didn't know. We kept our distance for a few days, neither of us having a desire to continue the disagreement. Godoy nodded toward Jeff and said something about he and I not being *socios* anymore, adding that Jeff and I were the real odd couple.

Everyone knew Jeff was trying to find a way to escape. The inmates joked about it all the time. "Jeffery *esta loco, no?*" they would say to me, as though I had something to do with his troubled state of mind. I shook my head and agreed with them, saying he didn't take well to the life inside and was having a difficult time. There was no reason for me to badmouth Jeff. It just made things more difficult between us, and he still had information that could cause me real trouble.

I tried to remain neutral when I was asked about him. Jeff was clearly going down a road from which there would be no return. Once you start telling everyone you're planning to do something, it would make you look weak, or even stupid, if you didn't go through with it. In any case, I could tell Jeff was sincere. He thought he was smarter than the Mexican officials and he could find a way out. He didn't think it was going to be difficult at all.

Occasionally, I bumped into him, and he mentioned this or that idea about how he was going to escape. I would tell him not to tell me, I didn't want to know. If he did try to escape – whether he was successful or not – I was sure it would fall back on me. I would be questioned as to whether or not I knew what was happening and how involved I was, so I asked him not to talk to me about it.

He could be seen jogging around the track every day for hours. He played tennis, really hard, almost like he was trying to injure his knees. He had his old knee injury and could use that in some way. All the jogging, jumping and twisting could re-injure it, but I couldn't see how it would assist his escape. He continued these actions all during the time we rehearsed *The Padre*. Everyone knew what he was doing. The inmates watched him and talked about him. They had a nickname for him, Jeffery *Loco*. Eventually, it became clear to me his plan involved hurting his knee badly enough that he could force the prison officials to take him to a specialist in town.

There was a clinic at the prison, with a nurse who could administer penicillin and aspirin, maybe set a broken finger or something like that. But if you were seriously injured, such as a stabbing or broken leg, you were taken to the hospital in Hermosillo. Jeff often went to see the nurse complaining about his sore knee and asking for pain medication.

Some of the inmates tried to talk him out of attempting an escape. They told him if he tried to run at the hospital, the guards would shoot him. Jeff was certain, because he was an American, the guards would not shoot him. He felt invincible. I tried to get him involved in *The Padre,* but he didn't want anything to do with it. He was confident in his plan to get out of prison, so there was no need for him to learn to accept the situation and make a life here.

I kept up my Spanish studies and soon was able to converse with people in simple conversations. Samuel and I had made great progress translating the scene from *The Odd Couple*. In fact, we were ready to start rehearsing it. I even got him to look at *Incident at Vichy*. He took a copy of the play to his wife, who started doing a translation of it.

Our next big challenge was to create a theatre space and we began working on the auditorium. There was so much to do, it was really a mess; a big concrete room with terrible acoustics and barely enough light to see. Standing on the stage and trying to project dialogue to the audience was a disaster. Even the most articulate speaker couldn't be understood and the critical details of a play would be lost entirely. Nor could anyone see the faces of the performers. We badly needed some kind of sound baffling and lighting. But that would be out of the question, not only because of the cost but how would we install it?

Ramon suggested I look at the dump. There were piles of trash and debris that had accumulated in an area inside the prison used as the dump. All kinds of stuff had been delivered to the prison for years. When people donated something or dropped off junk they no longer wanted, it would go to the guards first. They would take what they wanted and put the rest inside. It often ended up in the dump. So I met a couple of the guys there and we began searching for stuff that would help us create a theatre space.

There were piles and piles of discarded household and commercial junk. But as they say, one man's trash is another's treasure. We found a plethora of useful things. There was an old movie projector with a broken reel motor which rendered it no good, so we turned it into our spotlight.

We removed the unnecessary parts, mounted it on a platform we could turn back and forth and shift up and down. It was very clever; most of the guys inside had come from very low-income households and were accustomed to finding old cars, appliances, and furniture, then turning the discarded objects into useful things. Some of them worked in the shops where they made stuff for outside contractors, but could work on their own projects after the day's work was completed. In this way we created all kinds of props, sets, and equipment for our theatre, including lights and sound baffling.

There were mounds and mounds of paper egg carton flats. I couldn't believe how many had stacked up over the years. It struck me that we could stack up those egg flats and create columns, walls, and even archways for *The Padre*. And that's what we did. We created a courtyard with walls and an archway leading to a little hut upstage. It was perfect. We found dozens of discarded light sockets and screwed them to large pieces of wood, then hung those from the ceiling to create down lights on the stage. Together with the spotlight, it worked pretty well.

The main problem remained: the sound. You couldn't distinguish a word anyone said up on stage. The words echoed around the room, creating overlapping noise of the person speaking. They had tried to stage readings previously and it didn't work. It would be useless to try and mount a piece of theatre unless we could resolve the sound issue.

I stood there one day looking at the egg flats we used for scenery, then thought, *why not use them on the walls for sound baffling?* There were some discarded old sheets of plywood they had used for pouring the concrete walls. So we wired and glued the eggs flats to the plywood to make large sheets of sound baffling, then hung those sheets from the walls, both upstage and at the back of the auditorium, hoping the sound would stop its endless reverberation. It worked, and was perhaps the most ingenious project that helped create our theatre.

Even with just a few sheets of baffling around the auditorium, you could actually now hear the actors. Then the *comandante* got wind what we were doing and came to the auditorium to check it out. He, along with the other prison staff and even some of the inmates, had warned us it would be useless to present plays with dialogue because of the horrific sound problem. But when he saw, *and heard,* how well it was working, he beamed with amazement, then shook his head at all the work we were doing. He got as excited as we did and offered to help us by furnishing additional sheets of plywood. We continued gluing and tying egg flats to the sheets and hung them from the ceiling with wire. With the extra sheets, we were able to go completely around the room. It may not have been very attractive but it was a startling difference in the quality of the sound. Lights, sets, and sound... now we had the beginnings of a real theatre!

The day came to perform *The Padre*. We made a backstage area where we applied makeup and put on our costumes. One inmate's mother made me a hooded padre's cloak. It was perfect, that washed-out brown you see in old Westerns. The other costumes were mostly rags because all the other characters in the play were very poor, so that was easy. Much of the play takes place inside a prison, rather like *Man of La Mancha*, and there are flashbacks from one of the characters inside the prison. We created the time change by use of lighting effects with the spot, putting various pieces of colored cloth in front of it. They say creativity is born of necessity and so it was.

Many of the visitors had heard about what we were doing so the auditorium was jam packed for the performance. It was a smash! For the first time, the visitors really enjoyed a production in the prison auditorium. They clapped long and loud when we finished. Newspaper reporters came from Nogales, Arizona, to see the show because of an American in prison doing theatre. It was a very big deal. I was on the front page of the Hermosillo paper the next day with some headline about "PROFESSIONAL ACTOR AT THE *Centro De Redeaptacion.*"

The *comandante* was so happy he waited at the exit of the theatre as the audience and reporters left, laughing and complimenting him and the inmate actors. He shook hands with the reporters and told them they would see more of the same in the coming months. We were on our way!

Jeff hadn't gotten involved in any way. He poked his head inside during the performance and watched for a moment, then left to go play tennis. We were on two very different paths.

In Mexican prisons, the guards and the warden can make extra money aside from their salaries. It's considered a lucrative job to be the warden of a prison and the competition for the job is fierce. The job is as much about public relations as it is running the prison effectively. A warden (*comandante*) controls the flow of drugs and alcohol and can make a huge profit from it; he can short the inmates on their food and make a profit there; and he can take bribes from the inmates to work in the shops, pay them very little, and make even more profit there. The *comandantes* like to get any good press they can because it takes the attention off corrupt activities. And when the families of inmates see their loved ones receiving good treatment and support, it keeps them happy. Our single production made a big contribution to the *comandante's* good reputation and he was very complimentary to me.

After the play, the director from Mexico City was approached by a reporter from the local TV station asking if he would come to the station, accompanied by one or two of the inmate actors and be interviewed on a nightly news show. It was more of an *Entertainment Tonight* type show – not really hard news. Still, it would be good for us to have that kind of publicity. So the director asked the *comandante* if he could take me and one other inmate out of the prison to appear on the news show. This was a really big deal; inmates only left the prison to go to court and get medical attention. But the *comandante* agreed, and a date was scheduled for the following week.

I was ecstatic. So were the other guys. This would draw attention to our theatre group and maybe even get us some funding through donations. Besides that, I could get a copy of the show and send it home to all my friends who were thinking I was some kind of idiot for going off to Mexico and landing in prison. This would be my way of showing them how smart and creative I was. They would all say, "There he is stuck in a Mexican prison, and instead of feeling sorry for himself and whining about it, he's producing real theatre!" I immediately wrote to Kate and others, telling them about the play and my upcoming appearance on Mexican TV.

During the weeks I'd been rehearsing *The Padre* and building out the auditorium, Jeff was focused on his escape plans. I hardly ever saw him. He hung out with a different group of guys and we never crossed paths. I was working very hard, day and night, in the theatre all the time, either rehearsing or hanging sheets of sound baffling. During rehearsals for *The Padre,* we also started rehearsing for the Mother's Day program. There were three bands that wanted to play, and I helped them balance their sound and arrange themselves on stage. We finally translated the scene from *The Odd Couple* and started working on that with Samuel and Godoy. Everything was moving forward even better than I had hoped. It was like if Bad Luck had transpired to place me in prison, his brother Good Luck came to my rescue with the theatre group.

In my spare time – when I had any – I watched Mexican TV to keep working on my Spanish. My days were long and hard and I was always moving a mile a minute, only stopping to eat. It was, in fact, the hardest I had ever worked in my life. It's one thing to do that much work in a normal life, but add to it being inside prison, and having to learn a new language was triple the effort. Everything took longer, and there was always something we needed and couldn't find. Which often meant we had to make do or make the thing ourselves.

The fact I didn't speak Spanish fluently was simply a time killer. Every time I had to ask for something or direct someone or try to communicate a complex idea, it would take me three times as long. I kept a dictionary in my back pocket and used a ton of sign language to make general day-to-day discourse. My head was always spinning, and I hardly ever got a full night's sleep.

I lost a bunch of weight, and was not in particularly good physical shape because I wasn't eating well. Although it wasn't a World War II internment camp, I felt like a prisoner of war who was bedraggled and worn out. The language barriers and the cultural differences got to me most. I had only been speaking Spanish for three months and it wasn't enough time to learn to discuss complex issues and give instructions to inmate actors rehearsing a play. By the end of each day, I was exhausted.

When we finished performing *The Padre,* I slept for a whole day. We took a break from the theatre group for a couple of days so we could all catch up on personal things. I wrote some letters, played the guitar, and tried to catch up on my cooking.

Jeff had his plans too, and they were moving forward, as I was soon to learn. His strategy had paid off because he finally made his knee look terrible. It had become swollen and seemed awfully sore. He limped to the guards' office daily and begged to see a doctor. He did a pretty good acting job himself as I didn't really think it hurt as badly as he made out. But from the way he carried on, you'd have thought he was going to die.

Finally, they agreed to take him into town to see a specialist and an appointment was made at the hospital in downtown Hermosillo. I was lying in bed when I heard the loudspeaker proclaim "Jeffery Aldon Baye, *presente usted a la sala de guardia*," then it repeated. It was one of those mornings where I slept in, trying to catch up on my sleep. Whenever you had a visit from your attorney or had to go to court or there was a problem and you were going to receive some punishment, they would call your name from the prison loudspeaker, which could be heard everywhere. You were then supposed to present yourself at the *sala de guardia* and wait to be taken to wherever.

I laid there thinking, "Oh my god, this is it." It was about 7:30. Breakfast was wheeled around about 6:30 and the guards liked to get things done right after that. I could only imagine what was going through Jeff's mind, but I was certain about my feelings and they were twisted with anxiety. All I could do was wait.

I had run the gamut of emotions in the last few weeks; anger at Jeff for even thinking about trying this, guilt about not helping him more, concern over the theatre group and how it would be affected, and fear about what was going to happen to all of us, including Jeff. Would he try to run? Would he get scared and forget about it? I really didn't know. I had never seen him so distraught. Everyone thought he was deranged. His eyes were often frenetic and he looked crazy as hell at times. I was sure if he were in a normal frame of mind, he wouldn't try to escape. But in his current frame of mind, anything was possible. I really didn't have the right to rebuke him. I was the idiot who talked us into driving to Mexico to buy drugs, and that was as unimaginably stupid as what Jeff was going to attempt. The action we choose in an abnormal state of mind is almost inconceivable to us when not in that state.

After Jeff was called up front, the prison remained oddly quiet. I couldn't even get out of bed to get breakfast. I just rolled over and hunkered down against the wall. Ramon had already risen. He ate *yegua* every morning and usually hung out with some of the guys downstairs in the foyer. I knew they were all thinking what I was.

We just waited. Two hours went by. Then Martín rapped on my cell door. "Hey, *Gabacho*!" he shouted in a raspy whisper. He opened my door as I rose up and saw a wild-eyed face of serious concern. He had been at a conjugal visit the night before and was just coming back inside when he heard people in the administration talking urgently and running around the office. He heard one of them say that the American had tried to escape and was shot – but that's all he knew.

"*Esta loco*, Jeffery," Martín said, shaking his head and repeating it two or three times. Then he followed up with, "*Pero esta fuerte tambien.*" And then I realized what Jeff was doing. "But he's also tough," Martín had acknowledged. From the very beginning, Jeff had appeared weak to many of the inmates. He cried a lot when he talked with his girlfriend on the phone, and the phone was out in the open area of the *sala de guardia*, so anyone and everyone who was crossing through and standing waiting for something could hear him. But Jeff was undeterred. He didn't care who heard him and what they thought. He communicated with Arlene exactly the way he wanted to.

Guys in prison rarely let their emotions show. They try to remain tough, cool, and collected so the other inmates won't detect weakness and use it against them. But Jeff whined a lot to everyone about the prison and the conditions and the guards. It led many to call him names other than Jeffery *Loco*. They also called him a baby and a whiner. They thought he was overly emotional and consumed with sentimental feelings. Now this was a chance for Jeff to prove otherwise. He had been a high school football star, had played a lot of sports throughout his life, and had done well. He was 6'2" and 180 pounds of solid muscle. He worked out a lot and was in great shape upon arriving in the prison. He never thought of himself as weak or whiny. I believe he was determined to try to escape no matter what and that's what drove him.

Martín left and I fell back into bed. I was staring up at the concrete bunk above me when I heard my name called from the *sala de guardia*, just as I expected. My heart sank at the sound of those words, Richard Lynn Jewkes, over the loudspeaker. I knew what was going to happen. I quickly presented myself at the *sala de guardia*, and they immediately escorted me to the *comandante's* office. He was sitting in his chair behind the desk, reading a document when I entered, then he got up, walked slowly around and sat down on the front of the desk, a few inches from my face. This was not a good sign. His secretary had told me to sit in the chair right in front of the desk. He wanted to be close enough to look me directly in the eyes so he could see if I was lying.

By the time of Jeff's escape, I was teaching the *comandante* English. When we were building out the auditorium, he noticed how much Spanish I was able to speak and asked me to give him private lessons. From then on, twice a week, I went to his office and taught him English. It wasn't so much that he needed to learn English. He spoke my language much better than I spoke his. But he wanted me to correct his pronunciation and grammar. We would talk, and I would tell him the proper way to say things. He often had me join him for lunch too. In only two months, I had attained the level of a prison trustee, something that rarely happened to an American. We'd even shared a couple of shots of hundred-year-old tequila that a drug dealer's father had given him. We were actually becoming good friends.

But as he sat on his desk, staring into my eyes, he was very disappointed. I didn't need to ascertain that; those were the first words out of his mouth. "Richard, I'm very disappointed with you. Did you know that Jeff was going to try to escape today?" I tried to look surprised, but I don't think he bought it. I said I knew Jeff was talking about doing some crazy things, but neither I nor anyone else expected him to go through with it. I asked if he was all right.

"My guy had to shoot him," he said with sincere concern. He was very upset. Later today he would have to meet with the American Consulate and explain why Jeff was taken to the hospital and allowed to have an opportunity to escape. The *comandante* had sent his best man with Jeff, along with two drivers of the van. One driver stayed in the van, and the other stood at the front of the hospital while Jeff's guard, the *comandante's* top lieutenant, escorted Jeff to the doctor's office. There was just the one guard to accompany Jeff inside, and that was the mistake everyone would point to. All the way, Jeff had cried and limped and given the impression he could hardly walk. He even had the guards get him a wheelchair to go to the doctor's office. He had been shackled with leg irons so he couldn't run easily. The lieutenant went inside the room with him, but Jeff complained about his pain. The doctor didn't speak English and couldn't understand Jeff, so he asked the lieutenant to remove the cuffs so he could have Jeff show him the problem. The lieutenant did as the doctor asked, then stepped outside the exam room.

No one understood why the lieutenant did that. Perhaps he trusted Jeff was in too much pain to attempt anything. But as soon as the he left the room, Jeff slugged the doctor, knocking him to the floor. Then he busted through the door hard, and knocked the lieutenant out of the way. Jeff took off running down the corridor as fast as he could. His leg was swollen and hurt, but Jeff was strong and a very fast runner. He had planned all this, and somehow it all had come to fruition.

He had maps of the town in his shoes, and he had planned to make his way to the rail yard, where he was going to hop a freight train and go north to the border. Before reaching the border, he would jump off the train and simply walk through the border crossing. He was blond and light-skinned, so no one would see him as an illegal, and he thought he could just walk across without any papers or ID. But in order for all that to work, he first had to make it out of the hospital. Then he had to find a taxi or something and get to the rail yard. All this without speaking Spanish. It was a crazy idea but it was working for the moment, just as he planned. They all believed he was in too much pain to try to run.

The lieutenant was not only the *comandante's* best guard, he was also the best marksman at the prison. As Jeff ran down the corridor, he drew his .45 and called to the nurses and others milling around to hit the floor, which they all did very quickly. Then he shot four times at Jeff's legs, hitting him all four times, with Jeff on the run. This, as Jeff later told me, was completely unexpected. Jeff assumed the lieutenant wouldn't dare shoot him, there would be too much flak from the American Consulate. He didn't think the guard would be able hit him in the legs while on the run and didn't expect the guard to shoot him in the back. And he was right about that. But the lieutenant was a crack shot; he aimed low and hit Jeff's legs.

This could have been a terrible disaster for Jeff and everyone else. He could have lost a leg or had one blown apart so badly he would limp the rest of his life. He could have had his kneecap blown out or a bone fractured beyond repair. But, in fact, not a single bullet caused serious damage. Two bullets caused flesh wounds, passing right through muscle tissue. Another bullet hit the back of his knee, but it must have struck right as Jeff was throwing the leg forward in stride because the .45 slug stuck right there behind the knee cap, causing very little damage. The other bullet only grazed his thigh. All four bullets hit him, but not one tore through bone, ligaments, or major veins and arteries. If you added up all the possible ways he could have been shot, it's an improbability he emerged so unscathed, especially considering cops are trained to aim for center mass. The fact the lieutenant even landed a shot in a running leg in a hospital full of people is beyond extraordinary. But to hit all four shots... I don't know what you call that.

For most guys, that would have been the end of it. But Jeff was so determined and demented that even getting shot in the legs didn't stop him. He'd been a madman those last few weeks and taking four bullets, even in the legs, was not going to slow or stop him. He kept running.

He nearly fell, caught himself at the door, then continued right out the doorway. He ran into the street, and fortuitously, a cab was parked right there, near the front door. He jumped in and shouted "*Vamanos!*" By the time the guards got outside, Jeff was gone. He didn't speak Spanish, and couldn't have known there was going to be a cab there; it was like everything lined up for him. The bullets, the cab, the doctor removing the cuffs – everything was going in his favor. Except the bullets did finally take a toll. Blood began to fill his muscle tissue. Those four wounds were bleeding internally, not badly enough to bleed out, but certainly a problem. Though not a single bullet struck a main artery or vein, there was enough damage to cause bleeding into the tissue. Sitting in the back of the cab, he began to feel his legs stiffen. He could hardly move them and tried to lift each leg and massage the muscles. At this point, the cab driver began noticing something was amiss. I'm sure he saw the blood soaking through Jeff's jeans.

It aroused his suspicions and he started pestering Jeff with questions he didn't understand and couldn't answer. The cab driver became apprehensive and started to call in to dispatch. Jeff didn't understand the conversation but could see it wasn't in his best interest so he waited for the right moment, then threw himself from the cab with his last bit of strength. He ran as far as he could before his legs gave out and he collapsed into a field of weeds, thinking he could lie there until he got his strength back. He kept thinking if he could just hold out until dark, he could make his move to the train station.

But the driver had watched Jeff fleeing and kept tabs on him. He got back on the radio with the dispatch and told them what happened and reported his location. Soon there were cops all over the place and they captured Jeff, lying in the field where he had fallen. No fight left, he was bleeding badly and needed medical attention. It was all over.

They took him back to the hospital and this time cuffed him to the bed. Jeff stayed there two weeks recuperating and a guard was stationed in his room from that moment until they returned Jeff to the prison. Since all the wounds were flesh wounds, he was able to recover with no long-term damage to his legs or muscles. The outcome of the escape attempt had caused only minor harm to Jeff, and he didn't have to spend time in the *yeleta* as others had who misbehaved. The *comandante* convinced the American Consulate Jeff was emotionally unstable and needed help, so they went easy on him. The big change was to his reputation; from then on, Jeff was considered *un fuerte* – a real tough guy. All the whining, complaining, and crying had been a ruse and the inmates considered it part of a great escape plan.

When the *comandante* walked around and sat on his desk close to me, he was looking for the truth. He figured I should have known something about Jeff's plan. And since I did, I had been making it clear in the previous weeks to the *comandante* and everyone else that Jeff and I were no longer friends and had parted ways. We didn't share a cell, and Jeff was not involved in the theatre group. I looked the *comandante* straight in the eyes and did my best to make the case that I hadn't known anything about it. He seemed to accept that, but then looked at me with a measure of regret.

"I know you're expecting to go outside to the TV station for the interview tomorrow, but I'm going to have to cancel that. I'm sorry," he said apologetically. "It wouldn't look good now after all that happened."

"What about the theatre group?" I asked hopefully.

"You can keep the group, that's okay. And please continue with the Mother's Day program. But there will be no going into town for the interview with the TV station." Then he turned away and asked the guard to escort me back inside.

All the way back to my cell, I thought about Jeff. I no longer worried whether he was safe or crazy or even having a hard time of it. I was just plain mad. Mind-numbingly mad at him for doing this to me. That was the way I saw it. He had gone off the deep end and carried me with him. I wanted to throw him over the wall and get him the hell out of there. I was so bloody fucking mad. It was fortunate for us that he remained in the hospital for a couple of weeks to give me time to cool down. It wouldn't do either of us any good to fight over it. I would eventually have to let it go.

CHAPTER 13

WHEN I GOT to my cell, Samuel and Godoy were there rehearsing the scene from *The Odd Couple* where Oscar throws a plate of spaghetti against the wall. They could tell I was upset and stopped what they were doing. I'm sure their first thought was I would be mad at them for rehearsing in my cell without me there. But to see them going at it so diligently made my heart sing and I calmed down immediately.

"Jeff was shot while trying to escape," I told them blankly, trying to hide my anger. "He's in the hospital. The *comandante* has cancelled all off-prison excursions. There will be no chance of performing anything in the city or even going to the TV station for an interview. He got calls from the US Consul and the mayor. Everybody is upset. He could lose his job as the *comandante*."

"What about Jeff?" Samuel asked with sincere concern.

"He's fine. Nothing but flesh wounds, the lucky son of a bitch," I said, showing a little anger. "He was shot four times in the legs and not one bullet hit a bone or a vein."

"What about the theatre group?" asked Godoy, waving a copy of the translated *Odd Couple* scene. Godoy was so into it. I thought right there that if Godoy ever got out of prison, he'd join an experimental theatre company in Mexico City.

All the guys in the group were stoked, and feared the worst if Jeff tried to escape. There had been talk of us giving a performance in town at an arts festival, but there was no chance of that now. However, our theatre group was intact and unscathed, the auditorium was working well, and that would be enough.

"The *comandante* said he trusted Jeff because of me, and he thought I would know, or at least should have known, what Jeff was planning and that I should have told him. Or given him a heads up."

Samuel nodded, then said, "I think everybody knew, except the *comandante*."

"Well, in the end, I convinced him Jeff had been acting crazy lately and I was sure he did it all on his own. I suggested they send him to a psychiatrist instead of the *yelata*."

Yelata was the word for icebox, meaning something airtight and enclosed. It was also what they called the hole in the ground where they put the inmates who attacked a guard or an inmate or misbehaved horribly. Anyone who ever tried to escape always spent a week or two in the *yelata*.

"So, the *comandante* is going to let us do the Mother's Day program, but no inmates will be going out to the Sonoran Festival competition. And I won't be going to the TV station to do an interview. I guess the Consulate was pretty angry. They think the lieutenant shouldn't have fired at Jeff and just let him run out the door. Where could he have gone?"

Samuel explained, "They probably think Jeff tried to buy his way out and then something went wrong and he was shot. Your government helped build this prison, primarily to catch and contain drug dealers. They don't want them to get out."

"Yeah, well, I wish he would just buy his way out and leave me alone," I said, finally showing some sympathy for Jeff. "I'd be glad if he got out and left me here."

"He can't buy his way out now," said Samuel. "They will be watching him."

A few days later, I found myself standing next to Martín and Samuel at the gate to the *sala de guardia*. Martín had a fan and a bucket of ice with two Cokes. Samuel had only a bedroll. I was loaded down with my entire bedroll, a cassette player, a can of roach spay, a bag of odds and ends, and some plates of food. The gate opened and we passed through.

We entered a room filled with women who also carried bundles of supplies. The men and women arranged themselves in two lines, facing each other. We waited for our names to be called and to be issued a room. The men were dressed as cleanly and neatly as possible, and each of the women wore her nicest dress with lots of makeup. There were all shapes, ages, and sizes of men and women.

Kate was there. She was wearing a simple cotton sundress and carrying a Playmate cooler and a large bag. They called out the inmate's names one by one, and each was given a room number. I watched, trying to figure out which woman was paired with which man. I didn't know many of the inmates. Most of the guys in my theatre group were younger and unmarried, so they didn't get conjugal visits. Kate and I had not mentioned our divorce, so we were considered married. It was just plain screwy that you had to be married in order to be allowed a conjugal visit. You could smoke marijuana, have sex with the guys in cellblock five, even make your own fermented drinks, but you weren't allowed to sleep with your girlfriend.

I thought it would have been better to let everybody have conjugal visits. If an inmate could get a girl to visit him for the night, they should just let him have at it. It would make everyone much easier to get along with. They called my name and Kate stepped forward.

I smiled at her, and we walked down the hall to the room number they'd assigned us. I went in first and asked her to wait outside for a minute. It was a bare concrete cell with a sink, a toilet, and a barred window. I had been given instructions from Martín about what to do to make it a better, more romantic experience for Kate. I sprayed the floor with roach spray and the air with mosquito repellant. Then I rolled my bed onto the concrete slab and spread a rug to the side of the bed. I picked up any roaches or other critters lying around the floor and flushed them down the toilet. I tied a piece of heavy string from the pipes over the toilet to the bars on the window.

Then I brought in Kate. She opened her bag, took out a scented candle and lit it. I popped a tape in the player, one Diego had lent me, and punched play. Cool, sexy Brazilian jazz – Stan Getz and Joao Gilberto – filled the concrete room. I turned off the glaring overhead light, allowing the light from the outside to come through the small window. It complimented the glow from the candle and, all in all, it was pretty nice. I could, for a moment, imagine I wasn't in prison.

We took off our shoes and sat on the bed. It was a little tense at first. We hadn't said a word up to that point. We'd busied ourselves with small tasks trying to make the room pleasant. I brought a special meal I'd cooked in my cell, and she had some pastries she brought from Salt Lake. The whole thing was surreal. We had filed for divorce a few months before I left for Mexico and hadn't been living together as man and wife since then. I had gone back to school and she was busy performing theatre at night and working as a bank teller during the day.

I hardly knew anything about her life. And yet there we were, pretending to be a happily married couple getting ready for an evening of romance and sex in a cold, hard prison cell. We felt like strangers. I had seen her when she came with my parents a couple of months prior, but that was quick, and we didn't have much time to talk. I had been writing to her as though we were still married, and she had written back.

At some point in this ordeal, Kate decided to get involved. She would act as my wife, come down to visit, and help me with my case and other needs. She was a caretaker, had always been a person who cared more for others than herself. The kind of person who stepped in to help another with their struggles and challenges. Some years later, Kate would put aside her own comfort and equilibrium to help her sister with a completely disabled child who required 24/7 care. Kate lived with and/or near her sister for years helping care for this boy. It became a major focus in her life.

That was the woman who was sitting on a stone slab next to me with a stack of papers she had brought from the lawyer. "Rick," she said. "Can we take care of this paperwork first? I'm sorry, but I have to do something with this now." She brought out the divorce papers, which had recently become final, there were documents I was required to read and sign. I started to object, saying maybe we were too hasty and should reconsider. She didn't back down. It was one of the only times she ever fought back. She didn't let me get away with manipulation. She held firm and remained calm and steadfast.

With no recrimination, she said, "I want to continue with this now. I wasn't the one who wanted the divorce. You know that. I begged you not to do it. I loved you. But now that it's done, I'm okay with it. I don't want my helping you to be about us as a couple. You made these choices on your own. All of them – the divorce, this dumb idea to go to Mexico, everything. There is no reason I should help you. My friends and family think I'm crazy for doing it. But I have decided to help you. Not because I want you back. And not because I want anything else from you. I don't want to make this about you and me getting back together. I'm going to help you, Rick, because you're my friend. I've known you for ten years, since that first night in college when we made love."

She went on. "Then we got married. I was happy, but you, evidently, were not. So let's just keep things the way they are. We will finalize our divorce. We can see how it goes. Maybe you'll get out soon, and maybe we'll get back together. I don't know. And I don't know if I want to. But that will be another time. Another situation. We'll see what happens. For now, you can count on me to help you. I'll come down here occasionally and bring you things. I will meet with you for these visits, and we can make love if you want. But that's as far as it goes. Are you okay with that?"

I was the one in prison, but she was the one who had actually grown from the experience. She was stronger than I had ever seen before. And honestly, it made me fall in love with her again. At least that was what I told myself. "All right," I said, trying not show that I was a little hurt and maybe even embarrassed. I took the papers and just started signing them, one after another.

"Don't you want to read them?" she asked. I shook my head and kept signing where the little yellow tape pieces were. Then I put the papers down. She placed them back in her bag.

I asked her about Jeff and Arlene. She told me they were allowed to see each other for a few minutes in the hospital and he would be back in prison soon. I already knew from a phone call that Kate had driven down with Arlene. This was the first time she'd come to visit him. It was actually the first visit Jeff had. After being shot, he gained a lot of sympathy and notoriety, both in the prison and back home, and now all his family was planning to come and visit him.

I shook my head and told her how stupid I thought it was. Jeff was acting crazy and it was affecting everyone else. I started in on how he'd caused problems for my theatre group, and how our opportunity to go into town and perform and my interview with the TV station were cancelled. I was going on and on, then she finally stopped me.

"You haven't changed a bit, have you? You haven't been affected by this thing at all. It's like you're on some kind of sabbatical or you've taken on a crazy new project," she said with a bit of exasperation. "Jeff and Arlene are great friends, besides being a couple. You and Jeff were roommates. He's been shot. He's not doing well here. Just because you handle everything so well doesn't mean everybody else does. Why can't you have a little compassion for others, Richard?"

When she called me Richard, I knew it was serious. I rarely, if ever, saw Kate get mad. But here it was now, and I didn't want the evening to turn into a fight. I gave up and said, "Okay, okay, you're right. I'll try harder to understand what Jeff's going through." I don't know if I meant it or not, but despite everything, I was damned excited to have sex and I didn't want to lose the moment we'd created. I sat back and gave us a few minutes to cool down. Then I picked up a plate of the beefsteak ranchero I had cooked and took a bite. I gave her a taste, and she enjoyed it.

I smiled, she smiled. I put down the plate and put my arms around her and brought her close. Her head was resting on my shoulder. The sundress was thin and sheer. I could see the outline of her body easily. I dropped my hands to her hips and kissed her.

The sex was amazing. We had always been very sexual, and it was somehow even more exciting in prison. It was dangerous there. It had been long, arduous drive for her, and standing in line for hours compounded the stress and difficulty. We had argued over the divorce, lifting both our anxiety levels. Everything leading up to that moment of passion had been charged with a feverish, frenzied energy. We had stopped living together eight or nine months ago. I hadn't had sex since a couple of months before leaving for Mexico, when I slept with some actress from one of my classes. And it wasn't very good. I never liked, nor was ever good at, one-night stands. You didn't know enough about the other person to make it work very well; at least I didn't.

Katie and I had been married for several years, before that we'd lived together for a couple of years, and before that we'd dated. We knew how to have sex with each other. But it was never so furious, so passionate, so unbelievably exhilarating as it was that night. All the tension and fear and pain and hell leading up to that moment was expelled through hot, primal, physical sex. We were so goddamned good at having sex and that time, it was spectacular.

We really didn't sleep much that night. We just kept making love until about four or five. Then we fell into a daze, wrapped in each other's arms. It was hot, sticky, and the room smelled of mosquito repellant. But it was beautiful. Kate was dead tired; again, she'd driven twenty hours straight, then had to find the hospital in downtown Hermosillo, and after that, a hotel where Arlene could spend the night. Then she came to the prison and waded through the conjugal visit process with the other women. Then, for six or seven hours, she'd had prison sex with a madman. Kate dropped off like baby.

While she slept, I took our clothes and hung them over the line I had rigged to keep them clean and away from insects. I stood at the window for a moment and listened to the sounds of the prison: there was a chicken farm nearby and you could hear the roosters every morning; the main highway passed alongside the prison and big trucks and busses rumbled by all day long; and there was a stockyard across the road down by the train tracks where you could hear cattle being loaded, then shipped by rail. They burned the dung everyday, so there was the constant odor of burnt shit. It was a strange yet exhilarating cacophony of odor and noise ensnaring the senses each and every day. It was beginning to feel like home.

Quietly, I went around the room and tidied up. Then I carefully sidled in next to her, trying not to disturb her. There were many times I took care of her as well. Times before, difficult times at school and throughout our marriage. She relied on me for many things back then. I could be very tender and loving, so there was that. We'd had a good marriage up to a point. We were terribly in love for a few years and did everything together; we loved to cook and go to see plays and entertain friends. We liked the same movies and loved the Utah mountains for hiking and camping. There was so much we had in common. I laid next to her thinking about our life together and how it had all come crashing down so quickly. It made me sad. If not actual regret, then at least a humble sort of contriteness.

She was right: it was my fault, and the choices made were mine. But I instigated everything; including our first date, our first night of sex, eventually our marriage, and finally our divorce. That's who I was. That guy, the guy who never followed orders or did what someone else wanted to do. Perhaps I wasn't a thoughtful leader, and maybe I didn't help people the way she did. But there were things, things we did, places I took us that she would never have done or might never do again. Lying here in this Mexican prison, our clothes hanging from a line to keep the cockroaches at bay

– the sights, the sounds, the smells – it was raw and real and a long way from the antiseptic culture of Salt Lake City. At the least, it was an experience she would never forget.

What are the things you remember when you think back on your life? The straight *A*s you got, how gorgeous the campus was in autumn, the number of people you slept with? What's impactful, what triggers the big, brassy emotions? I think you look back at the difficulties and challenges you faced, and hopefully, what you learned from them.

I wasn't sure if we'd get back together. I did love her though, very much. And I loved making love to her, we were good together that way. But she couldn't stop me. She couldn't keep me from the wild things. And that's the kind of woman I needed. Perhaps I would make back to Utah, maybe I'd get my life going again. And if so, I wouldn't be able to survive too many more adventures like this one. Or I would never have a life. Someone had to stop me. Someone had to keep me from driving over the edge.

CHAPTER 14

THE WEEK LEADING up to the Mother's Day program was especially grueling. The whole idea started to seem hopeless; people weren't learning their lines, the lights were shorting out, the glue on the egg flats wasn't holding, and the sets were far from finished. It was just one thing after another. The gay and trans folks in cellblock five had agreed to make our costumes since they had the only sewing machine; plus, I think they liked being a part of the endeavor. They were trying hard to please me, but kept making real clothing rather than costumes that didn't need to be perfect, so they were behind.

I had assigned the building of *The Odd Couple* set to the wood shop, but when I went to check on it, they were constructing a house. I didn't have the language down well enough to make them understand they were constructing scenery for a play, not a real cellblock. The scene was set in Godoy and Samuel's cell and we were trying to make it look enough like a real cell so the audience would understand immediately what was happening. They'd constructed massive walls from 2x4s and sheetrock we'd never be able to move on and off the stage. So I spent a several hours showing them how to construct theatre flats from light wooden frames and muslin. Scenery is a different breed of cat and they didn't get it. I kept it from Samuel and Godoy, but I didn't think they would finish in time for the show.

Even the acoustics were troubling. I felt like I was losing my mind. The sound seemed okay for *The Padre,* but since I was in that play, I wasn't sure how it sounded to the audience. Now, standing in the back of the auditorium, I couldn't understand every word being said on the stage. After all the egg-carton sheets we'd hung, there was still a nasty echo. I was afraid no one would get the jokes in *The Odd Couple* or be able to hear Chabita and Soto deliver their poems. The excitement of the first couple of rehearsals was gone and I was worried we might fail.

We had three bands, three poetry readings, and the scene from *The Odd Couple.* Together, the cast and crew was about twenty guys, and they were disinclined to follow my rehearsal schedule. They showed up any old time and expected to have the stage. There's a class system, an inmate hierarchy in prison, sometimes based on wealth, sometimes on toughness. But everyone follows this unwritten code and knows their place. I tried to overlook it within my theatre group but it was impossible. Disagreements became arguments that nearly escalated into fistfights. In the end, I had to bow to the system and bend my rehearsal schedule to fit with the inmates' expectations.

People in prison are a combination of tired, frustrated, anxious, and uncompromising. They've learned to fight or manipulate or work the system to get a better life. One after another, they kept coming at me with unrealistic requests or frivolous complaints. Chabita was worried about portraying Paco, the little boy in his poem, the backstage crew wanted to dress in black like they'd seen in movies, and the *Norteño* band didn't like where they were placed in the program – they wanted to go last. In fact, everybody wanted to go last. They all wanted their piece to be the one the audience remembered.

When we started rehearsing, I had urged them to think about the show like it was a professional production, as though we were getting paid. My thought was that would motivate them to spend the time and effort needed to make the show a success. But I had created little monsters. They wanted to be treated like stars, like real professionals. And since I was the one with experience, I got dumped on. I had to find a solution to every problem, while, at the same time, making each performer feel like he was the star of the show.

I had deluded myself into thinking that simply getting an opportunity to do this kind of thing in prison would be exhilarating, and no one would complain. But in fact, it was the opposite. In prison, you're out of control of your own life. Each inmate is always trying to control something else. It might be another inmate, or they might try to pull a fast one on the guards by smuggling contraband into the prison, anything that would give them the sense of having more control over their lives. Most of the guys in Mexican prisons don't have release dates. Typically, they serve two-thirds of their sentence if everything goes well, but it doesn't always work out that way. The courts are fickle, the judges are often corrupt, and the system is faulty at best. It's a loose combination of discord and unconnected pieces, where anything can and does go wrong.

This sets up an underlying competitiveness among the inmates. They're always trying to get the best food, the best cell, the most attention from the nurses, and the most respect from the other inmates. The attitude was endemic in my theatre group and was certainly manifested in the Mother's Day program. Everybody wanted to have the best location on the stage, the best lighting, the most attention from me, and somehow, have the least amount of work to do.

I was the one ultimately in charge of making all those decisions – an outsider, an American, who barely spoke the language. Sure, I could tell someone to move to the left or right, or to slow down or face the audience a little more. I could even set rehearsal times and schedules and provide motivation for the entire program. But when it came to communicating with the cast and crew the subtleties of audience fatigue, balanced programming, scenery movement, lighting controls, the emotional arc of the entire show, and so on – it was impossible.

In the end, I was just like all of them, so I chose to position *The Odd Couple* last. I wanted to end the show with my clever writing and directorial work. At least they wouldn't be able to argue with each other over who went last. I took the final spot and that was that!

The night after our dress rehearsal, I dragged myself back to my cell and collapsed. I was dog tired. It had been a long, tedious day. The scenery for *The Odd Couple* didn't show up, the sound seemed to be getting worse, two members of the crew quit and Chabita wanted to cancel his poem. He thought it was boring, he thought he was too quiet, he didn't want to kneel by the grave, but mostly, he was afraid he might cry because the poem was too sad for him. He'd been teased and bullied many times in the past and he thought if the inmates saw him crying, it would begin again. He followed me all the way back to my cell, a hysterical mess. I finally turned to him and said, "*Esta bien,* Chabita, do it or not. It's okay with me whatever you decide to do." Then I went in my cell and toppled into bed, unable to recall if I had said it to him in English or Spanish.

The next morning, I awakened to Jeff standing next to my bed with bandages on his legs. He said, "Mind if I sit?" as he sat down on my bed. I was disoriented. I hadn't had my coffee yet, and I could barely understand what was going on. In a tone I hadn't heard from him in a while he said, "I'm still unstable on my feet, and so I have to sit whenever I stop or I'll fall over." He sounded almost sane again.

I mumbled a sympathetic remark, got up, and started to make coffee. I offered Jeff a cup, but he wasn't drinking coffee anymore. I didn't want to talk about what happened to him. I was still mad, I guess, and I was afraid I'd say something unkind and the whole damn universe would think me unfeeling.

He told me more about his crazy escape, filling in the details the *comandante* and Martín didn't know, like how he hailed the cab and dragged himself into the field, collapsing because his legs filled with blood.

As to why he punched the doctor, he said, "I could tell he was angry about having to see me. He wasn't very nice, and made comments to the nurse that sounded like he was making fun of me. He was a big guy. I think that's why the guard left me alone with him. I knew the only way to get out was to hit him as hard as I could and knock him down. So I jumped off the table and slugged him in the head. After that, it was all a blur. I reacted instinctively as things happened and moved accordingly. Next thing I knew, I was being hauled onto a stretcher with my hands and legs cuffed."

I shook my head. Jeff was courageous and tough at least, and had demonstrated that. Although I wasn't impressed, I didn't want him to think I was mad, so I let out an audible mumble that I hoped sounded like "wow." Then I let him know his escape attempt had cost the theatre group some privileges, and I wouldn't be going into town to do the TV interview. He didn't show any remorse or empathy for me, and I felt none for him. We each had our plans, our own perceptions of prison and how to handle the experience. Jeff envisioned himself in a Steve McQueen movie, where everything depended on escape. I saw myself in the *Bridge Over the*

River Kwai, and I wanted to build something magnanimous against all odds.

I suppose, in a way, it was that vision – *my* vision – that instigated the adventure and helped lock us in prison. I wanted to face an impossible challenge, an experience where my life would be on the line and I could make something great out of a trash heap. For a tiny moment, sitting there looking at Jeff, I wasn't sure that I hadn't hoped for this. Perhaps the underlying reason I tried to convince my friends to go to Mexico and buy drugs was just so I could end up in prison. Jeff, on the other hand, wanted no part of it. He wanted out, and he saw it as his right, even his civic duty, to try and escape. Unbelievably, after all that had happened, he was still hellbent on that goal.

I didn't want to hear any more so I changed the subject. He was annoyed, even a bit chafed that I was unimpressed by his escapade. I urged him to find something to do here, but he said nothing, just stared at me for a long, uncomfortable moment. I was afflicted with a disturbing thought: maybe he laid the blame entirely on me for all the injuries he'd sustained, both physical and emotional, and he wanted retribution.

I attempted to talk about our case, and told him that Pedro had a new idea for our defense. He was going to claim Jeff and I were drug addicts and were transporting the marijuana back home for our own use. I tried to sound more compassionate. "For some reason, we were charged with transportation instead of possession and Pedro thinks because of that mistake we might get our case thrown out." Jeff was unfazed.

I didn't really believe it either, but I hoped Jeff would. As usual, he let everything I said about our case and Pedro pass over him. He had a new plan; someone had given his mother the name of a well-connected lawyer in Phoenix who could buy his way out. His mother had flown down to visit him in the hospital and had brought a bunch of money so they were now committed to that idea.

I pleaded with him. "You'll never be able to buy your way out now. We both need to have a record of good behavior in case our truck is discovered. So they'll be more lenient in the US."

He looked at me with a sneer. "You mean if *your* truck is discovered. Not *our* truck."

"You knew about it, you were in the vehicle, and you used it to commit a crime right along with me. We're both guilty," I said, clarifying the situation.

"Maybe," said Jeff.

"What the hell are you thinking, Jeff? We both planned this. You were the one who said, 'yeah, let's do it.' We were *big* adventurers. Gonna find some drug dealers and trade a four-wheel drive truck for cocaine, come back, sell it, and start our own theatre! Have you forgotten that? What are you going to tell them... I kidnapped you?"

Jeff just stared at me, then at last he said, "I followed you here because I trusted you and believed in you, and when we got to the prison, you pushed me away. I was breaking apart. I needed you to help me but you didn't... you pushed me away. Now I don't need you." He got up and walked out the door, leaving me dumbfounded.

I didn't know what to think. Was I wrong? How could I have helped him *and* myself too? Didn't he need to accept some responsibility for his actions? How was this all on me? But maybe he was right. Maybe I should have done more to help him. But that was over now. We were headed down a bad road, and if we didn't hold it together, we could both be in big trouble. But it was all the time I could give to that issue, I had to run.

It was Mother's Day, the day of our program. My parents had driven down again, bringing money for Pedro and more supplies for me. And too, I think my mom wanted to see me on Mothers' Day. We had been getting along so well since I arrived in prison and, in an odd way, they were feeling like I was now closer to them than ever before. I ran straight to the visitor's area in time to meet them coming through the entry. We only had a few minutes before I had to leave them to get to the auditorium and prepare for the show. I had told them about the program and how much work it had been so they knew everyone was counting on me. The visitors would be allowed inside shortly so I left them with Martín and his family. They wouldn't be able to converse but at least they wouldn't be sitting alone.

I ran to the auditorium and found everyone unsure of what to do. The guys from the wood shop were installing the set. Finally! It would remain upstage and moved into place for the performance, so we covered it with black fabric. Godoy and Samuel were trying to rehearse on the set as it was being constructed but all the hammering and shouting distracted them. I went backstage to assemble the rest of my cast and crew, and ensure the correct program order. Chabita was still scared but was going to do it. Soto was rehearsing his poem, and Luis his reading, the three bands were practicing simultaneously; it was a giant cacophony. There was little more I could do now, it would come off as planned or fall apart, depending on how well the audience could hear and whether or not the performers could relax and have fun.

As we were positioning *The Odd Couple* set upstage and getting it covered, they opened the doors to the auditorium. Everyone came rushing in to the get the best seats, thinking the auditorium acoustics were so bad they had to be down front to hear. Press coverage and talk around the prison had both visitors and inmates excited and curious. I was afraid their expectations might be exaggerated, which made me nervous. What if we couldn't measure up?

With no time to dwell on it, I hurried to the door to meet my parents and Martín's family and show them the seats I had cordoned off. I hustled backstage to see the cast and crew one more time, and oh my god, they were terrified. I did my best to calm them down, giving each one a hand shake and hearty "good luck!" (They didn't understand the notion of "break a leg.") I went back out front to the check with the lighting guys and make sure they knew when to bring up the spot and the stage lights. The stage lights were controlled from the wall near the entrance, the footlights from just offstage, and the spotlight, of course, was controlled from the back of the house. I had to keep moving between locations to keep all three guys coordinated since we didn't have a comm system.

I turned the house lights off, the stage lights came up as planned, and we began with a musical number. The audience immediately let out a big *ooohh* and some even clapped. Diego, the classical guitarist, was revealed onstage with a guy on percussion and they launched into an up-tempo *bossa nova* piece. I was stunned - it sounded amazing. Then it hit me! I had forgotten about the effect of the audience on the room acoustics. The auditorium was packed; there were people sitting on the floor up front, extra chairs had been brought in and placed all around, and people were standing at the back and along the sides. It was a huge mass of humanity. The room had never been so full. There were cameras and reporters, the *comandante* was there with his people, it seemed like the opening night of a Broadway show.

The next act was Soto with the poem he'd written and the sound was acoustically perfect – just enough echo to enlarge the sound but not enough to impede understanding of the actors and musicians. I don't know how I had missed it. I knew the principles of acoustical physics, but had forgotten about the audience effect. I just stood there, jaw gaped, watching the show.

It went pretty well; the audience really liked the bands and poetry readings. Occasionally, there was a hitch, someone missed a cue, or turned on the wrong lighting. We had footlights, overhead lights with two colors, the spot, and a couple of side lights. I tried to use various combinations of our meager fixtures to set the mood for each piece. It wasn't the main stage at the U of U, but it wasn't half bad.

We came to the final stretch of the program: Chabita's poem, "*Soy* Paco," the wildly popular *Norteño* band, and going last, *The Odd Couple* scene.

The applause for band prior to Chabita covered the scenery change for "*Soy* Paco." We created a grave from egg cartons and papier-mâché, and made a rustic cross from old, weathered boards. I had planned to use only the footlights and spot on Chabita because he knelt at the grave and never moved. When the lights came up, Chabita walked slowly to the grave and knelt upstage of it. There were a few *oohs* and *aahs*, then it was eerily quiet. They all knew the poem. He placed some wilted flowers on the grave and began to speak.

The poem begins with "*Soy* Paco, *No Soy Basura*" (I'm Paco, I'm not garbage). It's a traditional Mother's Day poem that always brings tears. But Chabita's physical stature and personal history added a layer of reality that smacked everyone right in the gut.

Chabita is a nickname for *little boy*. And he *was* a little boy. Chabita was seventeen and had been in prison for a couple of years already, which meant he was arrested and put in prison (for weed) at about age fourteen or fifteen. He tried to hang around with guys who would watch out for him, and that's why he joined the theatre group. He had no family, at least no one ever came to visit him. I didn't know all the circumstances of his home life, only that Martín said it wasn't good. Chabita *was* Paco, a boy who had no mother, no one to care for him. Praying at the grave of his dead mother and pleading with her to help him was real for Chabita. Each stanza begins with "I am Paco, I am not garbage." The character can't find a way to keep himself alive after his mother dies. Everywhere he goes, people treat him like trash. He's discarded by all he meets. And Chabita felt like that too. Most of the audience knew this, so every time he said, *"Soy* Paco, *no soy basura,"* you could hear people in the audience crying and sniffling.

It was a perfect scene. The footlights cast an ominous shadow of Chabita and the cross on the back wall and the spotlight stained him in a wash of blue. The worn and tattered rags he wore were actually from his own wardrobe and had been further distressed by the gay guys. We hadn't rehearsed a lot with Chabita because he was so twisted about doing it, and the grave had only been finished the day before. But it was an unexpected theatrical moment, a moment of theatre magic. He let himself cry, and you could see the tears dropping from his eyes, even from where I was at the back. Soon, the entire audience was in tears. My parents didn't understand the words, but they were crying too. It was a moment that worked astonishingly well, not only because of Chabita's stellar performance, but because so many people in the auditorium felt like Paco. Some had lost mothers or fathers, and everyone had lost something because they had loved ones here in prison. It was a truer and more cathartic theatre moment than I had ever seen. And though I would likely receive a lot of the credit, I had virtually little to do with it.

Chabita uttered the last words, then remained on his knees. There was a moment of silence. No one said a word and Chabita didn't know what to do, so he slowly stood up. I guess he was waiting for a cue from me, but his confusion seemed real, like it was part of the character and the performance. As he stood up, he turned slightly to the audience, and there was thunderous applause. He got so embarrassed, he went running off the stage. Listening to the applause from backstage, his confusion changed to excitement. I ran backstage, grabbed him by the shoulders and shook him saying, "Good job, good job!" I said it over and over. Chabita was all smiles. He wanted me and everyone to tell him how good he was. He was a star, maybe for the first time in his life. That feeling, that accomplishment and validation, continued for weeks after because many of the inmates had watched the program and had also thought him amazing.

The *Norteño* band went on as Chabita came off, and began their accordion- and guitar-backed songs about *trafficantes* and corrupt cops. It was the perfect respite. Everyone wanted an emotional release after Chabita's poem, and it gave me a chance to get the actors and crew ready for *The Odd Couple*.

Samuel and Godoy were still very nervous. I had expected it, but had never seen either of them so fragile and dependent on each other for support. Godoy was pacing and rehearsing his lines. Samuel, who had helped translate the play, knew the lines, but he was sure no one would get the comedy. They were also nervous about how they would be received by the visitors – the two former subversives who'd fought with the police and army for a year.

They were once bright students with great promise but became involved in the student revolts of the late '60s and eventually joined the underground movement in the aftermath of the *Tlatelolco* Massacre of 1968. The Mexican government carried out a massacre of hundreds of students protesting authoritarian rule in the *Zocolo* of Mexico City. Following that, and aided by the American CIA, the government began a violent campaign against students across the country, executing, arresting, and torturing thousands.

The fear and hatred generated by the Cold War often played out in the streets and countryside of places like Hermosillo, where students, who basically wanted opportunity and education, were branded communists and hunted like animals. It was fueled by the belief that student revolts would turn into revolutions, which would become communist dictatorships. And there was plenty of evidence to support that belief. But the same movement played out in the streets and universities of America as students protested the Vietnam War and other social issues, and some might conclude, those protests brought about change.

Samuel and Godoy's activism ended with a gun battle in the streets of downtown Hermosillo as their group attempted to rob a bank to support their activities. Most of the students were shot, and a policeman was killed. It was never proven that the students actually shot the cop, but they were blamed for it, convicted of murder (rather than terrorism), and sentenced to long prison terms. Samuel and Godoy spent two years in solitary confinement before being put in to the main population. By then they'd lost out on an education and potentially successful careers. They were very smart, hard-working, and had completed their university studies and learned English from books brought to them by groups such as Amnesty International. The organization was also working for their release but the government refused to consider them political prisoners, because they were convicted of murder, not terrorism. Most people in Hermosillo, along with many inmates, were unsympathetic to their lost cause and thought of them as terrorists.

This was the situation that existed for Godoy and Samuel when they took the stage to present the fight scene from *The Odd Couple*.

In the original film, Jack Lemmon's character, Felix, is arguing with Walter Matthau's character, Oscar, about how he (Felix) is unappreciated, and how Oscar is such a pig. The conflict of the story is centered around the many differences in their two personalities. Felix is a neurotic neat freak and the fun-loving slob Oscar leaves cigarette butts and dirty clothes around.

In this scene, Felix tries to convince Oscar to be more sensitive and clean up after himself. But Oscar has had it with Felix and his annoying idiosyncrasies, and finally snaps. The tension explodes into a nasty argument with Oscar messing up the apartment and telling Felix to move out. During the argument, Oscar tries to make Felix understand how annoying he can be by telling him, "You leave me little notes on my pillow. 'We're all out of cornflakes... F.U.'"

When Felix (whose last name is Unger) composes the note, he signs his initials to let Oscar know who wrote it. But Oscar continues, "Who else would leave me a note like that?" And of course, in Oscar's world, the initials 'F.U.' would also be saying "Fuck You." Felix is clueless and doesn't get the double entendre, which only adds to Oscar's frustration.

It is one of the best jokes in the play and works so well because of the name Felix Unger, which is also a perfect name for the character. We had to come up with a way to make the joke work in Spanish, because there are no expletives in Spanish with the initials *F* and *U*. So, we gave Felix the name Chavo Tomás Manuel, with its initials Ch.T.M. In Spanish, *Chinga*

Tu Madre is a common expletive and everybody quickly understands it. Plus, Latin people have two last names so the name also worked for that. The problem was, we didn't know if the audience would make all the connections. First off, it was only a single scene, and there wasn't enough time to fully develop the plot, so the audience wouldn't have the background on the characters. Second, although we had written a reference to his name in the scene and we had it in the playbill, they could easily miss the fact that his full name was Chavo Tomás Manuel. And third (our biggest concern), it might be offensive to use the expletive *Chinga Tu Madre* on Mother's Day. We were all worried about it, but Samuel and Godoy were the ones who had to go onstage in front of people, many of whom weren't particularly friendly to them, and make it work.

It was nerve racking if you took a moment to think about it, which I did not, mostly because I didn't have the bloody time to care. I wasn't even sure if the audience would understand *anything* we did onstage, because I didn't think they were going to hear it very well. But none of those fears proved to be true.

By that time, the audience was hanging right with us. You could just feel it. After Chabita's poem and *Norteño* band, they were thinking the show was pretty amazing. The press, the guards, the inmates, the *comandante* were all having a great time.

The applause for the *Norteño* band, an inmate favorite, was long and wild, and easily covered moving the scenery for *The Odd Couple*. When the lights came up, the audience immediately recognized the prison cell and applauded for the set. Hoots and hollers came up from the inmates and laughter from their families. That gave Samuel and Godoy time to enter the stage and get settled.

We had rewritten the scene to be two guys sharing a cell in prison for many years, which was Samuel and Godoy's reality. We made the two characters tired of each other's idiosyncrasies and personalities, and their relationship was beginning to fray. We created events that paralleled some of the situations in the play but were the kinds of experiences inmates would have. Basically, we rewrote the entire scene using the two characters. It worked fantastically well. Everybody got it, right from the very first words. They were laughing all the way through, and unfortunately, I had forgotten to coach Samuel and Godoy to wait for the laughs. So they kept trying to go on with their lines while the audience was still laughing at the previous joke. We weren't even sure if all the prison-referenced jokes would play to the entire audience. We had written the scene mainly for the inmates but the entire audience was getting the humor, and evidently, understood the prison jokes. It threw Samuel and Godoy off for a few moments. Finally, they got the hang of it and began waiting for the laughter to die down before starting the next line.

When they got to the place in the scene where Samuel says the line, "You leave me little notes on my pillow… Ch.T.M.," he was afraid they wouldn't get it, so he took a little extra time and over enunciated. But they got it, and oh boy, they got it immediately. The crowd went completely nuts, laughing over and over again. Some didn't quite understand it at first and waited for their companions to retell the joke, and so the laughter started up again as the joke went around the room. Samuel had the next line, and he waited, then tried to start, then waited again, then tried to start again. He did that three or four times; it caught him off guard and he laughed a little. Then the audience laughed at that, as people do the outtakes of TV shows.

I really don't know why it worked so well. Maybe it was some kind of catharsis for the audience and the two activists. They were really good guys, and I think most people had come to change their thinking about the student movement and all that happened, even though some still felt strongly about the killing of the policeman. We had crafted the scene to portray some of the actual reality of Samuel and Godoy's relationship and what they had gone through together, even alluding to their student movement activities. There were layers of comedy, pathos, and satire that we didn't necessarily write into the scene but somehow existed, intrinsically, within the situation.

The scene ends when Oscar throws a plate of linguini against the wall, which we did, and It was a smashing finale. The lights dimmed to black, then came back up for Samuel and Godoy to take their bows. They relished in the near maniacal applause, then ran backstage out of breath, sizzling with excitement. It was the first time in years that people had applauded for them. All Samuel could say was, and he said it in English, "They wouldn't let me to speak, they wouldn't let me to speak... they were laughing too much hard. Laughing too much hard!" For me, it was one of those singular moments when you know something you did was special; not for you, but for someone else. You actually made a difference in somebody's life. I saw in Samuel's eyes how much fun he was having and how excited he was. And Godoy felt exactly the same. These two guys had endured so much pain and tragedy and were finally enjoying a moment of life as it should be.

The Odd Couple scene rekindled the emotion stirred up from Chabita's poem. Together, they were a rare and indescribably delicious moment of theatre magic, when a unique and unalterable connection exists between performers and audience. It's a thing you can't create or plan for and it's so deep, so rich that the resulting experience is foreign to whatever you thought it was going to be. It's magical. That's all you can say about it. I witnessed the power of theatre in prison that day and the feeling never left me. it would be something I would have to explore further.

The reporters interviewed Samuel, Godoy, Chabita, and some of the other guys. The *comandante* got in a few words. It was an indisputable success and I was exhausted. I didn't really have time to talk to anyone as I had to hustle to see my parents, who were alone and rather scared to be inside the prison. I caught up with them still sitting in the auditorium, not knowing what to do.

I had to admit, my little Mormon mom and dad were quite something. They had driven twenty-four hours, (always took them longer than Kate) to Hermosillo and had to go through all the rigmarole without speaking or understanding a word of what was said to them. They sat there alone, without understanding much of the show, and tried to be part of the audience. They were frightened and concerned about their son, and yet were really good eggs about it. I spent the rest of the morning (as long as visitors were allowed) hanging with them. I let my performers have the spotlight and I, for once, tried to be a good son. I was glad to draw back and let the cast and crew enjoy all the glamour of the moment.

The *comandante* let me take my parents to my cell so I could show them how I lived. That helped them feel better about the situation. They were still scared, but happy to see that things weren't as bad as they had imagined.

After the show, I was saying goodbye to my parents at the *sala de guardia* when Jeff walked up to us. He smiled, and bid an unusually friendly hello to my parents. He handed them a sealed letter and asked them to give it to the lawyer in Phoenix his mom had talked to. His mother had called my parents and told them about the new idea, so my parents were going to stop at his office on the way home and see what they thought of his plan. They were happy to take the letter for him. Jeff smiled at me and then at my parents, said his goodbyes, and walked away. He seemed rather odd though, but I couldn't figure out what it was.

The next day, I went to the *comandante's* office for his weekly English lesson. Hector Galaviz, an inmate and the son of a wealthy contractor, was having lunch with the *comandante*. Hector had been sentenced for drug possession; a huge amount, like major drug dealer stuff. But his father had gotten him a cushy situation at the prison. He often ate with the *comandante* and had his own cell apart from the rest of the population. I rarely interacted with Hector. He was from a well-connected family and no one could ascertain why he'd been involved in drug trafficking. We all assumed his family was not really in construction, and he had to take the fall for the crime in order to appease the DEA. He had everything you could want inside: his wife came to visit almost every day, he ate the best food, and his cell was more like a small apartment.

He and the *comandante* were drinking shots of hundred-year-old tequila and cooking fresh shrimp. They invited me to forget the lesson for the day and join them. It was the best booze I had ever had. It didn't taste at all like tequila; it was more like a really smooth cognac. Hector and the *comandante* were having a great time laughing and joking about things I didn't understand.

Then, out of nowhere, the *comandante* told me that today was his last day at the prison. He was being replaced. He thanked me for his English lessons and showed me a newspaper with the story on the front page about the Mother's Day program. He congratulated me on the show and the theatre group. Then he cautioned me to be nice to the new *comandante*.

"Because," he said, "he is much stricter than I am." Then he gave me an odd look, with his face scrunched up a bit.

As I sat there bewildered, trying to think of something to say, Thomas burst into the room. He saw me and said, "Well, goodbye, Richard, I'm getting out today!" He then said goodbye to the *comandante*. He was very excited. He was being released after three years because his case had been dismissed for lack of evidence. It was startling to hear all that at once. I was happy for Thomas, but he had been keeping an eye on Jeff, and that was helpful to me. The *comandante* was supportive of my programs, and the English lessons had enabled me to have some additional perks, like hundred-year-old tequila.

Now both those things were being taken away. I tried to show that I was happy for both of them, especially Thomas, but it felt like the world was changing around me – like my whole foundation was suddenly yanked out from under me just when everything was going great.

CHAPTER 15

ON THEIR WAY back to Salt Lake, my parents stopped in Phoenix to meet with the lawyer Jeff's mom had found. I thought Jeff and his mother were going to lose their money so I told my parents not to give him any. It wouldn't hurt to stop and meet him; they could see if he had a plan that might make sense. And they'd told Jeff they would deliver his letter, thinking it contained important information about our case.

I had never met Jeff's mother, but from the way he spoke about her previously, she didn't sound like someone we could count on. His parents were divorced, his father was not around, and I got the feeling his mother had not been a stabilizing force in his life. She'd taken a long time to get involved in helping Jeff, although he had some fault in that too. At the least, it was unfeeling of her, even negligent, not to have written him. Suddenly she appears, and miraculously has a clever attorney who claims to be able to buy Jeff and me out of prison. This seemed highly unlikely, not only because of what Samuel had said, but the total cost, including his fee, was unrealistic – a few thousand dollars was supposedly all it would take. The guy was baiting us and would keep asking for money, pretending to bribe officials until we actually made it on our own through the international transfer. It was a ruse, and the fact that Jeff couldn't see it indicated he was still living in a fantasy.

I mentioned Jeff's new plan to Martín and Samuel, who shook their heads, laughing. Several Americans had tried to buy their way out and not one had been successful. There was a Mexican inmate who bribed his way out because he had connections somewhere, but they'd never seen an American buy their way out. The DEA would never allow it. The US had provided funds to build the prison and the feds were on top of each and every case. I was sure they knew who we were and would follow us right through the transfer back to the States. This was one way the DEA fought the drug trade – keeping tabs on Americans arrested in Mexico. If they were just regular guys smoking weed, that was one thing; but if they were potential traffickers, that was a case to follow.

Even though we had ten kilos of marijuana, we were clearly not a professional operation. The weed was no good, it was bundled in an old box with plastic bags tied around it, and we hadn't even bothered to hide it. We had no prior criminal records, we were enrolled in college, and certainly didn't fit the typical profile of drug traffickers. But there was no way they would allow us to get out of prison illegally. We would have to follow the system through and end up in a US prison with criminal records.

A few days after my parents left, I walked down to the sala de guradia to get my mail and opened a letter from my parents that dropped me to the ground. I was so stunned by what I read I couldn't stand up. It was gut wrenching, heartbreaking, and disturbing all at once. It was all I could do to keep from throwing up, I was so sick. My stomach hurt, my knees gave out.

My parents had met with Jeff's attorney and given him the letter. He promptly read it to them and handed it back. I was reading that same letter because they had sent it back for me to read.

I found a place to sit, away from the crowd that gathered every morning, and started breathing slowly to try to calm down. I sat there, staring at Jeff's handwriting for a minute. Who was he? And who was I? Were we bad guys?

He had written to the attorney and ratted me out about the truck, claiming it was my fault and he had nothing to do with it. He claimed he and I had gone to Mexico for vacation and bought some weed, thinking it would be cool. When I told him about my truck, he was shocked and upset, and parted ways with me. He went on to say that the stolen truck story was the thing that drove him mad and pushed him to try and escape. He was willing to testify against me if it would help his case and get him out of prison.

My parents were understandably sickened and terribly heartbroken, and of course, deeply worried about me. Suddenly, their precious firstborn was into all kinds of criminal activities. I hadn't told them about the truck, and they assumed we drove Jeff's car to Mexico because they knew the story of my supposedly stolen truck. I was as angry at Jeff as much for dumping this on my parents as I was the betrayal. The thought of my mom so heartbroken made me feel like shit. I was more ashamed of that than the marijuana. I didn't think buying or smoking weed was so bad, but I did think reporting my truck stolen was a serious crime, and I was guilty of that.

I had been hoping the truck calamity would disappear. Insurance fraud had some pretty serious penalties. I didn't know for sure but I thought I could get a sentence of five years, at least, added to whatever sentence I got for marijuana possession. I sat there thinking, *how did I go so wrong?* I went from *A*-student to crook in a matter of months. My poor mother would have nothing but sleepless nights for days. I flashed on an event from my childhood she had always bragged about.

When I was around eight years old, I was shopping with her, and saw a woman reach for a bag of chips and accidentally knock it to the floor. She picked up that bag, put it back, and took another that didn't have smashed chips inside. She chose a fresh bag over the one she had dropped. I pointed it out to my mom and told her the lady should have taken the bag she dropped because now someone else would get a bag of broken chips. "And that's not right," I said to my mom.

My mom didn't talk to the lady or report the incident. She was consumed with joy at my sense of morality and ethics at eight years old. She boasted about it for weeks after. Even years later, she would recount to friends and family the story of how moral her son Ricky was. She was so proud of me.

And, in many ways, she was right to be. I had been a near perfect child: I didn't fight with other kids, I never cheated in school, I was a straight A student, always helped with the housework. Then in high school something inside snapped, and I started down a dark road. By the time I was in college, I began to feel like the only way to get ahead was to be a crook.

I convinced myself that the good guys finished last and the bad guys had great lives of plenty. That thinking was helped a bit by the fact that my parents couldn't afford to pay for college because they had four other children, and my dad was a shipping and receiving clerk. So I paid for college myself, along with living expenses, car, clothes, and so on. I was driving an old, late-model Chrysler gas-guzzler with a bad muffler. Every time I pulled up to a stoplight I felt like a big, fat, ne'er-do-well, dumb shit.

I wasn't a dumb shit, and I wasn't lazy – at least up to the point of deciding to go to Mexico – but I couldn't stand being so damned poor all the time, which may have been in part why I pulled the scam with my truck and reported it stolen. And now Jeff was ratting me out for it.

I suppose that was partly why I felt a responsibility for being in prison. I needed to make amends, accept punishment for the dirty deed. I felt a sense of duty to help other guys, teach classes, work hard on something, and try be an all-around good Joe. Unfortunately, the guy I should have helped the most was the guy who'd come down here with me. But he had made the same choices as me. I didn't report my truck stolen, *then* ask him to go to Mexico; we planned the entire caper together from the poker game on. He was as guilty as I. In writing that letter to the attorney, he could hurt both our chances of a shorter time in prison.

I eventually explained to my parents that his letter was all a lie. The whole messy thing added another layer of disappointment onto my hard-working and loving parents. I had gotten myself into a situation where I might have to stay in prison for years. And now Jeff, my once close friend, was turning against me and trying to sell me out to save his own skin. All of that hit me in the two minutes it took to read the fairly short letter.

It was like I had been kicked hard in the gut, almost as bad as the night we'd been arrested. In a daze, I looked up from the letter and, unbelievably, saw Jeff at the Coke stand casually buying a soda. I wanted to kill him. I walked straight up to him, barely containing my anger.

"What was in the letter that you sent with my parents to the lawyer in Phoenix?" I said, my eyes burning into him.

Jeff shrugged. I turned away to get hold of myself and took a breath.

"You wrote a letter to your lawyer telling him about my truck, and he read it to my parents, you fucking son of a bitch!"

"I had a right to do that. Why would I put myself in jeopardy if there were any repercussions? The truck was not my responsibility." Jeff defended himself with absolutely no remorse. He wasn't even slightly embarrassed. On the contrary, he seemed to enjoy the fact that I'd found out.

"You are a fucking rat! And you've fucked up your own case too because the lawyer in Phoenix will have nothing to do with either of us now," I said, letting him know he was not getting away with this shit.

That caught him off guard. He wasn't expecting the lawyer would be turned off by the fact that he and I were not working together and, in fact, were turning against each other. I'm sure the lawyer thought he needed both our parents' money if he was going to make enough for his trouble, so he refused to take our case.

Jeff sat down on the wall bordering the sidewalk, eyes darting back and forth, thinking hard. I noticed some guys watching us and realized we were creating a scene, so I turned and walked away. I was blinding mad and couldn't talk any more.

On the way to my cell, I passed Chabita, who asked me about auditioning for the role of the prince in *Vichy*. I abruptly told him no. Then I bumped into Martín, who reminded me that we had a game against the team from *pabellon uno* that day. We were playing intramural games with the prison teams, usually one from each *pabellon*. *Pabellon uno* was where Jeff lived, and he was on the team.

"I will be right there!" I told him, eager to play against Jeff, and I ran back to get my shoes.

The game was as fierce as the one with *La Pinta Vieja* and *El Mato Venado*, except this time it was Jeff and me doing the fighting. We pushed and shoved, elbowing each other, and fighting for rebounds and shots. Finally, he threw the ball at me, and I went after him, viciously. All the shit that had been building up between us surfaced and we went at each other hard, until the fight was quickly broken up and we were thrown out of the game. Jeff stayed to watch the end of the game because his team was winning and I went back to my cell, mad as a hornet.

A while later, Martín showed up and he was pissed off too. "Well, we lost the game," he said trying to gauge how I was feeling. Martín hated to lose at anything, but this time he was more interested in me. I didn't give a shit about losing. I was furious at Jeff for trying to sell me out for his own personal gain. I told Martín about the letter, the truck, everything. I told him what Jeff said and how I wanted to kill him. Martín shook his head and gave that wry smile of his. "*Estas en la carcel, Gabacho. No hay pedo.*" He always said that. You're in prison, and there's no use getting upset. "Anyway, your truck is long gone," he went on. "The *Federales* are driving your truck around some little town with new license plates and maybe a paint job. You or your lawyer or the DEA or even the local police will never find it. A four-wheel-drive Bronco, right?"

"Yeah," I said.

"That's a car in demand. Everybody wants that car. You can be sure the *Jefe* of the *Federales* is using your Bronco to drive one of his girlfriends around, or maybe he even gave it to one of them. You'll never have to worry about getting caught for that truck. That's all over."

That's exactly what I had been hoping for, but I wasn't sure I didn't need to be concerned. What would the US authorities do? Could I be arrested for the truck if they didn't have it? Would they go on Jeff's word? I had to be mindful of Jeff and what he might say or do.

As we were talking, Soto came into the cell and wanted to know about auditions. Once again, I didn't have time to worry about Jeff or my truck or how my parents felt about my tragic slide into crime. I had a difficult play to produce that was going to be much harder than the Mother's Day program.

Samuel and I had just finished translating Arthur Miller's *Incident at Vichy*. It was a huge amount of work, day and night, sometimes for hours. With each page or sequence, I would act out the scenario and try to convey to Samuel the emotional arc, the basic conflict, where the focus should be, what the characters were feeling, and the nuances contained in each moment. This I would do in mix of English and Spanish, and a lot of gesturing.

Samuel would translate a phrase, then read it back to me in Spanish. I would repeat it in Spanish, trying to make the rhythm work. If it sounded stilted or awkward, we would rethink the translation and come up with another way of saying the line. Plays are like poetry. There's a timing and rhythm to the dialogue. You can't lose that. We methodically worked through each moment and every line just like that. It took us several months, working nearly every day, and it was finally done.

Soto said he had read the play carefully and decided the parts that were best for him were either the prince or the doctor. *Incident at Vichy* is set in France in 1941. The Germans are arresting people who look Jewish. They measure noses and ears and ask questions that confuse the detainees. The play opens with several men sitting on a bench awaiting interrogation by German officers: a doctor, the prince who is a member of the Austrian royal family, a few working-class men, an artist, and a gypsy. The prince, being a royal, has the best costume and is the one who makes it out because he clearly isn't Jewish. The doctor also gets away but for a different reason than the prince. The prince and the doctor have most of the dialogue and are more or less the leads in the play. I knew all the guys would want to be the prince or doctor because everybody wanted to play the lead, so it was going to be very hard casting the show.

My anger and agitation faded as I chuckled to myself thinking how they would all count the lines to decide what part they wanted, rather than choose a character by how interesting or challenging it was. By this time though, I'd had a pretty good idea of each actor's capabilities and personality. During the translation process I had been thinking about who could play which character. I told Soto that he should read the play again and look at the part of the artist, Lebeau.

"It's the part I played in the States," I continued. "It is a good role and one that needs a good actor."

Soto said he would read it again and think about it. After he left, I looked at Martín and said, "All the guys read the play, counted the lines, and will want to play the prince or the doctor. Watch them come in one by one."

"Everyone wants to be a star," said Martín, smiling.

Next, Samuel came and asked what part I was thinking of for him. I asked what part would he like and winked at Martín as I said this. Samuel said it didn't really matter, but he did kind of like the prince or the doctor.

I told Samuel that I was hoping he would play the German major. It was a very difficult role and required a strong actor. I told him I didn't think anyone else could do it. He reluctantly said okay, then left.

I looked at Martín again. "The one I am really concerned about is Ramon. He's my *socio,* and has helped so much and I know he'll want to play the prince. But he's probably the worst actor in the group, and I can't give him a major role. I don't know how to tell him he can only handle the part of the captain or the guard."

"Maybe he won't care what you give him," offered Martín.

"I don't think I'll be so lucky."

Soon, Ramon popped in and stood there a minute, looking at Martín and I sheepishly. He shuffled uncomfortably, like he was afraid to state his purpose. At last, he said he had a question about the auditions. I looked over at Martín, rolling my eyes.

"You know," I started to explain, "sometimes actors want to play certain parts that they're not right for. We pick a part that we think is interesting or exciting or has a lot of lines. But all the parts have to be played in order to make the show work and often we have to play a part for that reason only."

"Well," Ramon said, "I was afraid you might say that. I know you probably want me to play the prince, but what I'd really like to do is play the captain of police."

At this, Martín burst out laughing and walked out the door.

"Okay, sure, Ramon," I said. "You can play the captain of police. That's actually an important part, and I'd like you to do it for me." Ramon grinned big and wide, and then he left.

I drew up a cast list and started penciling in names. Shortly, I heard a knock on the bars of the cell. I was expecting another actor that I would have to talk into playing a part he didn't want to play. When I opened the door, Jeff was standing there. He asked if he could talk to me a moment and walked away. After some hesitation, I followed him down the hall to the showers, my anger returning a little. He didn't seem angry, so I guessed there wasn't going to be another fight. Maybe he wanted to explain or apologize, I couldn't tell, so I tried to be nonchalant and give him the stage.

Jeff turned back to me and just stood there, looking directly at me for a long moment. I don't have the ability to stare right at someone's face for long . My eyes tend to dart here and there. I looked at the dirty shower stalls that had built up grime and mold over the years. The showers were no longer working. Water had only flowed to the cellblocks for a couple of months, then it was shut off. It came back on occasionally, but it hadn't been on for weeks, so guys used the shower stalls to eat or hang out or get high. They were filthy.

Jeff stammered, shuffled back and forth, then swallowed hard and began to speak. His voice was shaky and trembling a bit. "I don't know if you knew it or not, but before we came to Mexico… I loved you. Maybe the first time I ever really loved someone." He paused for a moment, and kept staring straight at me.

Of all the things I thought of walking down the hallway, I did not expect that. I stared at him, trying to recall occurrences or events in the past that might have clued me in to this. I didn't think he was talking about romantic love, sex, and all that. But he didn't clarify the comment any further. Can one guy love another guy? I never felt that before. At least in the way he seemed to mean it.

He went on. "Then we got into prison and you left me, just like everyone else in my life. You left me alone. You wouldn't talk to me, you didn't help me, nothing. I don't know if we can ever be close again, but if we do, it will have to come from you. And you will have to work really hard to get my love back."

For a brief moment, I felt like I wanted to strangle him, or at least hit him a few times, but he seemed almost pathetic. I had no words, no response for what he'd said. That was always my problem; when someone said something astonishing, I didn't have anything to say. No words came to into my head.

I just looked at him. "So... is that all?" It wasn't angry or mean, just void of emotion.

Jeff looked stunned. "Yeah, I, uh, just wanted to say that, that's all."

"Okay," I said, and then I turned to walk back to my cell. I thought I could hear him making noises that sounded like crying, but I didn't go back. I was so confused and completely taken aback, like I had the air punched out of me again. It was the very last thing I'd expected at that moment.

We had been at each other for months. Earlier that day we had gotten into a fistfight. He had written a letter that, if it got to the right people, could do me some real harm, maybe even keep me from going out on parole once we got back to the States. And here he was, revealing himself, like a jilted lover.

I wasn't prepared for what he told me and I didn't handle it well either. I couldn't roll over and forget everything that had happened in the last few months. We never spoke of that moment again. He didn't say anything about it and neither did I. We didn't fight after that. Eventually, Jeff joined the theatre group and took a role in *Vichy*. He worked hard after that and participated in the group classes and exercises. We weren't friendly, but we weren't enemies either. He got to say what he wanted and I guess he felt okay about it. And that was that.

It was another situation in my life where a guy wanted something from me I was unable to give. I never understood if Jeff had a thing for me. Maybe it was just brotherly love, I didn't know. Perhaps I looked slightly feminine, and that was part of it. I grew up on the truck-driver side of town and when I was in high school, I got made fun of for being a 'pretty boy.' But I never saw myself that way, I thought they were a bunch of Neanderthals. I heard, years later, from the rumor mill in Salt Lake that Jeff had an affair with a gay guy I knew, but I never confirmed it.

I had a distant and uneasy relationship with my own father. We weren't friendly or close in any way. He wasn't unusually mean, but there was no connection between us. We had nothing in common. I grew up without a father, really. And never learned how to interact well with other men. Oddly, there were several times throughout my life that a supposedly straight male seemed to have or indicated an attraction for me. I never delved into the situation nor did I pursue it further with any of the guys. Like with Jeff, I just turned and walked away and let it go. It wasn't appalling or aberrant to me, but I had no response. I felt nothing. Maybe a little embarrassment, but nothing more. From then on, I tried to be kind to Jeff and include him in conversations and activities, not for his sake, but the sake of our case. In my mind, he was a powder keg.

CHAPTER 16

THE NEXT TIME Kate came down, we had sex most of the night. It was different this time – hard and furious. We were both so exhausted afterwards, we feel asleep without a word. In the morning, I put on my clothes and asked when she might come down again. She said she wasn't sure if she could, that this time might be the last time before I was transferred to the States.

"But what if I am not transferred for some reason?" I was worried less about that than what might be happening with her. She ignored what I said and continued getting dressed. "And even if I do transfer, Jeff could sell me out, and I could be in prison for a long time over in the US. You have to come down and least see the play." I was pleading a little, trying not to push too hard.

"Richard." She turned to me with that clenched jaw she would get when something was difficult to say or she had to be strong. "You got yourself in here. You wanted a divorce, and you are responsible for whatever happened with your truck. I've driven down here several times, I've been paying for your collect calls, and I've been paying your bills. I have been drained emotionally and financially, and I don't have any more to give you. I don't mean to sound harsh, but you need to stop pushing me. I've got to catch up on my own life. You've made choices, and this is your life now. I can't devote my life to helping you."

I was roiling inside, but I held back my emotions as best I could. She was right. What could I say?

"I am not saying it's over between us, but I'm going to stop acting as though we're still married."

As she said that, I felt there was something more she really wanted to say, like she'd met someone or wanted to date or had been dating. I didn't want to hear it anyway. If that's what it was, I chose to let it go. I packed up our stuff and we headed down the corridor. She hugged me goodbye and left through the visitor's entrance. I watched her go but she didn't look back like she always had before. Something was going on, and how could I blame her? Still, I could feel the churning inside begin, that awful grinding you get in the pit of your stomach when you sense the person you love is loving someone else.

The next day, Jeff and I were called to the front office to meet the new *comandante*. Pedro and Gloria were there as well. The new *comandante* was taller, leaner, and more severe than the previous one. He was a no-nonsense guy who didn't care if the inmates were contented and complacent. Also, he didn't seem smart, which made him dangerous. Men in power who have limitations in one area will make up for it in another. He was the sub-*comandante* previously, so I'd had interactions with him already. He didn't like the theatre group; it didn't impress him at all. Thought it was a waste of money, even though it didn't cost the prison anything other than some electricity. It was the principle of the thing. He was a former soldier, but not from the upper class or an officer, merely a regular grunt. And now he had power. Power over dozens of staff and hundreds of inmates.

I kept watching the new *comandante* as Pedro told us we had been found guilty and sentenced to seven years and three months in prison. He went on to explain the sentence would begin from the day we entered prison. We had known this was coming because he had told us on a previous visit that we could expect that result. We just didn't know when. There was only one transfer each year. If you didn't get your sentence in time to submit the paperwork for review on both sides of the border, then you had to wait another year. A couple of times they missed a year, which would mean another two years in Hermosillo if we didn't get our paperwork done on time. And you couldn't apply for a transfer until you'd received a sentence, so that's where we were.

Gloria continued the explanation, saying she would submit our paperwork for the transfer but didn't actually know when the next transfer was. There hadn't been a transfer the entire time we were there, which meant one should be coming up. But no one really knew when – not Pedro and not Gloria. That's the way of life in prison, especially in Mexico; nothing definitive. We looked very disappointed, I'm sure.

The *comandante* jumped in; he sounded miffed. "Don't worry, you'll make the transfer. I've seen it many times. They will come and get you one day and you'll be gone. You Americans don't have to worry about anything. It all works out for you." He winked at Gloria, but she wasn't impressed. She smiled politely, somewhat embarrassed, then Pedro quickly stood up to shake hands.

I asked if they would come and see the play, *Incident at Vichy*.

"Oh, that sounds nice," said Gloria, not making a commitment. The *comandante* grunted. Pedro said he most certainly would, but he'd said that about the first two plays and didn't show up for either of them. Pedro was all about the money. He was honest, but he was not very smart. He probably couldn't have made a living as an attorney in any field but this. He only took cases where there was nothing to do except file paperwork and wait, and he was good at that.

I stood there looking at the three of them – Pedro, Gloria, and the *comandante*. It finally dawned on me; to them, I was a crook, one of the bad guys. An inferior element of society who had to be incarcerated and kept off the streets to protect the good people. Like the guys you see on TV shuffling into court, handcuffed, wearing orange jump suits. I was one of those guys. Pedro, Gloria, and the *comandante* – they were the good people. It hit me like a smash in the face with a basketball. I hadn't seen myself that way until that moment. Yeah, I was the bad guy. Just like the inmates I had seen on the news. I thought how sad and terrible they looked, but smugly I'd believed they deserved what was happening to them.

I knew I had to do something to be better, something that would make a difference, so society wouldn't judge me as one of the bad guys. I had to make a positive statement about myself. I wasn't really a bad guy, just a guy who did a couple of bad things. That's different. And somehow, I had to make everyone realize that.

Gloria had us sign some papers quickly. Then she reiterated how the transfer depended entirely on when the US government received enough applications to warrant making a plane trip to Mexico. Gloria and Pedro left, while Jeff and I stayed to talk to the new *comandante*. Again, I brought up the play we were working on and how much we wanted to present it. I thought about how I needed to do this now more than ever. The *comandante* said it would be fine as long as we worked within the regulations of the prison and ran everything past him for approval.

"Don't do anything without me knowing about it first," he warned. I took that opportunity to tell him the only thing we needed was a door for the set. The *comandante* said he would send a requisition for the door to the carpentry shop.

As we walked down the corridor to the *sala de guardia*, Jeff said he wanted a part in the play. It seemed more of a threat than a request. "Nothing big," he mumbled quickly. "Just a guard or something with no lines to learn." I shrugged, then tried to discuss it, but he quickly walked off.

As we passed through the *sala de guardia*, Jeff stopped and showed the guard a pass to use the telephone. He grabbed the phone and dialed. I went through the gate and wandered toward the auditorium, then turned and looked back. I could see Jeff through the bars of the door, talking and laughing. I supposed he was talking to Arlene; that was mostly who he called. He appeared confident, sure of himself, not as I had seen him for quite a while. I began to worry that he was planning something against me. And there I was, back at the place you never want to be – the place of not knowing, that insecure place of fear and frustration.

In that moment of creeping despair, Soto appeared and started going on about not wanting to play Lebeau. I turned to him, not in a good mood, and listened for a moment. I could hear his voice but I couldn't grasp what he was saying. It was like a gun went off near my head and my ears were ringing. All I could think about was how we might not make the next transfer. We didn't even know when it was. Jeff continued his strange behavior, but instead of being sad and weird, now he was cocky and rude. The *comandante* wasn't giving me the freedom the last *comandante* did. I didn't know if I could get the things we'd need for the show done. And now

Soto wanted to play the prince. Or maybe the doctor. What was it about these guys? Everybody wants to be king.

"No," I said quickly, inconsiderate of how he was feeling. I paused, and then tried reasoning with him. "I mean, why don't you like Lebeau? That's the part I played. And it's a great character. I won an award for best actor that year. Really, man, you can sink your teeth into this part. It'll be fun."

"But Leabeau's kind of whiny," moaned Soto, screwing up his face. "I don't want people to think I'm like that."

And in that moment, it was crystal clear why they all wanted to be the doctor or the prince. Not because those characters had more lines, but because they were the strong ones. Those two characters had less fear and were able to talk about their situation. That's why they had the most lines. The guys all wanted to be perceived by the other inmates, and their families, as the same type of *person* as the doctor or the prince. In a way, they were doing the play for the same reason I was. They wanted to impress people, let people know each of them was strong and smart; not some dumb shit who'd ended up in prison, but a good man who had been arrested for the wrong reasons. Like the Austrian prince, they wanted to be somebody important. It wasn't about the play, or having something to do to pass the time, or even learning a new skill. They wanted to be seen as something more than a prison inmate, more than just a fucking convict.

"Leabeau is not you, of course not. That's what acting is all about," I said to Soto, this time with sincerity. "You play a part that is not like you because you're a better actor. That's why I cast you. You can handle Leabeau. Everyone knows you're not whiny, they'll think you're a good actor, that's all." And I really did think he could handle the part. I thought he would be good at it.

Soto stood there for a moment, thinking about it in this new way. I put my hand on his shoulder and turned him as I said, "Come on, let's go to the auditorium. It's time for our exercises."

I started and he followed, then I turned back to see Jeff jumping up and down in the *sala de guardia*. He was pumped about something. I had to get my mind off it. Soto turned and was watching me watch Jeff. He saw the look on my face but didn't say anything. Everybody knew Jeff and I had issues, but I couldn't let him see how upset I was. That was my façade. I had to present the image of being in control, of being someone who could handle all the problems we faced. I thought to myself, *now I understand what they all need; I can finally get a handle on the auditions.* I had to make each actor think their part was the most important, and that everyone would see how good they were performing it. I would make them see that they were going to be big stars in the eyes of their friends and family.

In the end, I was just like them, insecure and needy. I wanted to be important. I needed recognition for my achievements. I wanted my friends and family back home to see how well I was doing – against all odds, doing amazing things. With all the challenges and difficulties of a foreign prison, I was accomplishing things no one else could. I was doing it for the same reasons they were.

Over the next few days, I began casting the show and planning the production elements. I needed to redesign the lighting and somehow find props, some scenery, and the costumes. That seemed impossible; two dozen characters in a play set in France, during World War II. Also, props would be a problem. German military would be carrying pistols and the French guards would have some kind of weapon. We would have to forgot those props because even a fake gun would not be allowed in prison.

As for the costumes, we needed clothing for an Orthodox Jew, German guards, French policemen, an artist, a doctor, an Austrian prince, a flamboyant actor, and some working class guys. This seemed utterly impossible without some kind of costume store, and trying to get it done on the outside would be absurd. I decided to forgo the costumes and have everyone wear their own clothes. We would put a note in the playbill so the audience would understand and just let them use their imaginations.

At our first rehearsal, the read-through, one of the guys joked about wearing a guard uniform in prison. Then another wanted to know how we would make a beard for the old Jew. Suddenly, they were all discussing the costumes and what they each thought their character would wear. That's when I mentioned my plan to wear our own clothing and just put a note in the playbill. After all, we were inmates in prison, so it kind of fit. Good hell, you'd have thought I said we were all going to remain in prison for the rest of our lives! They absolutely refused to wear their own clothes. Out of the question. And if I couldn't find a solution, they would.

That became my next challenge. My first quest was to find a beard, since I thought it would be both necessary and perhaps at least doable. Martín and I were sitting in the main plaza discussing my wardrobe challenge when I asked him for help. His mother and sister worked in downtown Hermosillo, and he'd see if they could find cheap beard at a costume shop or wig store. I started running through the list of characters and what we needed for each when he nodded toward the clinic. A bunch of guys from the gay/trans cellblock were hanging out and flirting with passersby, as they usually did. I didn't know why they chose the clinic; maybe the nurse took pity and gave them free stuff because most of them were very poor with no family support.

Martín looked at me with a sly grin. "There's the answer to your costume problem." They had on fantastic outfits: short skirts with tank tops, super tight cut-offs, and a couple were sporting a kind of Village People vibe with various accouterment from military uniforms. You wouldn't have seen anything more flamboyant or exotic on 18th and Castro.

I hadn't paid much attention to them before. "Where did they get all that stuff?" I asked Martín, beginning to grasp his idea.

He got up and started toward them. *"Vamos a ver."*

They had helped with the costumes for the Mother's Day program but it didn't require much - Chabita's rags and a couple of things for the musicians. I knew they had a sewing machine, but scrutinizing their outfits, I realized they must have a lot more than that. After a bit of cooing and flirting, I mentioned our situation with costumes for the new play and they got super excited. They couldn't wait to show me around their cellblock. It would be my first visit to *pabellon cinco,* and they were titillated.

Many of the guys were taking hormones and other drugs I didn't understand, neither how they got them or what they were. Some of the guys actually looked like girls, with breasts and other feminine features. I wasn't sure how each of them achieved their presentation, but it was a colorful and spicy condiment to the atmosphere of the prison. They hung out in a group, completely unabashed, and flirted shamelessly with everyone, especially me.

The situation of *pabellon cinco* was a curiosity for me, in a novel, even humorous way. I knew some of the other inmates, even those with wives and conjugal visits (Martín, for example), visited the gay/trans cellblock, and I supposed it was for sex. Or perhaps they just wanted to hang out and flirt; I never discussed it with any of them. I had no time to think about it or even care to venture over and see what was going on. I asked Samuel once why married guys would visit *pabellon cinco,* and he said that here in prison, as long as you're the pitcher and not the catcher, you're not considered gay, and it's acceptable behavior. To me, it was fuzzy logic but I didn't really care. The humorous part was this: while almost everyone called me *gabacho,* a couple of the guys, like Guero Rivera, called me *gabachita,* literally meaning *little white girl.* I got kidded for keeping my cell clean and decorating it with a feminine touch, as well as for the cakes and coffee I served. In a sense, I got kidded for being a *mariposa* (gay guy) because I did women's work like cooking and cleaning, while the guys who visited *pabellon cinco* for sex were macho men.

But now I had a very good reason to visit them and I was excited to see their "houses." On the way over, Martín recounted how charity organizations shipped boxes of clothing to Mexico, which often ended up at the prisons. Many of the clothes from organizations like the Salvation Army were so out of date that no one in the US, even the very poor, wanted to wear them. To make room for new donations, the charity groups got rid of all the old ones by sending them to places like the prison. After the guards and trusted inmates picked through the donations, the rest ended up at *pabellon cinco.*

Martín seemed to know his way around the cellblock quite well. As we walked through the corridors, catcalls and "Hello, baby" came from every cell. He was tall, with brown hair and light skin, because his father was of Basque ancestry. This made Martín quite popular with the guys in cellblock five. They took us to a shared cell they'd turned into a costume shop. It was a lot like the wardrobe department for the theatre at the University of Utah. There were several sewing machines, glue guns, buttons, and ribbons, bolts of cloth, racks of old clothing. It was amazing. This is how they did what they did. All this stuff had been donated to the prison over the years, and these guys made the best of it. It was their passion: creating and wearing the most outrageous and fabulous outfits. They weren't interested in sports, they didn't work in the shops – they made clothes and dressed up for each other.

They fell over themselves trying to show me everything they could do, and wanted desperately to please me and be involved with the show. Rarely did anyone visit the gay/ trans cellblock for anything other than sexual favors, and here I was, asking for creative help. They were so excited and willing to do whatever I needed, they promised to throw in a blowjob anytime I wanted. I smiled politely and said the costumes would be sufficient, "thank you."

We continued on through the entire cellblock, stopping now and then to see what each of the guys had in their closet. Everyone was so eager to help and kept pulling out the most outrageous thing in their wardrobe that had nothing to do with 1941 France. So I told them a little more about the play and incredibly, they showed me a couple of German military outfits and some jackets that would do for French police. I began to see that what I really needed to do was provide them with a list of the characters and the actors' sizes. I promised to return later that day and invited the first two guys we met to come to rehearsal one day and see what it was all about.

The costumes would become the serendipitous success of the play. Since the entire setting takes place on a bench in a bare room with only a door leading in, the costumes are visually the only thing to distinguish the time and setting. The guys sewed and created the costumes for all two dozen cast members, from German military and French police to the elegant prince and the raggedy gypsy. And it only cost me a few butt pinches and allowing the boys (and girls) to flirt and flutter whenever I stopped by. They were a bunch of flamboyant folks who craved attention. Most of them were very poor, had committed crimes to do with money, and had little or no family support. They loved being part of the show, doing costume fittings, and makeup and hair for the performance. I brought them a few gifts, like a can of Brown and Haley's Almond Roca someone had sent to me. Chocolate was a huge hit. I often wondered, if prisons in the US allowed this kind of thing to take place, would there be less rape and other violence?

CHAPTER 17

EVERY MORNING, I guided a stage movement class for anyone who wanted to attend. We'd start with stretching exercises and then evolve to more elaborate movements so they would begin to see their entire body as an instrument. It was a lot to throw at them but I wanted to help them feel secure and comfortable walking and talking on the stage. I had a cassette player with an Acoustic Alchemy tape, light jazz with a beat. It got guys out of their cells and gave them something to look forward to.

After half an hour of that, we'd break into groups, some reciting lines, some working on the sets, props, or lighting. Other inmates showed up with guitars or personal projects and there were jam sessions. The auditorium became a safe place to hang out and do something creative or different. Most of the guys were outcasts or oddballs, not unlike my theatre friends back in Utah.

The Mother's Day program and *The Padre* were much less challenging than a play like Arthur Miller's *Incident at Vichy.* There are a lot of lines, the dialogue is more complex and it's a large cast, comparatively – at least twenty-one characters, if I cut a couple of guards. A typical rehearsal schedule of four to six weeks would not suffice, so I planned a three-month schedule. That seemed a long time to the guys, so many weren't focused at first. I knew they would need as much rehearsal as I could force out of them, so I created an atmosphere that would slowly lead to the performance of the play. The daily routine of stage exercises, props and set building, and jam sessions kept them active and working toward the final event.

One morning, Jeff showed up and wanted to make sure he was in the play. He wasn't rude, didn't sound mad, but definitely gave me and everyone else the impression that he planned to be in the show.

Then he walked over to a corner of the auditorium and did his own exercises. When asked by the guys why he didn't join the group, he said bluntly I wasn't doing it right, and he had his own methods. One time, I was jamming with Diego and we were taking turns improvising. Chabita was standing there listening, and said, "Wow, Richard plays really fast."

Jeff replied, "Yeah, fast but not good. He doesn't play with emotion or finesse."

He said it right in front of me, evidently making a show of the fact he and I were no longer friends, but not necessarily adversaries. His comments weren't rude, but matter of fact, as though simply stating a truth. He was right, of course; my fingers were fast and I knew the scales, but I didn't play with the kind of emotion Diego did, and I wasn't very good at melodic improvisation.

He was also right about the exercises and the stage movement class – I wasn't teaching them correctly. I didn't push the guys too hard; I let them get by with simple, easy-to-do movements. I wanted to keep them involved and not dread coming to the auditorium in the morning, so I had to make it fun too. What could I say to Jeff's comments? He was right. But he was wrong too about what had to be done to instigate and direct a massive project like this in a Mexican prison.

From that point on, I never knew what Jeff would do. Would he testify against me? Would he try to convince them it was all my idea? When we finally reached the US prison – if we reached the US prison – would he tell them about my truck? Would it matter? Would there be any evidence? How would it affect my case for parole? These thoughts were running through my head daily.

Before we were stopped at the *aduana* and arrested that fateful night, I started thinking that if we got back to the States with the weed, I might just leave my truck in the desert somewhere and let it be found. It would likely be returned to me and I'd start making payments again. In fact, I was going over that scenario in my head when I saw the lights up ahead and nearly crashed into the *Federales* road block. During my time in prison, I began to recognize the importance of the rule of law. You can't choose which laws to obey in a civil society, because if everyone does that, you'll have nothing but chaos, and a bunch of guys will end up playing soccer with your neighbor's head.

In prison there is an unwritten law, things you do or don't do in your interactions with the other inmates. This is aside from the rules established by the administration. And punishment from the inmates can be much more severe.

I had made the wrong choices, twice at least: one, reporting my truck stolen, and two, buying marijuana in Mexico. I was currently paying for the second offense, and eventually, I came to believe I might have to pay for the first. I just didn't want it to be through several more years in prison. That thought was unbearable. The thing I hated most was not knowing. Our sentence in Mexico was seven years, three months; that was definite. What we didn't know was if there'd be a transfer to the States or when it would come or how long we'd have to spend in a US prison. There were rumors the US and Mexico might do away with the transfer. The two countries didn't agree on many aspects of the prisoner exchange. Mexico, for instance, doesn't have capital punishment and it was a big issue dividing the two countries. So there was the possibility of not even getting a transfer and having to spend our entire sentence in Hermosillo. That came to haunt me nearly every day. Jeff knew it and used it against me. This was how he got back at me for not reciprocating his, well… whatever it was he'd felt for me.

It was nearing showtime and I wasn't optimistic. We entered the final week of rehearsals with everything falling apart. As a scene got rolling, we'd hear a dog whining and whimpering beneath the stage. Lupe's, the auditorium caretaker, dog was evidently having puppies. We'd stop and wait, lose our concentration, then have to start the scene over. I became exasperated one night and made an off-handed comment, *could someone please get rid of that dog?* It was hard enough to rehearse the blasted play without adding obstacles. And part of my job was to eliminate obstacles.

The distractions and other difficulties were compounded by the fact we still didn't have a door for the set. The performance was a week away and the actors hadn't been able to work with a door. It was more than part of the set, something to open and close. The door was also a metaphor, an ominous portal through which you were set free or sent to a concentration camp. It loomed over the characters throughout the story. Every character referred to it, either in their dialogue or by turning to watch and wait for the door to open. We had to have a door, some kind of door. Even a simple cardboard door would have been fine.

The day we met with Pedro and Gloria, the *comandante* had promised me a door and sent a requisition to the carpentry shop. That was weeks ago. It was all I asked of him and he had virtually guaranteed me a door. Throughout our rehearsal period, I tried over and over to get the door to no avail. There were so many things unfinished, but the door was critical to the performance.

The saga of the damn door was a comedy of errors with a slice of malice and a dash of *go fuck yourself.* The shops at the prison were run by contractors from the outside. it was a lucrative concession because inmates were paid a tenth of the going wage and the products were sold at the market rate. There was machine shop, a carpentry shop, an auto body shop, an upholstery shop, and more. Each shop manager got their concession through political connections, bribery, or a deal with the *comandante.* They viewed the inmates as chattel, and me as a rich American drug dealer who was nothing but a nuisance.

I went to the carpentry shop a couple of weeks after the *comandante* delivered the requisition. They told me they had the requisition, but they didn't have any lumber. I looked around and saw lumber everywhere. I pointed to some pieces and they said that it was for other things, so I asked, "Doesn't the requisition mean everything, including the lumber? How could you build a door without lumber, isn't that part of the deal?"

They said there was no lumber in the requisition. They were only required to build a door, not provide the materials. Lumber was up to me. I went back to see the *comandante* and asked him to please let me build the door. He said no and told me he would take care of the requisition for lumber. Over the following weeks, I went to the shop every day to find nothing happening with my door.

Rehearsals continued and Lupe's dog had her puppies; they were crying constantly and driving everyone crazy. The actors were beginning to get mad at me for the door situation. They wanted a door to rehearse with and couldn't understand why I had failed to get one.

The next day, I went to the shop again. They'd constructed a doorway and a frame, but no actual door. They said that was all the lumber they'd been given. I didn't believe them and was starting to get angry, but I couldn't let it show or they might not do any more. I held my temper and told them to just make the door from cardboard. I went to morning rehearsals, the puppies were still whining and carrying on, Jeff was being difficult, and a couple of actors didn't show up. The stress was leaking through my façade.

Later that day, I went to check on the door and discovered they'd done nothing. They said they didn't have any cardboard. I pointed to a stack of boxes in the back; they said those boxes were for something else. I went to the café and asked if they had any empty boxes. They told me they had to give their boxes back to the distributors. Finally, I gave them fifty pesos for five boxes. You could buy two bags of weed for fifty pesos. It was just about all the money and patience I had left.

The actors had been complaining about the door for weeks. In fact, I could have derived a way to block the show without a door, but they wouldn't hear it. I tried staging the action to have them walk around a stack of egg cartons instead of walking through a door. But they kept complaining that in the script it stated that there was a door, and they didn't want to do the play without one. They didn't like miming a door and they didn't want to refer to a door that wasn't there. And somehow, they all blamed me for the goddam missing door.

That evening, Godoy was late for rehearsal. I yelled at him when he finally arrived. He got upset, told me no one could talk to him like that, and he walked out. I shouted after him it was fine with me and not to come back. That meant I would have to play the actor, which is the part Godoy was doing. I had intended to play the businessman because he didn't speak much. But now I'd have to play the actor and either find someone to play the businessman or cut that part. I walked around the stage for a moment considering how to cut that character while the cast stared at me, grumbling and complaining about a myriad of things, including the damn door and the incessant noise of the crying puppies. We continued to rehearse, but it was chaotic and sloppy. No one was into it; they couldn't recall half their lines. Jeff stood there and smiled, like he wanted the play to fall apart, and was happy to watch it happen.

The next morning, I went back to the shop again. They had covered the 1 x3 boards, making a door shape with cardboard, but it wasn't attached to the frame. So now I had a cardboard door and a frame to hold it, but no hinges or door handle. They said they would need another requisition for the hardware. I just stared at them, trying hard not to get upset or show any emotion.

"Why didn't you tell me that before?" I was beginning to lose control. They were deliberately trying to piss me off and stood there staring at me, hoping I'd lose it so they could report me to the *comandante* and I'd get nothing. I should never have allowed them to think the door was that important. They didn't know what it was, but they knew that it must have been important to me, and were doing everything they could to stall it.

I left, thinking the manager of the shop must have gotten his concession through political connections and not from the *comandante*, because he didn't seem at all concerned about the requisitions. And he hated me for some reason. I could tell he was trying to do anything he could *not* to deliver a door, and make my life as miserable as possible. He just had it out for me and there was nothing I could do but take his shit.

I went to the office and begged the *comandante* to let me have more control over the production; the play would be good for the prison, I reiterated. He said no again and told me to go to the metal shop for the hardware and that he would send a requisition. I could tell that he was starting to lose patience with me. "It's a goddamn door! What's the big deal?" he shouted.

That afternoon Godoy returned to the rehearsal and leaned against the back wall without saying a word. We were in the middle of a scene and the other inmates stopped rehearsing and watched me. Everything was driving me crazy. I couldn't seem to hold it together any longer. Each problem grew bigger and bigger, yet I knew it was just a silly play, in a Mexican prison. What was the big goddamn deal?

Finally, I said to Godoy, "Okay, you're back in, but no one can miss a single rehearsal from now on... that's final. We can't do this play without everybody being at every rehearsal from now on. We don't have our lines memorized, we haven't got our blocking down, entrances are late, and we only have a few days left. We may not get a door, and we can't let everything just fall apart. So please everyone, please be here for every rehearsal from now on!"

No one responded to that. They looked tired and frustrated, and I could tell they were not happy with me. We went on with the rehearsal, but it didn't go well. The tension was thick and I was unable to provide direction for anything: their lines, the blocking, their motivation, all fell apart. I had to let it go and hope for the best.

The next day, I waited an hour at the metal shop for the foreman. When he finally arrived, he said they had hinges, but no door handle, and that I should go ask prison maintenance if they had one. I hurried over to maintenance, but they didn't have a requisition for hardware. Only the metal shop had that. I started laughing. The *comandante* had told me not to bother him anymore, so how would I get a requisition for a door handle. It was a catch twenty-two.

There I was. I had a cardboard door on a wooden frame with some mismatched hinges and no handle. I didn't have any more money, couldn't get help from the *comandante*, and it was no use going to Martín or anyone else. I had to figure out a solution. This was not going to break me. I had to get a goddamn door!

"What about junk?" I pleaded with them. "Can I just look through stuff you throw away?"

One of them came back with a box of broken hardware. I rummaged through it and finally put together a door handle. It didn't turn, and it didn't look the same on both sides, but we'd screw it into the frame that went across the middle to hold the cardboard and the actors would at least be able to use the handle. We would have to make the door tight to the frame so it would stay in place while shut, and that would be the best we could do.

I took the broken pieces to the carpentry shop and asked them to put it together the way I showed them. They said they would. That was Friday. The play was Sunday.

Just before rehearsal that night, I got a letter from Kate. She told me that she wasn't coming down again. If I made the transfer, I would have to send my guitar and personal items home with someone else or give them away. My guitar was the only thing I really wanted, really needed. It was my last possession, a Guild D40, aged wood, but in great shape so it sounded amazing. I'd lost everything else, I couldn't lose my guitar. I was sick, my head was spinning. I couldn't believe she wasn't coming down again. I desperately needed to see her before going to the US because what if I didn't make it?

I wanted to cancel rehearsal but after my speech the night before, it was not an option. I had to drag myself to the auditorium and try to hold it all together. Nothing was working and I was sure the play would be terrible, so what was the bloody point?

I arrived at the auditorium to find out Chabita wasn't coming. They said he was depressed and was staying in his cell. He played the young boy, and though it wasn't a big part, only Chabita could do it because he looked much younger than the rest. I immediately announced to the cast that Chabita was out of the play and we would cut the part. I reminded them how the night before I had stated that if another actor missed a rehearsal they were out, and I meant it.

I launched into a quick explanation of how to get around the part of the young boy. "Anyone who has lines with the boy will have to wing it. Just cut those lines and go on." No one wanted to cut Chabita out of the play and they weren't sure if he had quit for good or was only missing tonight. I ignored their comments and began the rehearsal, reiterating what I had said the night before: anyone who didn't show up for the final rehearsals would be out. Chabita was out and that was it.

We began the first scene, and almost on cue, the puppies started whining again. Then the actors started bitching and moaning. How could we do the play without the door? They bickered with each other and complained about the door, Chabita, the costumes, the whining puppies, anything and everything. I tried to move forward and rehearse but it fell apart. Everyone was beat, frustrated, and mad as hell. We'd been rehearsing for three months, we had to replace several actors, there was no door, and the costumes hadn't shown up yet from *pabellon cinco*. *What the fuck!* I cancelled rehearsal and told everyone to go home and come back early in the morning. The following day was Saturday and the performance was Sunday. We would do two dress rehearsals, one in morning and one in the afternoon. Maybe we'd have costumes and a door by then.

They were actually glad to leave. They could get some sleep, get high, do whatever the hell they wanted. I went over to *pabellon cinco* to see about the costumes. To my surprise, they were looking pretty good. It was the first success I'd had. The gay and trans guys were doing a great job. They had built guard uniforms, the old Jew's costume, a chef's outfit, and a variety of raggedy clothes for the others. There was a younger guy who looked more like a girl and I asked if he wanted to be in the play. He was so excited, I told him he could take Chabita's place and be the young boy. He wouldn't have to say anything because he didn't have time to learn any lines. When anyone spoke to him he could nod and mumble, whatever seemed appropriate.

I worked with him for an hour going through the script, showing him where he came in and when he was called into the interrogation room. That was that. I was done. We had an actor for the young boy.

The next morning, the entire cast showed up together, along with Chabita, who announced he was back in the play. He apologized, saying he was depressed and upset and couldn't rehearse. I knew he had actually gotten stoned and couldn't get going, so I stood my ground. I told the cast there was no way. I introduced the guy from *pabellon cinco* and said he and I'd been working all night and that was the end of it. An argument ensued. They called me a tyrant and said I was trying to bully them. They didn't like the guy from *pabellon cinco* anyway because he had nothing to do with the theatre group.

Godoy accused me of trying to control everyone. Then he came up with this crazy notion; I was stealing the play from Samuel, who had helped translate it, and planned to take the translation back to the States, sell it for a profit, and not pay Samuel. He'd convinced the others that that was my plan all along, and I didn't really care if we presented the play which was why I wasn't getting things done. It was all about the money.

It was incredulous. I was dumbfounded. "Where did you get that idea? This play wouldn't make any fucking money in the States, and certainly not translated into Spanish. Why would anybody in the US pay for Spanish translation of *Incident At Vichy*, for Crissake! You don't know shit about theatre, here or there." I was so mad at them, and they were furious at me. As I spoke, they were shouting over me. It was a manic cacophony of bullshit.

Jeff stood with the cast members, but didn't say much because, quite frankly, he couldn't speak Spanish well enough to argue. I told them that I was the director and I was calling the shots. They came back at me by saying it should be done by a vote and I had no right to tell them what to do.

"Okay," I said. "If that is what you want, do it. Do the fucking play. I will finish my part as an actor but that is it. There is no director. The director is dead. I will present it with you on Sunday and that's it for me. You can finish the lights, sets, and costumes yourselves. You can figure out what to do about the fucking door. You have taught me something about Mexico; people here are lazy and irresponsible. You can have the translation, the play, the whole goddamn thing!"

I walked outside and as I left, I heard Jeff say, "Come on, let's rehearse." It actually felt good to lose my temper. After a few moments, I went back in and waited my turn to take the stage. We went through the rehearsal, and it didn't go badly. Everyone was alert and remembered their lines. They got their entrances and blocking right and we pretty much pulled off the first complete run-through. It was like makeup sex after a fight with your significant other, it was unbelievably good.

We had one more rehearsal in the afternoon so I went back to my cell and started taking down the photos of Kate as Ramon came by with lunch. He asked if I was alright.

Without turning around, I replied, "Yeah, I'm fine."

Ramon handed me a plate of food and then sat down to eat. He asked about Kate. I said, "It's not good. She isn't going to come down again and doesn't write much, but I'll be fine. I think she's seeing someone else."

"So, Mexicans are lazy, you say." He laughed. "Well, maybe that's true. But at least they got through the play for the first time."

I smiled. "Yeah, that was surprising. All we need is a door." I paused, letting down my guard. "That goddamn fucking door has driven me crazy," I said at last. "I did everything I could."

Ramon and I left early for the afternoon rehearsal to stop by the shop and see if the door was ready. But the shops were closed. It was Saturday, and they didn't work after noon. They hadn't left the door for me and there was no one to talk to or ask about it. Everyone was gone, and no door in sight. I kicked the shop door and mumbled a dozen expletives.

"Well, I hope they left it at the auditorium because there's no more time," I said as we started walking that way. We were the first to arrive and found the auditorium door locked. I knocked and knocked but didn't get any answer. Lupe always opened up for us. We waited, and I started to think maybe we weren't going to do the play. Finally, he came to the door, not looking very well. I asked if anyone had brought a door by and he shrugged. I bolted for the stage to see for myself. There was our bench, the stools, the flats we'd made to mask off the backstage area, a pile of costumes, but no door. This was making me crazy. It had been so easy with the old *comandante*. I asked him for things and they would happen. I was tight with him and everyone knew it. But now, no one paid any attention to me because I had no power. I didn't have enough money to buy things, and I had to rely on the new *comandante* to facilitate my requests. And he didn't give a shit.

It was Saturday, the performance was Sunday, the shops were closed, and we had no door. That was the last straw for me, and I started shouting at no one in particular, just the whole shitty ass world. Ramon backed away and let me have the stage for my tantrum. Everything had built up and I finally snapped. Kate wasn't coming, the actors were angry, Jeff was trying to undermine my authority, and I wasn't sure we would make the goddamn transfer.

It seemed insignificant, but the door was the part of the set that really mattered. The door represented so many things: hope, despair, escape, the outside world, both brutal and hopeful. The door was more than a piece of scenery, it was a symbol of the prison gates. I had chosen the play because I thought it would be a reflection of life in prison and a text the inmates could relate to. And so it was. But I hadn't imagined the kind of emotional twist that followed. They had all suffered, been tortured or beaten, lost so much from incarceration. In the play, those who are judged harshly are escorted through the door to a death camp. Those who escape the clutches of the Nazis walk out the door free men. It was almost too real for everyone, including me. Not getting a door left a huge hole in our endeavor. How would anyone escape without a door? My failure in getting a door underscored the complete lack of control, the fear one has of being incarcerated forever. It's a recurring nightmare I had: never getting out of prison. There would be no transfer, I would have to remain incarcerated in Mexico, and who knew what would happen after that. We had to have a door.

I started throwing things and screaming, "This fucking prison! This crazy fucking madhouse!" I kicked the bench. I threw a stool into one of the costume racks, knocking it over. I took another stool and began banging it on the floor. Then I swung it round and round and was about toss it through the flats that established the back wall leading to the outside when Martín appeared and grabbed the stool from my hands. I turned to him, still furious and ready to take a swing at him, when there was a loud disturbance at the entrance to the auditorium.

Two guards entered with burlap bags; one had a bat and the other was fighting with Lupe, who was trying to keep them from entering. Lupe was screaming and crying. The guards were yelling at him to back off. Lupe's dog came out from under the stage and barked at the guards defensively. One of the guards kicked it away and reached under the stage and pulled out a box with the puppies. He shoved them in the burlap bag one by one as Lupe was still struggling. Lupe screamed louder and tried to grab the box away. The mother dog went back at the other guard, who clubbed the dog over her head and placed the limp body in a burlap bag. They pushed Lupe away, broken, shocked, and utterly heartbroken. He crumpled to the floor, a blubbering, crying mess as the two guards quickly left with the bags of yelping puppies.

It all happened so fast I couldn't understand what was going on. I was in shock. I looked at Martín, held up my hands, and said, "What the hell?"

Martín explained, "A guy was bitten and got rabies. They don't know how many dogs are infected or which ones, so they're taking them all away."

I was still shocked. "But why? They have tests for that. And injections for rabies."

"Too expensive," said Martín. "They don't want to spend the money, and this is easier. This is what happens in prison. Dogs are expendable. I thought you wanted the dogs removed for the show anyway. You asked for someone to get rid of the dogs, didn't you?"

"Yeah, but I didn't mean that! Just taken somewhere for a few days. Something... I don't know."

Martín said, "You don't know, *Gabacho*. You think you know what you want. So you work hard. You make everything a big deal. It's prison, it's useless. Your guys are mad. You don't have your door. The play isn't ready. And so what? What will happen if it all goes to shit? You think you'll be nailed up there on the wall with your egg cartons?" He paused and waited for me to answer.

At that moment, the *comandante* and a guard entered, carrying the door. They set it against the wall. He looked at me, then at the stage, and said, "I got your door for you. They closed the shop early today." Then he left.

"You see, *Gabacho*, no big deal. Take it easy. *Calmete*, or you will go crazy." He walked out and Ramon stepped outside with him. I sat down on the overturned benched and listened to the silence. I could hear Lupe crying backstage. I had asked someone to "get rid of those damned dogs." I did that. Godoy, Chabita, Martín, they were right. I was a tyrant. I should have been the one they clubbed and put in the gunny sack.

CHAPTER 18

PRODUCING *INCIDENT AT* Vichy in a Mexican prison was the most important achievement in my life, and no one from my world in the US would see it. It could turn out to be the most challenging creative project I would ever do. It took three months to translate the play, one month to get copies and cast it, and three months in rehearsal. Over six months struggling and working to do this one play.

There had been a lot of press and hype over the production, which brought a tremendous number of people to the auditorium to see it. The play wasn't well known in Mexico; in fact, no one I met had heard of it. I thought it must have sounded important to them, or perhaps they were captivated by the notion of prison inmates portraying detainees who would be sent to concentration camps. The auditorium was hot, people were sweating and fanning themselves. It was September in the Sonoran Desert and the temperature outside was well over a hundred degrees.

The cast had shown up way early to get ready and go over lines. They were fussing with their costumes, busy applying makeup (which they didn't need) but said it helped them get into character. They were becoming actors, and like actors on opening night, they were nervous. We designated a guy to watch the script and cue the cast if they lost their place or forgot a line. I couldn't help but notice the barking and whining of the dogs was gone, which made me feel sick.

Everyone seemed to forget the day before, with all the arguing and name-calling. We slapped one another on the back and offered compliments and best wishes. It was as if nothing had gone wrong: no door saga, no fighting, no name calling. Prison was like that. Guys got fighting mad for no good reason and the next day it was over. Although I was still bruised, I let it go as well.

The lights went down, and the initial characters took their places. The lights came up, and Lebeau, the first to speak, began the dialogue before the audience had settled down. The first few lines were shaky, it was hard to hear for a moment. The characters of the doctor and the prince continue the dialogue, but hesitated, because the two actors weren't sure if they should wait for the crowd noise to die down. This wasn't a comedy or a musical, like the Mother's Day program, the audience had to listen to the lines in order to enjoy the performance. Almost at once, the crowd recognized that, quieted down, and the actors dived into it.

My character was on stage for about half of the play. A businessman and clearly not Jewish, he was a rich man who had been arrested by the French police more out of spite than for being a Jew. After my character exited, I sidled around to the back of the auditorium to watch the rest of the play. It went off without a hitch. A few lines didn't get said in the right order, but it made little difference. The audience understood the story, seemed to relate to the characters, and were able to grasp the complexities of the central themes: the right to life, and complicity and guilt with the forces of authority. Arthur Miller attempts to explore how and why it was so easy for the Nazis to perpetuate the Holocaust for so long with such little resistance. Each soldier, officer, or policeman was under the gun of a superior above him.

Set in German-occupied France during WWII, in the play Arthur Miller explores the themes of complicity, guilt and whether to acquiesce to authority in hopes of survival, or to struggle against a perceived threat with the risk of danger. The detainees are awaiting inspection by the German officers with little information as to why. The communist, the flamboyant actor, the titled nobleman, the bohemian artist, the rational psychoanalyst, each has a perspective on what the Nazis are doing, influenced by their own fears and expectations.

I thought the play might be boring for some who would tire quickly and walk out, but I was wrong. The families of the inmates found it easy to identify with the central theme and the characters' reactions to their situation. And as in any good drama, it was aided by the stellar performances of the actors. They never broke character and remembered their lines and blocking like pros. They looked the part too: gritty, sweaty, eyes wild with fear, in costumes that were near perfect. Even the bare concrete auditorium served to highlight the cold reality of the situation.

The audience has the benefit of hindsight, knowing in abstract what a horrible fate awaits those sent to the camps. This heightens audience emotion as the characters argue and cajole each other to act in the face of the unknown.

The inmates and their families had experienced similar emotions through different circumstances. Many in the prison were convicted on evidence obtained through torture or coercion. And, in the minds of most, the Mexican government was complicit with the US in its so called *war on drugs,* the fallout of which was so many young Mexican men were sent to prison for very small amounts of marijuana.

Martín was serving a five-year, six-month sentence for a single joint. While in the US, possession of that amount of weed would have been a misdemeanor and an individual would likely have been given a fine and probation.

It was a double standard, and most felt it was unfair to Mexicans. Racial injustice, complicity, cruelty were underlying themes for all these families.

At the end of the play, we got a standing ovation that went on for some time. We had touched the audience, and they appreciated the story we chose and all the work we did. Some people were even crying, and nearly everyone was discussing the characters and the choices they made as they left the auditorium. It was earthshaking for me. I had wanted to do the play because I thought the inmates would have an affinity for the characters, but I hadn't considered how much it would resonate with the audience. They were right with us all the way, and could feel the danger and presence of the German SS behind the door who caused so much trouble. Some in the audience even booed as the German guard (played by Jeff) ran after one of the characters who tried to escape. I was emotionally drained by the end of the play, but supremely satisfied. Despite all the chaos, anger, and confusion leading up to the production, it was successful beyond any of my expectations. And in that moment, it no longer mattered whether my friends and family saw the work.

After the play, all the inmates gathered in my cell, laughing, talking, and congratulating each other. They were happy and proud. All was forgotten about the events of the preceding days. We had a hit. And nothing that had been said in our fighting ever came up again. No recriminations, no rebuttals.

Godoy commented on how Soto had made the audience cry with Lebeau, and Luis described how he felt actual fear of Jeff as the German guard. Jeff even joined in the congratulations, adding a couple of comments about how well the other actors did. He seemed unexpectedly sincere.

Chabita looked at me and asked what play we were going to do next. "How about *Jesus Christ Superstar*?" I said, thinking there would not be another play. I was hoping to be gone by the time we could mount a new production. There were exclamations of excitement all round. Martín was there to take part in the wrap party. He thought we had the perfect actor to play Jesus, and nodded toward me. The others agreed. Somehow success overcomes everything, even in prison. No one seemed to recall how, only yesterday, they were all ready to throw me to the sharks.

I looked over at Jeff. He stared back at me with no expression on his face.

Just then Guero Rivera came running down the hall. "Hey, Martín! They are calling you to the *sala de guardia*. *Vamos, rapido*." Guero hung around the guards' area and relayed important information. He had no money and used this as a way of obtaining favors from the inmates.

Martín sped away without saying a word. We all knew what it meant: he was getting out.

Later that day, I was standing at the *sala de guardia* with a bundle of Martín's clothes. Guero was there, along with Arturo. Martín turned to me and said, "Remember, *Gabacho, calmete*! *Estas en la carcel*."

We bade farewell and good luck to Martín, who was so happy to be out that he hardly took time to say goodbye to us. After five years in prison, he was anxious to go home. It was hard for me. I wasn't sure when I was going to leave, and Martín had been a great friend who had been very helpful. I wasn't sure how well I'd have done without him. I felt lost and alone. He had provided feedback and friendship that I often needed so badly. And there he was, walking out through the *sala de guardia*. I didn't know if I'd ever see him again. How strange that was, to be so close to someone and watch them walk out of your life, perhaps forever. Prison was that way.

A few days later, we were notified that the US/Mexico prisoner exchange was going to take place. It would be the last week of September. We weren't told a specific day, just a window of about ten days, but we were definitely on the transfer. This was it. We were going home.

I called Kate to let her know I would be making the transfer to San Diego. A week later, she sent me a letter saying she and Arlene were coming down one last time. They wanted to see us before we left for San Diego and pick up our belongings for us.

It was great to hear from her. I had been so sad thinking about her, and how much I missed her. But there was some melancholy as well. She didn't sound happy, so I called her again that weekend. She was distant, like she was forcing herself to come down. I could sense it was Arlene's idea and Kate wanted to help her. Arlene was not the kind of person to have made the trip alone. I suppose I couldn't complain; at least she was coming to visit one more time. I had a few things I really wanted to keep: my journal, all my letters from friends and family and from her. And, of course, my guitar. Everything else I would give to Ramon. But I wanted to take those things. I wanted to remember this experience for the rest of my life.

There was little time to see her. She spent the night for a conjugal visit, but she was tired and we hardly talked. We didn't even make love. We had some minor words, then fell asleep, and the next day she drove off. I didn't see her again for several months.

LA MESA PENITENTIARY, TIJUANA, MEXICO

PRISON TWO

CHAPTER 19

A FEW DAYS later, about mid-afternoon, I heard our names called from the loud speaker announcing Jeff and I should present ourselves at the *sala de guardia*. There was no time to do anything but leave. I said goodbye to Ramon and left him with my keys to the cell. A couple of days prior, I made him a gift of my *casa* and its remaining contents, and thanked him for all the help he'd given me. He wasn't sad, really. Rather, he seemed glad to have me gone, as he'd have my cell to himself and could sell it or the contents for good money. I owed him much and was glad to repay him with my well-appointed cell. He had no family that he spoke of and never got visitors, which meant no money to make his life better. The cell we'd shared for the past few months was a valued property and the gift changed his life. Years later, I learned from Martín that Ramon sold the contents off and eventually the cell for what would have been a lot of money for him.

We weren't allowed to take anything except a few clothes and a bedroll. Jeff was already at the *sala de guardia* when I arrived. A few of the guys from my theatre group were waiting to say goodbye. Karin, who'd been Jeff's roommate since Thomas left, and had been friendly to both of us, leaned in and said, "Watch out, *cuidadenos, La Mesa esta duro.*"

They put us in a van and drove us to the local airport. I asked Jeff what Karin was talking about, and he said, "*La Mesa* is the old prison in Tijuana and Karin says it's very different, because the inmates are in total control. It could be tough for us if we have to stay long."

He wasn't particularly friendly, but definitely more polite than he'd been. We were shackled together with our legs and hands cuffed, and it's futile to be angry at someone you have to walk in stride with. The van pulled up to a small prop plane and we waddled toward it. There were eight other guys, cuffed and already on the plane, who'd arrived from other prisons further south – Mexico City, Oaxaca, Guadalajara. It was strange, being cuffed to Jeff in such a rickety old plane; if it went down, we'd die shackled together. I wondered, if that happened, would we be chained together in the misery of some strange afterlife?

We flew directly to Tijuana about three hours away and were immediately taken to the old prison, *El Centro de Readaptación Social de la Mesa*, or *La Mesa* for short. Once located on the outskirts of town it was now in the middle of the congested narrow streets and a jumble of shops and markets. As the families of inmates moved nearby to support their loved ones, the community surrounding the prison grew. *La Mesa* was (and as of this writing still is) a small city within the city of Tijuana. It's an underworld of drug lords, violent offenders, inmates' families, petty thieves, and a mass of undesirables. Like any city, *La Mesa* is divided into boroughs and sectors: skid row, a marketplace, areas of town where as a newbie you go and don't go, the homeless sector, the main plaza, and the super-rich penthouses. There are families with children playgrounds, sex workers, and lots of petty crime. The super wealthy who run *La Mesa* keep crime to a minimum because it's bad for business. And punishment is harsh.

A lot of Americans end up at *La Mesa*. They go to Tijuana to party, buy narcotics, indulge in wild sexcapades and sometimes get caught doing something stupid. And like it was in my situation, there's no bail so they wait in prison, sometimes months or years, for their case to progress.

The idea behind *La Mesa* was to establish a prison where none of the normal rules applied. Not only were inmates free to abandon their prison cells, but their families were free to come and live with them in the prison. The stated reason was giving prisoners a sense of normalcy would make rehabilitation and reintroduction to society easier, but it was basically a cheaper way of housing inmates because their families would shoulder the burden of necessities like food and medicine.

Over the decades, the prisoners and their families developed enterprises and small businesses within the prison walls. Entire criminal rackets arose, establishing a price on every commodity imaginable. Not only did the guards turn a blind eye to the drug rings that emerged, but even innocent items became pricey and rare commodities. Whatever an inmate needed or wanted, somebody found a way to get it inside and sell it. There were times when water was going for as little as $1.20 for five gallons and a two-room shelter could cost as much as seven thousand dollars. If I'd been there for the last eight months instead of Hermosillo, I could have sold my little apartment for a couple thousand dollars. But, of course, it would have cost me that much to buy it in the first place. It really was a small city, or a "little village" as its nickname *El Pueblito* translated to. Everything was available inside, including any kind of sex and every kind of drug. It could have served as an example in a thesis on capitalism: private property, capital, wage labor, a pricing system, and competition.

As we drove up to the entry gate, I caught a glimpse of the exterior walls through the front window of the van. It looked like something out of a James Coburn movie: old, rough-plastered concrete block walls ran along a side street with pedestrians moving beneath multiple guard towers. Every so often, guys with automatic weapons walked atop the walls, peering over both sides. This place looked like what our friends thought of when we said *prison in Mexico.*

They marched us out of the vans and through rooms that were as old and decaying as the walls outside. We were all pretty nervous, and as we sat in dark little rooms for processing, a couple of guys from the plane recounted wild stories they'd heard about *La Mesa.*

We were ushered along narrow and ever darker corridors that felt like catacombs. We could hear people shouting and screaming nearby, then passed a holding tank and saw what the commotion was: men were jammed into extremely cramped and dirty quarters, more like cages really, fighting and struggling for a bit of territory or scrap of food.

Fortunately, they pushed us passed that holding tank into an outdoor area with the same type of narrow corridors. There were doors to rooms all along the corridors, and occasionally, someone would go in or out. Sometimes they looked like staff or guards, and sometimes they appeared to be inmates. It was hard to tell people apart, and no one looked like an authority figure.

Suddenly, there was a commotion up ahead, and the guys further in line looked horrified. As I got closer, I could see what they were reacting to. Three hefty guards were beating on a young kid who looked to be about seventeen. They were pounding him hard, heedless of his grunts, groans, and screams This kid's face was ashen and bloodied, as he cried and begged for help. We were only a few feet from him as he crumpled into a doorway. Someone up ahead told me not to watch. "Don't look at that guy," they warned. I tried to avert my eyes, but it was impossible. Each time they smashed a fist or baton into the kid, you could feel every gut-wrenching, bone-crushing blow.

I didn't understand what was happening, I thought they were doing this for our sake, maybe to frighten us. It was sickening and terrifying. The kid couldn't defend himself. Besides, he was about half the size of any one of the guards, and there were at least three beating on him. After we got inside, one of the Americans in our group, who was Hispanic, told us the kid was a pedophile and had raped a little girl. In prison, that's the worst crime you can be in for. In the US, pedophiles are called "short eyes" because they have "eyes" for short people, meaning kids. They're usually removed from the main population and put in solitary to prevent this kind of beating from other inmates. In Mexico, they get dumped into the main prison, where they don't last long. This kid was going to have to face the guards first, then the inmates would tear into him once inside. It was brutal, but then so's the act of raping a little girl.

At the end of the line, they stamped our papers, took some quick photos and handed us our bed rolls (which had been brought from the plane), then assigned us to a building for sleeping quarters. Evidently, there were Mexican prisoners arriving in San Diego in the next few days, so we had to wait for them before the transfer could take place. With no escort or guards to accompany us, and no small amount of fear and trepidation, we walked into the main plaza of *La Mesa*.

I'd never seen anything like it; it was a combination of Turkish bazaar and Mumbai slum. There were people everywhere, walking quickly one way or the other. All kinds of shops and front-facing stores selling anything and everything. There were women dressed like sex workers alongside pregnant mothers with kids playing in the mud.

La Mesa is the kind of place where anything is available; from a steak and lobster dinner accompanied with fine wine to a night of exotic sex with multiple partners. All you need is the money and you can have whatever you want. Very little is provided to the inmates; you have to buy a place to sleep and bedroll to sleep in. A small cell or "apartment" could run from one hundred to several thousand dollars a month. Property is sold and transferred as any real estate business. There were at least fifty restaurants and dozens of markets and shops selling electronics, kitchenware, furniture, clothing, and if you didn't see what you wanted, they could get it for you the next day.

There had once been cinderblock cells and other constructed buildings, but they had been completely taken over by the inmates. Dwellings were built wherever anyone could find a space big enough to lie down. All the old block buildings were hidden by layer upon layer of wildly diverse and ingeniously designed human dwellings. They were stacked up three or four stories high, some supported by others below and each holding onto a small bit of territory. What would be a food bar during the day was converted into sleeping quarters at night. The owner would drop down part of the front wall and put out a couple of stools. He would sell coffee, fruit smoothies, tacos, grilled meat, anything, then just fold up the wall and sleep right there in the same area where he had been preparing food during the day.

A guy could create a small space in between two dwellings where he could make a bed and put up a piece of corrugated tin to form a sleeping chamber just big enough to lie down. Guys hunkered down any place they could find a space. The front-facing shops were the area of the prison you would consider the middle class. The upper-class inmates lived in rooms or apartments hidden by the smaller front-facing spaces, and the super-rich were up on the third and fourth stories. You couldn't see the fronts or entries, or see inside those houses and I supposed just about anything took place inside the hidden spaces. Ex-politicians, drug lords, and young guys from wealthy families lived in those spaces and, evidently, ran the prison.

Throughout the little city were myriad pipes and wires. People needed power, water, and waste removal, and how they got it depended on how much they could afford. Guys made money running pipes and wires to provide water and electricity, some carried things or transported stuff like cinderblocks, mortar, and lumber. People would do anything for a fee. Dwellings hung out over the walkways and wires and pipes ran in hundreds of different directions, carrying electricity, water, or waste in one direction or another. The corridors were narrow as over the years shops and dwellings had consumed most of the space between the old cellblocks so there was just enough room to pass through with a cart or a wheelbarrow.

The women's prison was right next door, and a gate allowed women to pass into the men's prison. Some of the women who came into the prison during the day worked in the little shops and cafés. They also mended clothing, cut hair, and provided cleaning services. Even the person who managed the gate between the women's and men's prisons was collecting a fee, and then he paid someone else for the "concession" to do that. A very powerful inmate, somewhere above all this mess, was the "city mayor" and established the laws or rules of the prison, which most seemed willing to follow. It was a functioning city with all its vices, utilities, food services, transportation, servants, labor, and police. The police, of course, were just badass inmates hired by the guys who ran the prison to keep order and make sure no one crossed into someone else's territory.

As we stepped out of the dark corridors we entered the main plaza of *La Mesa*. If you stood in the center, you could turn around and see everything else. After spending most of the day shackled together in the plane and two vans and having just witnessed the beating of the young kid, we were utterly knocked off our feet by a giant Diego Rivera-style mural painted on the side of the concrete block inmate building. It was at least seventy-five feet wide and three stories high. An artist who'd been incarcerated there for a number of years had painted it by himself. The inmates adored the mural, it belonged to them, and depicted the exploitation of indigenous peoples by Spanish conquistadors with Native miners being whipped by their overlords. It had all the Rivera ideas captured in a giant seventy-five foot mural, including scenes of Poncho Villa, Mexican independence, socialist workers fighting factory owners and slave laborers. You could stare at it for hours, discovering bits of Mexican history. The mural was the first thing you saw upon arriving, and the image never left you.

Inside the building with the mural was shanty town, skid row, tenement housing; where the guys who had no money or family and didn't belong to a gang lived. That's where we, the transferring Americans, were assigned. It was a large, three-story cinderblock building that stood off to one end of the plaza with the mural on its only front-facing wall. The top two stories were rows of individual cells. New inmates and those without money lived in those cells. They were the workers who handled menial jobs and transported supplies throughout the compound. The bottom floor was a big open space where guys slept on makeshift beds of cardboard and piles of trash. Those inmates were usually brand-new guys, or those who had mental issues or other disabilities.

An inmate's quality of life depended on how much money he had or who he worked for. Life was miserable for many people.

The inmates there begged us for cigarettes and money, and pleaded for our bedrolls. But we didn't have money, or anything of value, except the bedrolls. When we made the transfer to San Diego, we all left our bedrolls, but for a few days, we had to roll them up each morning and store them with the administration before going out into the main prison.

It was late afternoon by the time we got inside that day, and I wandered around and stared at everything. I tried to stay out of the way and not bother anyone, but a couple of times, I clearly crossed some invisible boundary and nearly got my head chewed off. Then someone came up behind me, grabbed me by the shirt, and told me to follow him before I got hurt. He was small and slight and, though Hispanic, spoke perfect English. I followed him to a little café where we sat down and had tea and pastries.

He introduced himself as Bili. Guillermo was his real name, but he went by the American nickname of Bili because he was actually a US citizen. After tea, he took me to his dwelling, his *casita*. It was a room that had been specially built far away from the main plaza, tucked into a group of buildings that appeared to be connected to the administration, but occupied entirely by inmates. These were the inmates who attended the daily routines of managing the prison, the city employees working for the mayor and city council living high above.

As I walked inside Bili's house, I stepped into another world: a shiny black grand piano was the centerpiece with an exquisite Persian rug beneath it; all around were cushions and pillows for sitting and lounging; a large brass incense burner sat upon a Balinese-style wooden coffee table, and prints of Salvador Dali and Picasso paintings, along with artwork from Mexican artists, graced the walls. It was reminiscent of a '60's style artist pad, like a loft for Grace Slick or Jerry Garcia.

The incongruity of it all had me reeling for a moment. I thought I was hallucinating. When I prodded him, Bili said he had a *situation* with the administration that allowed him these perks. He wasn't required to be there, because he was not incarcerated any longer. He had been released, then had come back on a minor offense which would have required a short stint. I got the impression that his first incarceration was from of a crime of passion, as though he'd hurt somebody. When his second sentence was over, he refused to leave. He provided something they wanted in exchange for his situation, but I never learned exactly what it was. He'd simply found a perfect place to live. He was happy, albeit lonely. He taught art and music to the inmates, instructed the guards in English, and smoked a lot of weed. He described his life as perfect and he seemed, on the surface at least, to be one of the happiest people I ever met. But I was unable to identify what seemed to be apprehension, or even torment, underlying his happiness. When he wasn't stoned, which was not often, he was ill at ease, as though afraid of an impending doom.

Bili was admittedly gay, yet no one accosted or propositioned him and he didn't have a lover. He wouldn't say why or how he came to exist in *La Mesa* this way and I didn't push him further. We sat for hours talking about existentialism and Shakespeare, art and music, and how living in prison changes one. I wiled away most of the time I spent at *La Mesa* sitting and talking with Bili. That first night, I fell asleep on his sofa after smoking hash, and in the morning, he came in and woke me with one of the best cups of coffee

I'd ever had. It was Moroccan-style, thick and rich with a touch of cinnamon.

Bili had found paradise, nirvana, in a fantastically ludicrous environment. If I had been incarcerated in *La Mesa* instead of Hermosillo, I could have written a full novel about Bili and his marvelous yet incongruous life inside *La Mesa* Prison.

Bili played the piano for me; he wasn't good but played with emotion. He liked having it there as a piece of furniture more than anything. Mostly, he enjoyed reading and discussing philosophy, especially the existentialists like Nietzsche, Sartre, and Dostoyevsky. I'd read *The Brothers Karamazov* in college, and *Crime and Punishment* while in prison. I myself had become fascinated with existential notions, and I loved discussing the fundamental doctrine that existence precedes essence. We were inmates, prisoners, but that did not define our existence. We were independent, responsible, conscious beings – not labels, stereotypes, or preconceived categories. We discussed gender labels, what it means to be gay or straight. Is there such as thing, really, as black and white? Gay or straight? It was fascinating for me, especially after experiencing everything I had up to that point. I finally had a chance to talk it over with someone who saw the universe the way I did. I'd witnessed "straight" guys going to *pabellon cinco* to have sex with other guys, then saw them heading off for conjugal visits with their wives. I myself had been called *gabachita,* "little white girl," because I liked to cook and keep my cell clean. Yet I'd never even considered visiting *pabellon cinco.* Then there was Jeff, and whatever it was he'd felt for me. I'd been thinking about notions of identity, essence, purpose, and existence, even in college. And so had Bili, here in prison. I found myself wishing I'd been in prison here instead of Hermosillo, even though it was much more dangerous for Americans.

Yet Bili's underlying sadness plagued me. He belonged, had a place and a purpose, but didn't seem to have anyone. But that didn't seem to be the source of the deeper sadness. He could have left prison and gone back to the US, but he chose not to. Perhaps he was wanted in the US on another charge, or maybe he'd gone through a terrible tragedy that kept him away. There was something he couldn't face, either emotionally or legally, and wouldn't say what it was.

Without Bili, I would have been faced with Jeff the entire time because Americans had to stick together to be safe. While I was hanging out with Bili, Jeff made friends with a couple of guys who were with us on the transfer. One in particular was Carlton; he had come from Oaxaca and had been there over two years awaiting transfer. He was cool, easy going, and had the kind of temperament that helped him get along with everybody. A pilot who'd been arrested for transporting appliances, Carlton spent two years in prison in Oaxaca. It struck me as paradoxical - here in *La Mesa* where you could buy anything, Carlton wasted in jail for flying toasters and blenders into Mexico.

The Mexican government had placed high tariffs on things like electronics and appliances, so transporting them illegally was about the same as transporting drugs. You could sell appliances in Mexico for a much higher price than what you paid in the US because the brands sold in Mexico weren't very good. Rich Mexicans would pay a premium price for illegal appliances, and Carlton thought no one would really care. Toasters? Blenders? Why not?

He pleaded not guilty and spent the two years fighting the charge, which was his mistake. He finally got sentenced and went on the transfer where in the States he would go free quickly.

The best thing about Carlton was he kept Jeff away from me for those few days and it was great. I didn't have to worry about placating Jeff and keeping him company. Jeff now had a new friend: Carlton from Montana, who had a backcountry, easy-going nature. He could listen to anybody's problems with the appearance of highly-engaged empathy, something I never had. Even when I had empathy, my face just didn't register it. I was one of those guys who looked like I couldn't give a shit about your problems, and maybe that was just a little bit too true.

After five days, we were loaded into a prison van and driven across the border to America, and to the federal prison in downtown San Diego.

METROPOLITAN CORRECTIONAL CENTER, SAN DIEGO, CALIFORNIA

PRISON THREE

CHAPTER 20

THE METROPOLITAN CORRECTIONAL
Center, or MCC San Diego, is a United States federal
administrative detention facility that holds both male and
female prisoners of all security levels. It's basically a large
holding tank for inmates moving somewhere else – such
as being transferred to or from Mexico – or serving short
sentences. It's a twenty-three-story tower on the edge of
downtown San Diego that houses 1,300 inmates. From the
outside, it looks like any other tall metropolitan building,
albeit more mundane and uninteresting, and I imagine it was
by design. Most people walking around the streets below
have no idea it's a prison.

Each floor is a cellblock, separated from the other cells and
inmates, so the administration can keep certain inmates
isolated from others. There is a large open area in the center
of each floor, and the rooms (or cells) are situated around the
outside walls. The elevator is located in the administration
area on one side of the floor, along with medical and food
service. The central eating and hangout area resembles a
food court in a shopping mall, with plastic tabletops fastened
to heavy metal legs scattered around the room. Each table is
a hexagon, which enables an inmate to sit alone on one side
without having to sit beside or too close to another inmate.

Each cell, about the size of a large bathroom in a mid-sized American home, accommodates two inmates. Two bunkbeds are situated against the window of the room where, through a long, slender window, you can look out over San Diego Bay or the downtown area, depending on which side of the building you're on. There's a closet, a sink, and a small desk, with communal showers located off the central court.

All inmates arriving at the prison, no matter their crime or sentence, are immediately placed into twenty-four-hour lockdown, with an hour a day alone outside in the main court to shower and exercise. The prison administration must wait for every inmate's paperwork to clear so they can be sure of an inmate's identity, where they had come from, and what their crime and sentence is. They have to protect witnesses, separate violent gang members, and make sure people who are high risk are properly managed before being moved into the main population. It took at least a month for paperwork to clear. There was no choice of who they put you with; they went down a list and the next two arrivals were bunked together. We were all treated as maximum security risks from the moment we arrived.

Jeff and I were on the list one after the other so they put us together. Our relationship was strained, at best, and mostly adversarial, and now we had to spend twenty-three hours a day together, for a least thirty long days.

Upon arrival we had a good idea of the parole situation: in 1980, in the United States, possession of marijuana was a federal crime. For a first-time offense, the penalty was zero to five, meaning that, at most, you would spend five years in prison. Usually, people were out in less than a year. Almost anyone convicted of a zero to five crime was eligible for parole after eight months.

Today (2019), folks are serving life in prison for smuggling a few ounces of weed or cocaine. But those laws weren't changed until the tough-on-crime era of the Reagan-Gingrich years. And of course, in 2019, there are states in the US where marijuana is legal, so that has changed as well. We were federal prisoners, not in the State of California's jurisdiction, so we wouldn't have benefited from the changes in the laws for California anyway.

Jeff and I were now under the jurisdiction of US law, no matter what our sentence had been in Mexico. That was the purpose behind the prisoner-exchange program. Inmates from Mexico arrested in the US would fall under Mexican law upon returning to Mexico and vice versa for US citizens returning to prison in America. We'd already spent a number of months in Mexican prison, so as soon as our paperwork cleared, we would be assigned a case officer who, likely, would recommend parole for us. That is, as long as there were no outstanding warrants, misbehaviors, or pending investigations. At some point, without discussing it, Jeff and I realized neither of us wanted to jeopardize our parole, so we endeavored to be on our best behavior with each other. If he said anything about me or I said anything about him, it could hurt us both. He could tell them about my truck; I could tell them about his escape attempt. Then we would have to wait for further investigations. The best thing for us both would be to say nothing, and though we never discussed it, we both understood it.

There I was, in that small room, walking around, sleeping, eating, sitting on the toilet, reading, writing letters, doing everything you do all day long, with someone I didn't trust or even know any longer. Someone I thought wanted to have me arrested for another crime and put in prison for a long time.

We were assigned a parole officer and a psychologist. The administration wanted to know as much as they could about the new arrivals in case someone was a nut case. We could apply for parole, but we had to wait to speak with someone about it so we would know what to do when the time came.

For a couple weeks, we just sat there, day in and day out, not saying anything really, trying to talk around the big issues. We were polite. I pretended to care about his problems with Arlene, and he pretended to care about my issues with Kate. By that point, both women were just plain tired of the whole shitty mess. We'd dragged them into this debacle, relied on them over and over to bring supplies, and pay for our phone calls.

Neither had much money or great jobs. Kate was working as an actress in Salt Lake City, and Arlene was still in college. A fifty-dollar phone bill for one month was outrageous in 1980, and that's often what they had to pay due to our international collect calls. Neither had enough money to pay all their bills. Both were starting to question what they'd gotten into and whether they'd done the right thing helping us. Kate and I were definitely falling apart. Jeff thought Arlene was placating him, so he told her to forget him, but she kept at it.

The days dragged on. I mostly sat in my bed looking out the small window and reading. I caught up on some of the classics – Mark Twain, Charles Dickens, Shakespeare, and even some Stephen King – since that's what they had in the prison library. We weren't allowed to go to the library room, but trustees would bring around a cart with books we could check out. Sometimes we could request something if they were in the mood and occasionally, there was a guitar I checked out. One guitar was passed around all the floors and I rarely got it.

The tension between Jeff and me in that little room was heavy, and we endeavored to stay above it. We had the same parole officer, since we would both be released into the custody of an officer in Salt Lake City. Our officer covered that area, but was more of a case officer who would file our paperwork for parole and either recommend that or more time in prison, based on the basic regulations about parole.

The idea is to convince an officer that you are a good egg, that you can be trusted on the outside not to repeat your crime. You've learned your lesson and have been rehabilitated, as well as have a potential job and someplace to live. That's how parole works.

We'd been a couple of college guys who tried to bring weed into the US. It wasn't that big a deal in those days, except that we had ten kilos with us (about twenty pounds). By any appearance, that was no longer "personal use," but "drug dealer" status. Our challenge was to convince the parole officer we were not drug dealers, it was a mistake and we ended up with that amount of weed because we were trying to buy some cocaine for our college break.

I don't think he believed us, but he had a lot of other fish to fry. Each parole officer has a huge caseload and the easiest thing for them to do is release people. When a couple of guys like Jeff and I come up for parole – guys with no priors, guys who have families and either jobs or school to go back to – we're a good bet.

The very nature of prison generates fear, intimidation, and greed. With precious little space and almost no freedom or power for most inmates, everyone battles to get the optimum situation, and *survival of the fittest* kicks in automatically. It's innate, we all have it. Reduce the area where you live, or reduce the resources, and competition for control of territory and resources becomes a strategic focus. And it's more intense in prison because there are few resources and most of the people are more aggressive, so everyone fights hard to get the best deal. The guitar was a good example. There was only one other guy I saw who could play the guitar well, but a dozen guys would check it out and keep it for as long as allowed, just so they could have that little bit of power. It was a small thing, but it was something.

While Jeff and I were in that tiny cell for twenty-three hours a day, the shared territory was greatly reduced. You long to think quietly without hearing the breathing and ruffling of the other person, but there's nothing you can do to stop it. The other guy's energy, noise, body movements, every little scratch is ever-present and suffocating. There's no escape, and at times, you'd like to strangle them. And cellmates often hurt or kill each other. I lost myself in books, falling deeply into the story, lying in my bunk for hours upon hours, reading, thinking, and daydreaming.

Jeff wasn't of that ilk, he needed to talk, and would talk incessantly. Again and again, talking about the same damn thing over and over, and I believed, trying to drive me crazy. I had to listen to him or it would be considered a rebuke, which could lead to him spilling his guts to the parole officer. I couldn't help but think Jeff was almost on the verge of slipping into some kind of unstable psychological or emotional state. He rambled at times, and made almost no sense. I faked listening to him and occasionally offered a comment or suggestion.

Finally, after a month, we were released into the main population. They took us to another floor where the inmates were serving short sentences, mostly drug dealers and "coyotes," the nickname given to guys who bring illegals into the US. Most had been arrested along the miles and miles of the US/Mexican border with a van of people trying to get in to America in order to have a better life. These guys were ruthless, and left people stranded in the desert without water and took advantage of younger, lone females. Inside, they were thugs, what you imagine when you think of a convict.

We were randomly placed into cells, and I got bunked with a Mexican coyote who didn't speak much English. He was icily stoic, didn't talk much, and never once endeavored to introduce himself to me. But on the other hand, he didn't bother me either. He stayed outside the cell most of the day and only came in at night to sleep. That left me some time alone where I could think, write, and read in peace. He clearly didn't like me, but it didn't do either of us any good to argue, so it was always a matter of who got to the cell first. The other guy would leave and find someplace else to hang out.

One program they offered was a class taught by an art psychologist who came to the prison almost daily on a federal grant, to work with the inmates on personal art projects. She taught mostly visual art, as that was her field, but she tried to help us with writing and even music, despite the fact she had little or no experience in either of those disciplines. I had been writing songs, documenting the events of my life in prison through music. I had some vague notion of creating a musical when I got out that would give my career a boost, so I asked her to listen to my songs and give me some feedback. She did. It was at this point I started thinking more about how art could help prison inmates. The songs weren't any good, but she helped me a great deal just by listening to them.

A couple of weeks before our parole release, Jeff and I were granted trustee status, and we were allowed to go outside for a couple of hours each day. We picked up brooms, shovels, and cleaning supplies, and were let out onto the grounds around the prison. It was the first time in nearly a year that we'd actually touched US soil. Well, it was mostly concrete, but there were pockets of real earth. We were on free ground and nothing was holding us or keeping us fenced in but our own recognizance. It's done as test to prepare you for release and become acclimatized to the freedom of the outside world. If you run, the authorities will eventually catch you, and they'll know you weren't ready for parole. If you do anything like buy drugs or bring drugs back inside, then you'd lose your parole and have to wait another couple of months or more.

Jeff and I hadn't been talking much since we were moved into the main population. He spent most of his time with Carlton and a couple of the other guys who came with us on the transfer. I spent most of my time reading or casually talking with just anybody. I didn't mix well in that prison; Jeff was more at home. He liked speaking English and eating American food, even if it was prison food. There were TV sets, and half the guys were in one corner watching NFL, NBA, and NASCAR, while the other half were in another corner watching Latin League soccer.

Going outside that first time was strange; I had to fight the urge to run as fast as I could and get away from prison forever. There wasn't much cleaning to do. The grounds were sparse, mostly concrete, with patches of bushes here and there. We picked up trash and scraped pigeon shit off the walks underneath the ledges where they liked to roost. The rest of the hour or so we sat on the concrete, backs against the building in our orange prison outfits, and made attempts at conversation.

By then there was little to say. We'd both been through our individual parole hearings and received our approvals. We knew we were getting out soon. Not the exact time and day, but we knew it was over. He hadn't reported me for anything, evidently, and likewise, I hadn't said a word about him. We had kept quiet about the things that could hurt either one of us.

There was still a lot of shitty stuff between us, stuff we never talked about, even after prison. I ran into Jeff once after we got out, each of us living back in Salt Lake City. I was still unbelievably mad at him. It was a couple of weeks after we got home, and we'd both gone to the Sundance Film Festival. With dozens of movies and multiple venues all over Park City and Salt Lake City, we happened to run into each other at the same movie. I was with Kate and he was with Arlene. In some odd way, it was like we'd never been to prison; we were just doing the same old shit we'd always done before. But it was only two or three weeks after getting out, and the past year still weighed heavily on me. All the shit that had happened, the accusations and recriminations, the vituperation, and downright hatred we'd both felt was like a dinosaur sitting on my shoulders.

I saw him and Arlene, they saw Kate and me, and started to walk toward us like nothing had ever happened, like we were old school chums. I was blinded by utter disbelief and unbridled anger. He had been a cruel thorn in my side for a year. I fretted and worried about him going crazy, about him turning me in, about him making my life as miserable as he could. That's all I could think about in that moment, so I turned and walked in the opposite direction. I didn't want to see them. And I couldn't talk to them either.

I saw the look on Jeff's face as I did that. He was immediately angry, maybe hurt. He had tried to make up and repair the relationship by approaching me first, and I had rebuked him… again. Kate was upset at me and wanted to reconnect with them. She'd spent a lot of time with Arlene driving to Mexico and they had become friends. She thought I was being an ass and said I should put it all behind me and move forward.

I wasn't ready to forget and forgive. I never saw Jeff again and I don't know what happened to him. I should have tried to forget. I should have tried to meet him that day and get past it all. It would have been better for me, for Jeff, and for everyone involved. But I didn't do it and I always regretted it.

UTAH STATE PRISON, DRAPER, UTAH

PRISON FOUR

CHAPTER 21

TWO WEEKS LATER, they put me on a bus for Salt Lake City. Jeff took a different bus; he'd planned to visit his mother in Northern California before heading back to Utah.

The bus depot in Salt Lake City is on the west side of town, the indigent area of the city. Stepping off the bus reminded me of the day I walked into the main plaza at *La Mesa*; I was scared, not sure of what would happen. This was oddly similar; a diverse assortment of people traversed the depot where my parents, a couple of my brothers and sisters, and Kate were waiting to see me. All smiles and hugs, it was a cheerful welcome, though my mother thought I looked thin and tired. On the long bus ride from San Diego, I fretted the entire way, wondering what my life would be like now.

We had dinner near the depot, where I mostly listened to everyone else talk about what they were doing and how their lives were moving along. I went home with Kate to her tiny apartment where she'd been living throughout my ordeal. On her last visit to Mexico, she had transported a few of my belongings, like my Guild D40 acoustic guitar I'd had since I was a teenager - the guitar had helped me endure the ordeal, and by then, it was about my only possession. I walked in and immediately looked for it. That's when she told me a burglar had broken into her apartment after she got back from Mexico and had stolen my guitar, along with her TV set and some other things.

I dropped to my knees, my heart sank. The loss of my guitar left me dangling, disconnected, and shaken. I don't know why it was the straw that broke me, but I began to unravel. I questioned her, like it was the death of a friend, I had to know more about what happened. She snapped right back, reminding me of the shit she had to go through, how long it had been, and that she too had lost important things from the break-in. She was angry about something else, I could sense it. Her tone was icy. "I'm in no mood to hear about your fucking guitar!"

I shut up. She was right. From that moment, the tension hovered over us like a guard tower. We backed away from the messy issues and things remained stagnant. Neither of us cared to discuss the real issue, so we tried to get along and let sleeping dogs lie.

But after a couple of weeks, there was no getting around it. I knew something was troubling her, we finally sat down and discussed it. A few months before, she'd fallen in love with someone, a producer she'd worked with on a commercial. I knew him, slightly. He was very successful, made good money and, I thought, rather a dickhead the way he treated people on set. She needed someone stable and secure, someone with whom she didn't always have to be strong. This was the thing that hurt the most; he was strong and successful and I was the dickhead.

She broke it off with him just before I came back. In order to get parole, inmates are required to have a place to live, meaning someone has to offer you a home. It would either have been Kate, or my parents, who lived in a small mining town in eastern Utah. That was hardly an option because there would have been nothing for me to do. I wouldn't have been able to find a job, at least not in my field. And you need that too. Kate reluctantly agreed to let me move in with her, and because of that, she broke it off with the producer. He was pretty upset, I learned later from an acquaintance, which meant they'd gotten pretty close. But she held to the agreement and stopped seeing him so I could move in with her. But that was the problem: she resented me being there and I felt like a burden, so our relationship was doomed.

I had been offered a job at the university theatre where I worked previously, building scenery and doing tech work. It wasn't a great job for me; tech work and scenery construction weren't what I wanted to do. But it was immensely helpful of the management to provide a job for my parole. It's a requirement that every convict reentering society – and that's what I was, a former inmate, and convicted criminal – have a place to live and a job. I had to visit my parole officer weekly and report on my activities, including any progress or setbacks. I'd sit in the foyer of his office and watch the other convicts come and go. Yeah...I was one of them now.

Kate and I eventually became completely estranged and I finally got my own apartment. I asked the theatre for an advance on my salary, and they obliged, but it shorted my income in order to repay the loan. I had been in prison for a year, and although I'd had a couple of conjugal visits with Kate, I longed for female contact. I started hanging out at bars to try and meet a girl. Fat chance. I was thin and pale, my voice was weak, my confidence was nil, and I had no money. I bought an old gas-guzzler for a couple of hundred bucks, and after paying rent and buying food, it left me enough cash for one beer a night. So I'd sit at the bar nursing that one beer, trying to strike up a conversation with anyone who had breasts. But I couldn't even get a conversation, let alone get laid.

A lot of my friends had graduated and gone off to work or graduate school. I did a play as an actor, but it was a disaster. I couldn't act anymore, I was insecure and didn't have the openness and sensitivity you need to be a good actor. I was closed off, stuffed up. I was sinking lower and lower.

One night after another failed attempt at meeting a girl, I had a severe panic attack. I woke up in the dark, fumbling for my concrete bunk, thinking I was still in prison. I thought I was dying and shouted for the neighbors to come help me. It was embarrassing, and I felt stupid afterward. It was a recurring nightmare I had for years; stuck in a strange prison with no way out. Like a damaged guitar, I couldn't get myself in tune, I was sliding into emotional hell, drowning in a sense of uselessness.

And then it struck me why prison recidivism is so high. The average rate of recidivism is about seventy percent. People who spend time in prison usually go back. Sure, they're mostly people who have been inside longer than I was, but there's still some kind of cultural phenomenon that pushes people back inside. That's why the people who manage our criminal justice system are always seeking ways to improve recidivism rates. It can save taxpayers money and lower crime rates.

While inside, you have an intense and singular focus on quality of life and your very survival. There's no job to go to or corporate hierarchy to please, no school, no teachers, nothing to distract you. And though you live in close quarters with hundreds or even thousands of other inmates, you're on your own. All that matters is grabbing hold of something to increase your quality of life, while you strive to get out as soon as possible. That's an acute focus you lose once you're back in the civilian population. Even though I'd only been inside a short time, comparatively, I was falling into the same damn trap of despair.

It was about that time, Steve Dent, a close friend of mine with whom I'd shared a house in college, threw a party for me. A lot of people from school came, including Scott Wells, who by then had graduated and was working in the Artist-in-Residence program at the Utah Arts Council. Scott did plays as an actor and director, but got his degree in arts administration. During the evening, I went on and on about my theatre program in Mexico and the plays we did. My friends couldn't really empathize with the formidable difficulties of developing a program like that in prison, but were fascinated by the idea of inmates doing theatre. Later, Scott pulled me aside and told me he was working with two nuns doing an outreach program at the state prison, and partially funded by the Arts Council. Inmates were accumulating high school and college credits for the courses the nuns taught. Through his work with the nuns, Scott had genuine affinity for my experience and we commiserated over our respective challenges.

It was the first time someone had been interested in the work as a social services experiment or an inmate rehabilitation program. I was so excited to share with someone, my eyes were alive and I could feel the surge of energy in my body. Scott was intrigued and kept asking more questions. I told him about the art psychologist in San Diego and thought we might use that as an example. Of all the people to run into at that party, Scott was the one person I really needed to see. He loved theatre, was working in arts administration, and had connections to programs and money. He agreed, we had a gem of an idea here and promised to arrange a meeting with Julie Grant, director of the Artist-in-Residence program, and Susan Boskoff, head of programming.

A few days later, I walked into the old mansion on South Temple that served as headquarters for the Arts Council, and met with Julie, Scott, Susan, and a couple of others involved with the Artist-in-Residence program. They were intrigued, and began to develop a strategy to get a program off the ground. We'd have to submit a grant to the Arts Council board, then approach the administration at the prison and the Utah State Department of Corrections. First, I had to apply, and be accepted, into the Artist-in-Residence program at the Arts Council. Though I hadn't graduated from college, Susan planned to convince the staff that this was a unique opportunity; a former inmate with college-level arts training and experience would be going into a prison to work with inmates on art projects. Her plan worked, I was accepted, and we were off!

The next challenge would be to sell the idea to be Ken Shulsen, Warden of the Utah State Prison. If he didn't like it or see a benefit to the inmates, it would all be over. There were plenty of reasons to say no to an ex-con requesting to come inside a maximum-security prison and do plays with inmates. How would that benefit them? How would that rehabilitate or prepare them for re-entry into society? It was unlikely that any of them would ever work in theatre, so career training was hardly relevant. And wouldn't teaching inmates acting lessons just help them fool the authorities better the next time they were arrested? Hadn't most of them lied or presented a false case to keep from going to prison? These were concerns offered by some on the Arts Council.

But I'd seen the results of inmates working on artistic projects and could testify to the benefits. My plan wasn't to teach inmates to act or perform just so they'd have something to do or have some kind of respite from the harsh life of prison. It was something deeper.

The day I walked into the warden's office, I didn't have a clear understanding of how to accomplish my goal. I knew little about him or the prison, but I hoped my enthusiasm would sell the idea. Sitting across the desk from a stone-faced Ken Shulsen that day, I tried to gauge who he was or what he thought of me. He wasted no time on small talk and after a few comments about my incarceration, he asked me what I intended to accomplish. I launched into my diatribe about why criminals make the choices they do and how lack of focus and direction is a catalyst for crime. It's not always about getting easy money, I said, but something deeper, a kind of angst, a need for adventure, an underlying disquiet or edginess. I'd encountered the same types of people in three different prisons, in two different countries, and had found that theatre had helped us develop focus. I believed I could make it work here at the Utah state prison. He looked me straight in the eyes and without committing to the idea, gave me a couple of warnings. " No candy-coating, Mr. Jewkes, here's the deal; if anything were to go on inside your program that even smelled like trouble, I'd cancel it immediately. And you would work within the existing prison structure. I have a director of inmate programs, Dean Hobbs, and you'd work with him, from his office, using his inmates, and with him as your boss. Understand?"

I said I agreed, but I couldn't tell if he was saying yes or not, so I decided to push it further with one more request. "I'd also like to go to the women's facility and do the same thing there." Hoping I hadn't ruined my chances by asking too much.

He looked at me for a moment and then smiled. I'd said the right thing. I hadn't tried to offer excuses for my crime, or claim I was innocent. I didn't complain about his directive of try to find a way around it. My first request was to expand the program even before it began. He saw that. I told him I wanted to perform plays, ordinary plays, and it would require men and women actors. He understood that as well, but I think, more than anything, he sensed I was in for the long haul. Many well-intentioned folks go to the prison to help reform, rehabilitate, and/or "give back," but they tire quickly and soon leave. I was in for the duration of the program, whether for my own aggrandizement or whatever. He didn't really care. He thought I looked to be someone who would stick around for a while. And that's what he wanted. It was a go! He'd confer with the women's facility director, but was sure it'd be fine since the women didn't have as many programs and opportunities as the men.

A month later, I arrived at the main guard gate, entered the prison, and was met by Dean Hobbs, who took me to his office and introduced me to his inmate assistants. They were developing several programs at the time and were suspicious of my intentions. Dean hurried off to deal with a problem and left me with the three inmates: Mark Gotcher, John Harney, and Joe Ward – all convicted of armed robbery. They'd tried to initiate many projects but had been shut down over and over. Mostly there weren't enough inmates who cared to become involved, or if they did, it was only perfunctory to appear as though they were rehabilitating themselves. They complained that the prison didn't contribute enough money. Plays required sets, costumes, and lighting — production elements they didn't have. I could see I had to win over these guys, and told them about my Mexican prison group and how, with very little support, we produced some great shows. I mentioned my connections with local theatres and production people, and said I could do a lot of the tech work myself, along with their help. I didn't candy-coat it to them either; I offered no grandiose promises, told them it would be a lot of hard fucking work, and they might even hate me at times. They got it. By the end of the day, we were planning several plays, including *Twelve Angry Men* by Reginald Rose, *The Curious Savage* by John Patrick, *The Night of January 16th* by Ayn Rand, and *American Buffalo* by David Mamet. They were fired up and eager to get going.

The people I had met in prison were often smart, sometimes hard working, and artistically talented, but also impatient and expected results and/or success immediately. They're the kind of people who don't have the ability to envision what the future could bring if they focus hard on one thing. I thought if I could show inmates another way, another approach to finding happiness and satisfaction, then that could be helpful to them after returning to society. It was the first time since being released that I began to feel I was involved in something important, like my life had a purpose.

It had taken six months to get the program rolling. It was late in 1981, the year Ronald Reagan took office. He implemented sweeping new political and economic initiatives, including an escalated War on Drugs and greater efforts at fighting crime in general. But that was the first year of his presidency, and the sweeping changes didn't begin until Newt Gingrich took control of the House a couple of years later. So I got in under the gun, so to speak.

The work I did with the theatre group in Mexico was a huge help and inspiration in managing the program. I began by teaching classes to both men and women, arranging schedules for each facility separately. We read plays together, worked on scenes, and watched a few plays on TV. After a few months, I asked the warden if I could bring the men and women together. It got to the point where, when I walked into his office, he'd start shaking his head before I even sat down. It was reminiscent of my days with the old *comandante* in Hermosillo. Shulsen had a clever idea regarding the co-ed group though; before we brought the men and women together, he wanted to ensure the program was restricted to the guys already in the group, the guys who really wanted to do the work. Once we let the women into the men's prison, every guy inside would beg to join the theatre group, and by then it would be closed.

A few months after my first meeting with Mark, John, and Joe, I quietly introduced the women to the men's group. We met in one of the school classrooms near the administration offices. Men and women were already taking classes together for school, so it wasn't out of the ordinary to have both men and women meet there. At that first rehearsal, I announced we were going to do the play *Twelve Angry Men,* and we would all work together, men and women. It caused quite a stir, and the next day, over a hundred guys applied to be in the theatre group.

As requested by the warden, only those who had taken part in the theatre classes up to that point could be in the co-ed group. I assigned two of the women, along with the three original guys, Mark, Joe and John, to form an admissions committee. Together they would decide who could join the group. It would be inevitable that we would lose people through attrition, those going out on parole or transfers, so we had to create a process for new members.

About a month later, they allowed me to bring the women to the auditorium in the men's facility, right in the heart of the prison. The only way to get to it was through the main corridor, which was open to all inmates during the day. Guys going to school or to work in the shops or on the farm, and guys returning to their cellblocks walked that corridor daily. Everyone passed through the main corridor. There was one long stretch right down the center of the building, then a right turn for a few yards to the auditorium, where we'd be out of the sight of the main guard gate. It was those last few yards that were the problem.

On rehearsal days, I'd stop by the women's prison – a couple of hundred yards from the men's prison – and pick up eight to twelve female inmates. We'd walk across the yard, with the tower guards keeping an eye on us as we entered the men's prison. It was a new idea no one had tried before. Women went to school located near the front office, but never entered the security double-doors into the main corridor of the prison. It made a lot of the guards nervous, and they complained about it. I could tell there were some who wanted to get rid of me, a "bleeding heart do-gooder coddling the criminals." But the warden recognized the need to address the long-term problem that plagued the criminal justice system. Most inmates eventually leave prison and mix with the civilian population; we have to find ways to help convicts returning to society live productive lives within the law, and we have to reduce recidivism.

That was the intent and focus of my grant proposal, and the reason I got money and the opportunity to start the program. I think many believed that I, as a former inmate myself, might be able to reach these folks in a way that perhaps others could not. And if the program worked for even just one inmate, that could save as much as eighty-five thousand dollars a year, in addition to the contribution that person could make through holding a job, paying taxes, and maybe raising a family. The amount of money the program cost over the four years of my endeavor didn't amount to even a quarter of what it cost to house one inmate for one year.

Inside the prison at the main security gate, the guards would give me the keys to the auditorium. Then, along with Dean Hobbs and another guard, I'd walk the women down the corridor about a hundred yards, turn, and walk the few more yards to the door of the auditorium. Male inmates lined the corridors and called out to the women as they passed by. The guys in the theatre group would be waiting at the auditorium door, and we'd all go inside, with the help of the guards who kept the other inmates from sneaking in with the group. Then I'd lock the door from the inside and remain there alone, without guards, for three to four hours of rehearsals with twenty-five male and female inmates.

Occasionally, I knew shady things went on behind my back, like sex and drugs. But it never got out of hand and no one ever hurt anyone. None of the women complained, and, of course, neither did the men. So, honestly, I didn't care if a few of the girls and guys got a little on the side. After all, they were regular people with needs and desires. I made sure, with the help of my three trustees, no one was coerced or raped, and that was that.

We rehearsed three or four times a week, working really hard for those few hours. It was interesting how the competition between the men and women accelerated the work. The first time an inmate showed up to rehearsal with all their lines memorized, it built a fire under the others, and then next time more had their lines down. There's something to be said for having men and women in prison working together, and I believe we proved it to be successful.

I was giddy with excitement every day I went to the prison. After all my angst and depression, I had finally found something to sink my teeth in. My experience in theatre and the work I did in Mexico all came together to form a single-minded purpose. I belonged there, was comfortable and happy, and in a way, free to be creative. I could say anything to these people. I could swear, get mad, challenge them to work harder, and not worry about offending anyone. They knew I worked really hard to help them, and no one ever confronted or threatened me.

The guards, for the most part, let me be. Some thought I was in over my head and would get myself killed. Others thought I was crazy to even try to work with convicts, certain I was being fooled into believing the inmates would actually accomplish something. But there were also guards and staff who believed in and supported the program. They could see the potential benefits and, in the end, I had enough support (mostly because of the warden) to make it work.

To understand and better engage with the inmates, I ate lunch with them before rehearsals or classes. It was some of the worst food I'd ever eaten, but doing that accomplished the objective of letting them see I was one of them, and they appreciated and respected that. They knew the food was rotten, and yet I ate it alongside them. Sometimes I'd eat lunch with the women before we went over to the rehearsal, and sometimes I'd eat with the men before I went to get the women. I treated them like regular folks, and they granted me respect; I was one of them, ate with them, had a record like they did, and didn't take any shit from guys who tried to strong-arm me.

They knew I'd been in a Mexican prison, and tended to trust me more than they would have some "straight guy." It was a lot of work that I was asking from them, and they had to give up time from other activities. Some of their friends were angry because of all the time they put in. I kept telling them we'd eventually perform the play and they'd see how amazing it would be. But it required a lot of work, and I wasn't going to put them on stage unprepared and looking silly. I didn't want to bring outsiders into the prison to watch a bunch of sorry-assed convicts work out their psychological problems. I didn't want the audience to feel sorry for them or think of them as people who needed help because of their tragic upbringing. I wanted the play to work artistically, to show the inmates that there was something they could do in the straight world that could be as exhilarating as crime.

This is basically what I said to them at our very first rehearsal of *Twelve Angry Men.* "Look, man, I know the deal. You wanted some money. Quick cash, without going to a stupid fucking job where your boss is a shithead and you can't even make up enough to pay your rent. You stole a car, you sold crack, you hooked, you robbed a bank, you shot some kid at the 7-Eleven. You did it. I did it. We all did what we're in for. I haven't heard one fucking word from any of you saying you didn't do the crime. And I'm not going to ask a bunch of people to come out to the prison to listen to you whine about your problems and complain that you had a bad childhood.

"So let's do this right. Let's do a real fucking play, that only we know and understand. You've all been in court. You've been judged and sentenced by people just like the characters in this play. You understand better than all the upper-middle-class rich kids I went to school with. They're just acting. Pretending. You are being. You can become these characters because you know them. We can make this work. But it will be a lot of fucking work! And you will get so goddamned pissed off at me at times you'll want to choke the ever lovin' shit out of me. Forget about it. Let's just do it! And fuck 'em all!"

About six months later, we presented *Twelve Angry Men* in the prison auditorium to a civilian audience. We announced it in the local papers, noting it was *Twelve Angry People* because we were using both male and female inmates. It got a lot of attention. No one had done this before. School or church groups had gone out to the prison and worked with inmates in various programs focusing on rehabilitation. But to my knowledge, and to the warden's, no one had done this kind of thing; presented an ordinary play, performed by inmate actors, to a civilian population for the same reasons anyone would do a play in school or church. It was like a community theatre group, but inside a walled compound.

We had to postpone the performance a couple of times due to prison security issues and fire code problems, and for a couple of weeks my people didn't think it was going to get done. They were accustomed to disappointment, but I wouldn't let it go. I kept pushing, and then on January 16th

– almost two years after I'd been arrested in Mexico – we opened the prison to the outside and presented the play.

I understood the main reason people came to see it was because it *was* in prison, *with* inmates. They expected to see something out of the ordinary. Something they wouldn't see at a community theatre or high school. But I didn't characterize it that way. I let the news say whatever they wanted, and we presented the play as it was written, with limited scenery and human beings pretending to be people they weren't.

I wasn't sure what to expect. We had plenty of guards and staff to help in case a lot of people showed up. We were going to bring civilians into the main heart of a maximum-security prison. I was pretty sure virtually none of the audience, outside of prison officials, had ever been inside a prison before, yet alone that far inside. All the rest of the prison inmates were locked in their cells (which caused quite a stir and much criticism), so the prison corridors were empty except for guards and staff. The general public entered through the double security gate, then walked down the corridor where inmates usually played out their days. It was unprecedented and rather amazing.

My cast was crazy nervous, they didn't know what to expect. Earlier that day they were concerned no one would actually come. After all, most of these inmates had been raised in broken homes and bad environments: abuse and neglect was simply part of their lives. We were sitting on the stage wondering and worrying when Dean Hobbs came running into the auditorium and said there were dozens of cars driving into the parking lot. People were starting to form lines outside the security gate. "Lots and lots of people!" he cried.

I gathered the cast backstage as the public began entering the auditorium. There were dozens and dozens of all kinds of people. They filled the entire auditorium, and the guards had to run and get folding chairs. It was a madhouse at first and the crowd was nervous. Even the guards were nervous; no one knew what to expect because this had never been done before.

Local government officials came, all the press came, the Arts Council people came, and university students came. The warden and the director of the board of pardons were in the front row with their wives and friends. People wore suits and dressed like they were going to the opera. It was unbelievable. Before long, the auditorium was filled to capacity, and the fire marshals had to turn people away.

I had come out front to help seat people and bring in chairs and just stood there for a moment, gape jawed and wide eyed, as the auditorium filled. By that time, Kate and I had become friends again, and she showed up with a couple of friends. As I was talking to her about the event, she asked me how the cast was feeling.

"Oh my god! I forget about my actors!" I ran backstage to find them frantic, they were so nervous. None of them had experienced anything like this, and hadn't anticipated the fear that would overtake them.

They'd been imprisoned for murder, assault, armed robbery, fraud, bad checks, prostitution, drugs, burglary, just about every crime you can think of. Most had been in prison more than once and all had faced peril and danger that could have resulted in death. And now these tough-as-nails criminals were huddled backstage, scared to death of an audience that had no power over them. I had to laugh and cry all at once.

One of the younger women there for prostitution and drug crimes was about to faint. She clung to me, pleading to let her out of it and not make her go on that stage. I hugged her for a long moment and told her how important she was to the show. She couldn't let her friends down, she couldn't let me down, she had to go out there and do the show. She kissed my cheek and turned to the others and said, "Okay, I think we're ready to go on."

I went out to the light booth and slowly brought the house lights down, then the set lights down, and then it was black. You could feel tension in the room, so thick it was smothering. There were over three hundred people sitting in the middle of that maximum-security facility, waiting to watch inmate actors do a play. Now they were in the dark, in a prison, with several inmates up on the stage and in the tech booth.

I thought to myself, *my hell, everyone here is scared to death*. After the play, my colleagues confirmed how spooky it was for a few minutes. What a fantastic moment: guards, inmates, and civilians all in one room, all on the edge, scared of an unknown threat.

I slowly brought the lights up to half, which the cast knew as their cue to enter. The assistant director backstage ushered them out. Quietly, they took their places in the chairs around the table and I brought the lights up to full. You could hear a pin drop. But nothing happened, they just sat there. For months, I'd worked with these folks in classes and rehearsals, including several dress rehearsals. One thing I forgot was how much they'd relied on me. At every rehearsal, I was always there to say, "Okay, let's go." I had always started them off, and now they were silent.

They looked around, waiting for me to say "go." But I wasn't there, I was out in the auditorium by the tech booth. The audience started fidgeting nervously, thinking something had gone wrong. I was about to run to the stage and get them started when suddenly, Mark Gotcher spoke up. He'd assumed the role of assistant director, helping with schedules, etc., and finally realized I wasn't there to get them started. So he just mumbled something, not his line, but enough to get the dialogue going, and the play began. The audience relaxed, the actors took over and performed the play as rehearsed.

Twelve Angry Men depicts a jury considering the guilt or innocence of a man accused of murder. As the play opens, they have a nearly unanimous decision of guilty, with a single dissenter of not guilty. That character wants to talk it through one more time because he doesn't feel they should sentence a man to the gallows, or life in prison, without a thorough discussion. They argue and discuss the merits of the case both for and against a guilty verdict. That's the entire play – a bunch of people talking to each other about the guilt or innocence of a young man on trial.

The inmate actors had been through it before. Not as a jury, but as defendants. They had watched the jury, witnessed the outcome, but from the other side, like the kid in the story. Sometimes they were innocent of the crimes they were being tried for, but usually not. They'd witnessed both sides and could identify with the story. They weren't actors, had little training, but they had a different kind of connection to the material: they had empathy. That's something a lot of actors, especially the ones I'd worked with, couldn't possibly have had with a lot of characters or stories. Actors often go through a play or film saying lines as characters they would never know, or portraying situations they would never experience. They're good at it because they learn to utilize a personal experience or emotion to help them imagine the situation, conflict, or what the character feels. They're good at the make-believe part, but it's a stretch sometimes since it's not a real-life experience that informs the character development.

These inmate actors had little training, no previous experience, only their gut-level emotion – the feelings they'd felt many times sitting in court or being arrested or waiting in jail. They remembered those emotions when they said their lines. It wasn't perfect, It wasn't fine acting or what one might call great theatre, but it was excellent entertainment. The experience for both the audience and the inmates was truly amazing. At the end of the play, the audience remained still for a long moment. They didn't quite understand what had just happened to them. Then suddenly, all at once, they erupted in applause, jumping to their feet to emphasize their appreciation.

I ran backstage to get the actors because they didn't know to come out for a curtain call (I hadn't gone through that with them either!). They went back out to the stage, somewhat embarrassed and scared. The audience was still applauding madly, and finally, the cast began to feel it. This is what I wanted them to experience, recognition of a job well done. I came out with them at that point. We stood there together and accepted the applause for as long as it seemed appropriate, and then I ushered them backstage.

They hugged each other and jumped for joy like children at a birthday party. Of course, they wished they could all go out for cocktails and a wrap party, but that wasn't going to happen. I got hugs and kisses from the women, and hugs and handshakes from the men. We'd been instructed to wait backstage until the audience exited the prison, then I said goodnight to the men and walked the women back to their building. This time, I got to go home with the regular citizens.

They talked about it for the following two weeks. We didn't rehearse or conduct classes, just talked about the performance, the evening, the audience, and the play. Exactly as it should have been.

Shortly thereafter, we started another play. It was called *The Night of January 16th*, which seemed like an appropriate title for our next show. It was another courtroom drama with an unusual feature: volunteers from the audience take the parts of jurors and decide the ending. That was an interesting moment, bringing civilian audience members onstage with inmate actors to decide the verdict of a murder trial.

The third play was *The Curious Savage*, which we mounted as a touring production to the Egyptian Theatre in Park City, home of the Sundance Film Festival. It took a year to get that one off the ground. It's a full-length play, not a one-act like the other two, with multi-layered characters that require genuine acting technique. Since it was a comedy, we had to work hard on character building and timing. But we did it, with a prison bus and twenty armed guards surrounding the theatre. It too was an amazing success, and the Park City theatre was packed, including people sitting in the aisles. I lost some actors during that year as they were released on parole, so we had to keep adding new ones. That, of course, was the intent of the program: to work with inmates until they went out on parole and, hopefully, provide the support and tools they needed to cope and adjust to the outside world. And perhaps find a way to live within the law and not return to prison.

Over the four years of the program, I worked with some fifty inmates. I kept up with eight of them who left prison during the years I directed the program. Not one that I followed, for as long as I followed them (about two years), went back to prison. That's not absolute evidence of success, since I didn't do a thorough scientific assessment. I wish I could have followed all the inmates who got out and tracked what happened to them. From my perspective, the program was working. I witnessed the effects of transformations on several people. There weren't grandiose changes in personalities, but it doesn't take a great leap forward. Sometimes a little nudge will do.

The program was cancelled after four years. We presented three productions to the public and worked on two additional plays. We were about to present *Incident at Vichy* at a lab theatre at the University of Utah when three violent convicts escaped from the prison wearing street clothes. We were doing dress rehearsals at the time and our costumes were locked in a closet in Dean Hobbs' office. Someone reported to the press that the convicts must have stolen the theatre group's costumes, so the warden – a new one by then – suspended the program the day of the escape and wouldn't allow me back into the prison until they found the escapees and resolved what had happened.

A couple of weeks later, they caught the three convicts and brought them back to the prison. By that time, the prison administration had decided to cancel the theatre program altogether and focus on more structured programs that would teach inmates a usable trade. Reagan's tough on crime policy was pushing the public in a different direction: don't coddle inmates by providing them access to fun activities; make them work hard and learn a trade. That was the new mindset.

When they finally captured the three convicts, the news reported they were actually wearing street clothes taken from the prison industrial shops. The escapees had managed to steal the work overalls and blue jeans that instructors from the outside had left in the shop lockers. All my theatre costumes were intact and untouched.

It had been over four years since that first meeting where I convinced Mark, Joe, and John to help me start a theatre group. Within a few months of the end of the program, all three got out on parole. I stayed in touch with them for a couple of years, and none went back to prison during that time. John remained in Utah and finished his college degree; Mark returned to Montana and went to work on a farm; Joe hung around Salt Lake City for about a year, then went back to Pennsylvania.

I can't say as to whether any of the three ever went back to prison after that, but if ex-cons don't go back within the first six months, the odds of them staying out for good greatly increases. They were doing pretty well the last time I spoke with each of them.

As a nation, our view of criminal justice – how we think about crime and punishment and how we manage the judicial system – has changed dramatically since then. Prisons are overflowing, with five times the number of inmates per capita than in 1981. We still have a major problem with our system of crime and punishment and it costs taxpayers a lot of money and wastes lives.

According to a 2014 report by Human Rights Watch, the tough on crime laws adopted since the 1980s have filled US prisons with mostly nonviolent offenders. The policy has failed to rehabilitate prisoners, and many are worse after release than they were before incarceration. The report also noted that rehabilitation programs for offenders would be more cost effective than the high cost of incarnation.

I don't know what the answer is nor do I claim that my little program is a model for inmate rehabilitation and better reintroduction of convicted criminals into society. Every one of us is different, and we each need a different solution for a good life and happiness. Perhaps that's the way it is for inmate rehabilitation – each convict requires a different kind of solution to help him or her lead a productive life.

There was an inmate who joined my program and remained a solid contributor for a couple of years, actually one of the best actors. Apprehended with a truckload of cocaine, he was an independent drug dealer who made deals with various cartels. I said to him once, "If you devoted half the effort into career like investment banking or sales, you could make a fortune!" He vowed he would never give up his criminal enterprise – his business, as he called it, made more money, provided more extraordinary things than I could possibly imagine. He was willing to give up a few years in prison to enjoy his fabulous life of private jets, luxury hotels, and a bevy of exotic women.

And then there was this.

During the months that Joe and John lived in Salt Lake City, we got together now and then. They found jobs and began to rebuild their lives. One night, the three of us went out for beers and ran into Steve Hunt, a theatre director I knew from the university. He'd seen the play we did at the Egyptian Theatre in Park City and wanted to congratulate us on the performance. He sat down, ordered a round of beers, and began extolling the benefits theatre could bring to people in a variety of situations. He was excited about our work and wanted to contribute to the story.

Joe watched him for a while, nodding here and there, then added, "You know what it is for me? I have something to talk about. I can talk to my family, people I meet at work…I can tell them about the plays I've done. Not about prison. I'm more than just a convict with a rap sheet. I have something to say that people want to hear. Guys get out of prison and have nothing to talk about. Just their crime and their time.

But I can talk to people about David Mamet and *American Buffalo*. It's a thing. And I feel good doing it."

I'm sure for some there's no possibility of rehabilitation, they will never fit into a civil society. For me, it was a matter of finding my place, developing my own philosophy. For Joe, John, and Mark, they needed direction, and, I suppose, something to talk about.

It didn't escape me that I could have been in a similar situation as the inmates from my group. Easily I could have served a much longer sentence. I was fortunate. I spent a year in prison and, all in all, it wasn't terrible. I made bad choices and more mistakes than I had to pay for. But I was a lot like them. A lack of focus and no goals early in our lives had led us to become lost. Most of them had grown up in difficult or challenging situations – raised in families where they didn't fit, or no family at all. What most of us want is to fit in. Be accepted, be part of a group, a family. It's the reason so many young guys join gangs. People need focus, they need purpose, a direction. That's what the theatre group provided. For a short time, we had focus. There was a goal and a purpose. The work was difficult, but creative, and the artistry helped round off the edges.

We're sixty percent water. Our cells are round bubbles floating about in water. Water is fluid, it's resilient, strong dynamic, and yet soft and malleable. You can't destroy it. You can boil it and freeze it but it always returns.

Our lives are like that. We can be strong and resilient, dynamic, and yet soft and malleable. We are aqueous. Our lives and the way we live them are mutable, reversible, transformable. Like water.

Art is also like water. There's a kind of fluidity in its creation as well as its appreciation. It enhances our experience as human beings in amazing ways. Our fluidity is our strength, because it is so complex and multi-layered, just like art.

I had told the prison authorities I wanted to do plays with inmates as ordinary theatre, not as an exercise in social services or to pursue deep intrapersonal evaluation. I wanted to do plays with them, like they might see at a local community theatre to demonstrate the performing arts could provide another way to think about life. They might work at a fast food diner or drive a delivery truck, but they could always find a way to have art in their lives. And just maybe, they could find a way to make a living doing art. The creative, artistic work I did in a Mexican prison certainly saved me.

I've thought many times about the performance of *Twelve Angry Men,* when the inmates came back on stage for the curtain call, and the audience was applauding madly. They'd stood there, embarrassed, most with tears in their eyes, not quite sure how to react. Then they began to feel really great about what they had accomplished. The embarrassment faded and they were proud.

That's what I wanted them to experience; the simple recognition of a job well done. Something we could talk about.

VERY SPECIAL THANKS TO:

Brian Whitney
K.E. Norek
B. George
J. W.
Martín
Susan Boscoff
and my wife Debra

ABOUT THE AUTHORS

RICHARD JEWKES IS an actor, writer, director and musician living in Costa Rica where he sings and plays in the local beach bars. As a writer, actor, director he has been involved in over a hundred theatrical productions and currently teaches creative content development at a private school in the jungle.

BRIAN WHITNEY HAS been the author and co-author of numerous books, including RAW DEAL: The Untold Story of NYPD's "Cannibal Cop" (WildBlue Press 2017) co-authored with Gil Valle. He also writes for many websites including Paste Magazine, Alternet and The Fix.

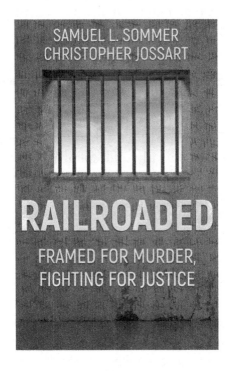
1.

Stolen in Suffolk

THREE MEN IN sharp suits briskly walked toward Sam Sommer's car. Sam looked down at the D on his automatic transmission console inside his Chevy station wagon, grabbed the door handle with his left hand, and poised his right hand atop the horn. His vehicle slowly coasted with one foot on the brake. He wasn't sure whether to squeal out, park and run, lay on the horn, or just keep coasting and jittering.

For someone who made a living making decisions that affected dozens of people each day, Sam couldn't decide what to do in a flash for his own good. His 150-pound furry backseat driver did a better job on demonstrating some damn decisiveness than he did. Sam figured the hell with indecision; it felt better to freeze and hope they would go away. He parked the car—stopping just inside a driveway from a well-travelled street. The unorthodox position of the vehicle appeared foreign to structured rows of parking stalls that filled the lot.

One of the men shouted, "Sommer!" This was all business whomever these good ole' boys were, and the unfolding encounter made Sam realize it included a one-sided agenda. One guy looked familiar from a recent civil, yet macho-style encounter he experienced with a member of Suffolk County law enforcement almost a week ago.

Sam quickly caught a glimpse of an unmarked car parked on the other side of the lot near Walter Court, which runs next to Long Island's busy Jericho Turnpike. The observation of the car parked away from everything else made Sam's already sweaty predicament even more of a salty horror.

He pulled into a Dunkin' Donuts parking lot adjacent to the freeway in Commack, New York, with his big St. Bernard dog. The 2073 Jericho Turnpike establishment opened in 1964 and was a favorite destination for a blossoming community. It was within blocks of Sam's house. The donut shop still stands today near the long-running Mayfair Shopping Center.

Sargent started barking wildly at the sight of oncoming strangers. Sam squinted out the window in an attempt to muster some last-second negotiation to slow the men's collective pace. The way the men marched spelled trouble.

"Who are you and what do you want?" Sam contended. Nothing but steps for an answer, now a few feet from his car.

The pleasant distraction of sweet dough aroma in the air moments earlier was now history. It was replaced with the stench of something dirty going down around 8:10 p.m. on Wednesday, May 22, 1968.

Sargent's momentous fit temporarily distracted the three intruders from their pursuit. The hiccup in an imminent showdown of three-against-one (plus canine) gave Sam an attempt to slide across the seat and exit the passenger side. It was too late for man and best friend. One of the three men had already swung around that side of the car to guard the passenger door.

The man who was shouting "Sommer" identified himself as Detective Thomas Gill with Suffolk County Homicide. The officer, a bit older than Sam, commanded him to join his men in going to the homicide division fourth precinct in nearby Smithtown.

The guy that Sam believed he met days earlier was another detective, Thomas Mansel, who piggybacked Gill's command. "You heard him, Sommer, let's go." Mansel was with the County's Homicide Squad as well.

Sam boldly said he wasn't going anywhere until he learned why.

"Let's go, Sommer," Gill said. He and another man opened the door before Sam could roll up the window and lock his vehicle. They clutched him by the shoulders.

Two men yanked Sam out of his idling station wagon head first in waning daylight at Dunkin' Donuts. Sam thought for a second that the orchestrated grab-and-go was a bad joke somehow tied to a call he received around dinner time to meet someone at the donut shop. He winced in pain from the deep grabs that latched into his sunburned skin. The men rolled Sam to his side on the concrete and cuffed him.

"What the fuck?" cried the thirty-one-year-old family man and business pro in feeble resistance to a kidnapping. Sam's five foot, eight inch frame fell prey to two taller kidnappers. "Stop!" A chorus line of pleas continued during the out-of-the-blue confrontation. While resisting he received a kick in the back of his knee from one of the detectives while being prone on his side for the wide open target. The men quickly dragged Sam across the parking lot toward the unmarked car.

"All right, all right," Sam yelped. Mansel and the other detective following Gill let go of Sam. They lifted him up and let him walk on his own toward their vehicle after a hard shove from Mansel. Sam resumed the journey to the police car voluntarily.

It was still bright enough to notice a man being dragged against his will. Some teenagers had been hanging out in the store for quite some time. Less than a minute before the men left their car from across the lot, Sam entered the Dunkin' Donuts property to meet another man for a meeting concerning one of his business associates, a family relative. The man had not yet arrived, but Sam arrived expecting to wait for him.

Sam slowed his pace toward the car and glanced at the men, expressing concern for Sargent. The dog was left alone in a running car with the driver's side door partially opened. A response came in the form of another shove forward.

Sam looked back again toward his station wagon without breaking his stride to catch a glimpse of Sargent. The car bounced like a modern-day pimp mobile from Sargent's display of protection toward his master.

Within feet from the unmarked vehicle, Sam switched his cadence from a defensive tone to one of cooperation. "What's this all about? Please, stop."

Gill opened the back seat door and the other men chucked Sam into the car. After avoiding a brush with his head against the far side door, Sam tried to roll on his back. He was instantly lifted up to a sitting position and buckled. While vehicles zoomed next to one of New York's busiest thoroughfares, a group of men allegedly sworn to serve and protect were stealing a man's freedom amidst the roaring engines.

The door closed to the back seat while Sam realized there were no inside handles. His capturers were in a hurry. The car instantly hit the turnpike and in no time it merged with traffic.

Sam was shaking too much to play eye games with Mansel and Gill, who were seated on each side of him. He just closed his eyes and prayed for the best—whatever that meant. The car quickly exited the turnpike and within a few blocks ended up parked in what seemed like a bumpy lot right next to a main road. That made Sam breathe a little better knowing he wasn't going somewhere far—a self-fulfilling means of fabricating hope.

The driver got out, and Sam asked Gill what this ordeal was about. Gill said he'd find out soon enough and told him to shut up. The driver came back and in less than five minutes the journey to purgatory resumed. No more freeway. Sam arrived in what appeared to be an alley by the narrowing of a street between two lit buildings. He then realized he was at the police station in Hauppauge, a suburb of Smithtown to the south.

It was dusk when the three men placed Sam to his feet in the parking lot of the back entrance to the Suffolk County Fourth Precinct. The whole thing about being around cops suddenly didn't feel right. Sam was supposed to find comfort at a police station; yet, he felt increasingly scared while the three men assertively escorted him toward the back entrance. Once inside, they led Sam down a long hallway to a room on the right.

The average-sized room, about twelve by twelve, was filled with some office equipment, a stool, a couple of chairs, and a square table. It resembled an interrogation room but with a more office-like feel to it. The men immediately shoved Sam against the table and then dropped his fumbling body onto a hard wooden stool and removed his cuffs. They seemed to be setting a tone of play along or it's gonna get physical. The three men convened with a fourth badge from the station outside the room while the door remained open. Sam mulled the connection of a few dots.

How in the world does one go from hooking up with someone in a parking lot to finding a home in a Suffolk County police station in the snap of a finger?

He tried to link learning about the sudden death of his business partner and relative, Irving Silver, to the current madness. Sam flew home last Wednesday, May 15, from Florida by himself while his family remained vacationing with both sets of in-laws. Sam had to deal with a dilemma Silver was having with Sommer's businesses, in particular a man named Harold Goberman.

Goberman was the one who called Sam around dinner time to meet at Dunkin' Donuts regarding Silver's death. Sam recently hired Goberman, who went with an alias of a Harold

Masterson, to do some work at his deli in Commack, the Deli-Queen. His hiring was the result of a recommendation from Silver to help Goberman get reacclimated into society. He retained a vast criminal record and was out of prison on parole. Sam wanted to give the man another chance at life.

Detective Mansel rather forcefully asked Sam to help Suffolk County police identify Silver's body on the afternoon of Friday, May 17. Silver was apparently killed during the early morning on the same day. His body was found on Wheatley Road, a rather unfrequented rural artery off the Jericho Turnpike southeast of Commack.

"You're going to confess, Sommer, right now," instructed Gill in the interrogation room. No identification given of the other men. No reading of any rights concerning a kidnapping called an arrest. The door slammed from the hallway and the same two men who nabbed him plus another stood behind Gill in the crowded room.

"About what?" Sam inquired, still cuffed.

The new man on the scene from the precinct grabbed Sam under his arms and lifted him off of the stool. Gill then pushed Sam head first into the wall and proceeded to shove him onto the floor. Still cuffed, Sam was then harshly seated and punched across the left eye by another officer. His sunburned skin absorbed the beating with needlelike pain.

Another greeting with the concrete floor. Picked up again and placed on the stool, Gill got in Sam's face.

"Want a lawyer, Sommer, or you gonna fess up?"

"For what?" Sam shouted.

"Killing your business buddy," Mansel shouted. "We know you wacked him with a lead pipe and then ran him over. Son of a bitch."

Stunned by what he heard, Sam offered a left-to-right head nod that suggested a nonverbal "No" in reply to the men's accusations. Bewildered with the name Harold Goberman taking over his mind as the centerpiece part of a jigsaw puzzle, Sam started to describe his phone call to Gill tied to a meeting at Dunkin' Donuts.

"A Harold Goberman is behind this" … stars—a galaxy of pain. A thump on the head by an undetected detective from behind with a telephone book while Sam was held down on the stool blurred his vision. Another whack on the neck from the phone directory ensued in what seemed to be a one-sided conversation. The Goberman mention obviously set off the detectives.

More pounds from the phone book behind Sam's head continued until his ability to sit upright in the stool gave way to the hard floor. Sam laid with his hands over his head and shook enough to trip a Richter scale. His fear couldn't muster any words.

The persuasive techniques used in the basement of Suffolk County's Homicide Unit didn't stop. The men of the badge kicked and yelled at Sam while he curled up on the floor. Realizing there was no other choice but to possibly die, Sam begged to tell the officers about the Goberman phone call. They would have nothing to do with the Goberman thing.

The four men huddled together as if it was fourth-and-goal on the one-yard line and Sam was on defense all by himself. Too pissed off to think about a lawyer, Sam wanted to fight the assholes head on. It was evident there was no more hope for textbook interrogation procedures; it was now all about survival—in a damn police station.

Further beating might have killed Sam. Why didn't they just kill him? That question is still debated today by people who know and love him. God's grace allowed for his story to be told for the benefit of others in the name of justice, Sam offered in retrospect.

"Think about what comes out of your mouth before we come back, Sommer," asserted Gill. The men then left the smoke-filled whipping chamber to the hallway with the door still open. In a cloud of chaos sat a man who a couple of hours earlier left home to learn something to aid in the case of a loved one.

The origination of Sam Sommer's fateful trip to Dunkin' Donuts came with risks and uncertainties in dealing with Goberman. The disgruntled Goberman set Sam up, or so it appeared.

To this day, dear friends Phil and Susan Cirrone from Long Island remember that day more than fifty years later. Philly, as Sam coined the nickname of his close friend, detailed the circumstances leading up to the kidnapping and subsequent aftermath.

A personal recount of horror:

I got a call around 8:00 from Elaine Sommer to come over earlier than planned the evening of the twenty-second of May. We were going to leave shortly anyway to see Elaine's parents visiting from Florida, but Elaine said it was important. We heard earlier in the week that a family member died unexpectedly.

Susan and I are the type of friends to Sammy and Elaine that wouldn't question them in a time of need. We got a babysitter in light of the urgent development and headed to their house.

Upon arrival, Elaine greeted us by the front door. We could tell something was up. She told us that Sam didn't return yet from a meeting at Dunkin' Donuts near the freeway. Elaine didn't have time to go into detail. All she said was that Sam had been involved in trying to find out what happened to her uncle, Irving Silver. She was beside herself; Susan and I were barely inside the door.

Sam was going to meet some guy who had information about Silver at a donut shop. She said Sam drove the station wagon to Dunkin' Donuts with their dog and that something felt wrong.

We didn't know Irving Silver, but Elaine quickly filled us in about his connection to her family and that he was dead. Regardless, friends are friends, and there was no need to pry at the moment about what happened to him. Shocked and saddened by the news, we kept listening. Her parents hugged us and just remained silent the whole time.

Elaine asked me to kindly take her to check on Sammy at Dunkin' Donuts. Of course Susan and I agreed, but first I told Elaine to call the store. She did so and learned Sam wasn't inside the establishment. We then left, determined to find out where he was. Her parents remained at the house for the kids.

The three of us arrived at a nearby Dunkin' Donuts off the turnpike and immediately saw the Sommer's vehicle barely inside the lot from the road. We cautiously circled the car to get a pulse on the situation and noticed their dog going berserk in the back seat.

Creepy shit, yet we remained calm for a horrified Elaine. The lot was well lit and a couple of cars were parked near the store's entrance. Elaine jumped out of our car and yelled to us that Sam's vehicle was still running. We could see, too, that the driver's side door wasn't closed all the way either.

Unquestionably, this was a spine-chilling scene. The dog increased its barking likely from recognizing Elaine. Susan and I both hesitated to go near the car. We advised Elaine *not to touch anything and told her that we were going inside the donut shop to see if anyone knew anything. Susan and I sped to the entrance of the donut shop and ran inside for answers.*

Inside the store we couldn't find Sammy, but we found the sight of curiosity all over the joint from the way a couple of workers and a group of kids looked at us. They all appeared dazed.

I was working as a corrections officer at the time and learned a few things when it came to reading people. Susan kept an eye on Elaine while I asked the manager what was going on. Sweat drenched my shirt. Where in the hell was Sammy?

A few teenagers congregated around the counter in front of the manager. He said the person in the car who parked weirdly in his lot was taken by some guys. One of the teens chimed in and said the man he thinks we were talking about was dragged out of his car and taken away (pointing in the direction of the turnpike). Another teen described the dog in the back seat running around so wildly that the car bounced.

Susan and I grabbed hold of one another. "What?" we collectively bellowed. "Like kidnapped?" I piggybacked the disbelief with a question to continue the inquisition. We froze with jaws on the floor. The first kid said they were like gangsters and asked if we knew the guy who was taken.

The store manager indicated that the men, unable to recall how many for sure—a few he proclaimed, looked like a bunch of wise guys. Another teen said that they looked like bad asses and one of them carried a gun. The same youngster believed there were three men working together against one victim.

I asked the manager if he called the cops. He said no. I got the impression he wanted to look the other way, so to speak.

The kids were kind enough to wish us well and they split, too, likely not wanting to stick around much longer. The described mobster-type men had everyone on edge.

On the verge of calling the police, I noticed a cop car pull into the lot. It felt comforting, yet odd. If no one called the police how would they know what was going on? Maybe someone else around the neighborhood or store called, I thought. Anyway, Susan went outside toward Elaine, who quickly grabbed the officer's attention for obvious reasons. I made a quick call to a lawyer friend of mine to explain what was going down and then joined the commotion outside.

The front driver's side door was part way open. A slimy mist, like dew, covered most of the windows, probably from the dog's cries. It didn't look like Sammy was around. All eyes fixated on the cop for answers. Car running. Dog freaking out. No Sammy. The officer then did a quick search of the car.

Elaine then left with the officer to go across the way a short distance to the Mayfair Shopping Center to use a phone. We just stood by the car trying to comfort the dog without being able to touch anything. The biggest thing we couldn't touch was reality. We were scared and more so for Sammy.

The officer said that he and Elaine would be back in a matter of minutes. Their poor dog's barks grew hoarser. I told Susan that I called Joe Scibilia, and that he might be able to help Sammy from a legal standpoint, if needed.

Like the officer promised, he returned with Elaine. She looked as mad as she did worried a few moments ago. I asked what was going on. The officer informed us that he called the station to see if there was anything on Mr. Sommer. I could tell Elaine was pissed. She then insisted that her husband was kidnapped. Just hearing that word sent shivers through my body.

The officer said that she would need to fill out a Missing Persons Report at the police station in Hauppauge. He told Elaine that she could take the car home (for perceived concern about the dog). The cop's intention appeared heartfelt toward the dog; yet, I found it strange that he would release the car back to its owner so quickly. Theoretically, this location and the vehicle itself could still be considered a potential crime scene, I thought.

Here's what else seemed screwed up. The officer didn't write anything down up until this point. From my years in corrections, documentation means everything. Writing something down gave an impression of importance and focus. How do you dismiss a running car with the driver's side door left open and a dog going nuts in the back seat as anything not related to foul play?

Nonchalantly like another day at the office, the officer reminded us of the Missing Persons Report and departed the scene. His calmness drove me nuts. No urgency. It was going to be a long night.

Susan skillfully excelled in the field of empathy. She was a gentle offset to my dealing with hard asses all the time. I thanked her for comforting Elaine. I trusted her more than myself to handle Elaine the best way possible given the circumstance. I was too upset at this farce of an investigation.

We both agreed to bring the vehicle and dog back to Sam's home. It might buffer the heart-stopping news a bit for Elaine about her husband, and frankly, the dog was pretty messed up. Susan and I followed Elaine back to her house where she parked the car and took the dog inside. A neighbor was watching the Sommer kids, and the three of us proceeded to the fourth precinct.

Susan guided a tear-drenched Elaine into the back seat of our car, and in a flash we took off to get this report done.

Maybe then we could start to get somewhere concerning Sammy. There we went... into the waning abyss of hell known as May 22, 1968.

***

Gill and his men quickly returned to Sam's abuse chamber from just outside the room at the Suffolk County Fourth Precinct Homicide Division. A day etched in lawlessness against a hardworking young man, husband, and father of seven came close to an end—at least based on the time of day. Sam didn't know if these sworn men of honor were just getting warmed up for an all-nighter or maybe an amateur form of execution.

Sitting with his head resting on a small table, Sam fielded a command from Gill to get up and pay attention. He gingerly rose and hunched over in a state of pain and stood as attentive as possible. A slap to the back of Sam's head and neck with a phone book now serving as a weapon staggered him from wall-to-wall in another round of late night captivity. He felt like dying. Gill felt impatient, like he didn't want to be there and would rather have the whole thing over with.

Lowered back in the chair, Sam's head tilted toward God in prayer of something to happen—heaven or home. Surrounded by folded arms and smoky drags around the table, Gill leaned into his helpless prey. "Fess up, Sommer."

The verbal onslaughts that previously followed with a physical bashing took a different turn this time. Two men behind Sam rather gently lifted him upright. What should have felt comforting seemed creepy to Sam. After he was lifted, the stool beneath him was removed and the detectives laid him on the ground. The men ripped his t-shirt and removed his clothes. Sam curled into a ball on a cold floor, stark naked.

"Gonna speak now, Sommer," one of the detectives asked pompously in a new twist of torture. The room succumbed to silence. Suffolk County's interrogation techniques were building in stunning infamy. "Come on, Sommer," insisted Gill or Mansel based on Sam's aged recollection. "Fess up."

"Florida," Sam uttered from his shell. No response. No punches. No accusations. He prayed for even a belch in the room. The stillness defined a level of fear that Sam never fathomed. He believed the next phase in this scheme was death. He knew that protecting himself was even more of a fairy tale since he wasn't wearing any clothes.

Sam lifted his head a smidgeon to see that the men walked away from the table. In the first act of a humane tone since getting seized from a donut shop parking lot, Gill calmly inquired, "Tell us more, Sommer, about Florida. What the hell does that mean?"

Sam as a suspect suddenly had a voice in this assumed interrogation proceeding going down in the final hours of May 22. The interrogators welcomed his voice for the first time outside the realm of being toyed with to make a false confession. "Took my family to Florida… came back early to help Silver deal with a matter about the business," murmured a drained Sam.

"You told me last week you were going to meet Silver, and that was around the time he was wacked," Mansel reminded Sam.

"We were working together on some bad shit with Goberman—you need to talk to Harold Goberman," uttered the helpless suspect.

No reply. Sam heard some shuffling of feet and a whisper or two. He could sense growing frustration in the room among the badges. He predicted that these guys weren't going to leave him alone until they got what they sought—a confession to the murder of Irving Silver. His prediction materialized. In so many testy words, Gill told him that he needed to give them what they wanted so they could wrap up the investigation.

At one point the detectives moved Sam into a basement room for a few minutes. His state of confusion disallowed him to really make heads or tails of what was going on. Since Sam was so weak, he kind of went with the flow during this peculiar little tour of the precinct's lower level. The detectives didn't say much—it seemed like they were hiding him. Within moments, they returned Sam upstairs to his original interrogation room.

The smell of judicial corruption took over. Whoever was orchestrating the targeting of Sam Sommer was friends with the devil. 'What the...?' Sam internalized while wincing in pain moving his exposed body to the floor. 'This is serious shit. First, a dead relative. Then a phone call from a guy we were trying to help get his life together, followed by getting nabbed from my own damn car to having the shit kicked out of me and stripped. Why ask me about Florida and then disregard it?'

***

Phil Cirrone and the two ladies arrived at the same Suffolk County precinct near Smithtown where Sam was getting tortured. Unaware of that coincidence upon arrival, Philly tried to work over the officers by way of influence as a member of the New York City Department of Corrections. He started to flex his relational muscle for the Sommers to get some real answers.

Bingo, but not on Philly's card. No more than a couple of minutes after the three entered the station, Susan recognized a friend of her brother, an FBI special agent. He was there conducting some business related to a case on Long Island.

"Remember me?" asked Susan. "I'm Marvin's sister."

"Yes," replied the agent. "You're"…

"Susan, Susan Cirrone."

She briefly small talked about her brother after shaking hands with the agent. She then reintroduced her husband, recalling their paths crossed before through her brother. Phil was consumed in watching over Elaine so Susan could converse with her brother's friend. Elaine wanted to speak to someone in charge, ASAP.

"What brings you here? Is everything OK?" the agent asked Susan.

Phil introduced Elaine to the agent, and she explained the situation to him with reference to Sam's name. Expecting support related to the process of reporting a missing person, the three instead hear an Orson Wells-caliber revelation.

"I think he's down the hall, locked up."

Paled and going through her own version of abuse from yet another bomb dropped, Elaine darted toward a long hallway, the direction in which the agent glanced when he made the claim. Phil grabbed Elaine's arm and slowed her enough to allow Susan to thank the agent and apologize for the trouble. The three citizen investigators of Sam heard the word "locked," and an aura of injustice dismissed the conversation.

The agent embarrassingly gathered that he shouldn't have disclosed Sam's whereabouts. He added out of desperation to deflect the situation elsewhere, "They've moved him to another precinct. It's common to rotate someone… uh." The agent stopped talking and left abruptly.

Whether he was lying or inferred "elsewhere" as being a hospital remains unsettled today. The agent could not later testify to such a claim for obvious reasons of conflict of interest. Incidentally, Sam was moved from his first-floor interrogation room to a similar room in the basement at some point between 10:00 and 11:00 that night. He believes to this day the move was made out of fear by the police that three people were there looking for him.

http://wbp.bz/railroadeda

AVAILABLE FROM LARRY SELLS, MARGIE PORTER AND WILDBLUE PRESS

She Was The Darling Of The Indy 500 Teams...
Until She Was Murdered

RACE TO JUSTICE

LARRY SELLS
MARGIE PORTER

RACE TO JUSTICE by LARRY SELLS
AND MARGIE PORTER

http://wbp.bz/rtja

Chapter 1

NOVEMBER 15, 1992

THE MEAT LOCKER bite of November winds chafed the flesh of the three rabbit hunters. Dreary skies cast a haunting fog through stark branches. The hunters were having no luck. An army of bunnies could nest beneath the slender trees, camouflaged amongst millions of windswept leaves.

DeMotte, Indiana police officer Kevin Jones, and his two neighbors, Bill Whitis and Terry Ward, kept a keen eye on the landscape that Sunday afternoon. Where there were rabbits, coyotes and wolves also roamed close by.

The rural wooded area, owned by a local woman named Mrs. McFarland, lay a mile from the interstate, one quarter mile west of County Line Road, and along a dirt path. The place was good for hunting but also frequented by daredevils on all-terrain vehicles. It was an illegal dumpsite too, as evidenced by aging appliances and outcast furniture.

Jones, Whitis, and Ward wended their way through naked tree limbs, marking the air with ghostly breaths. Then Jones spied what appeared to be a discarded mannequin about twenty yards away. The men stepped closer. Maybe not a mannequin? It looked so real. Maybe someone drugged or drunk? Possibly. There was a nudist colony a mere mile down the road.

The ivory limbs peeking through the leaves were no passed out nudist. This was a young woman, clearly dead. None of the men recognized her. There had been no recent reports in the area of a missing woman.

The body was that of a nude, slender white female. She appeared young, twenties or early thirties. Her pale skin wore a crust of fallen leaves and slivers of snow. One arm lay to her side, the other flopped across her abdomen.

Animals had come to sample the corpse, leaving nibble marks in the flesh on both feet, her upper right chest, and her left upper arm. Tan lines showed she had worn both a bikini and a one-piece swimsuit. Knobby knees projected from her slim legs. Her left ankle was adorned with two delicate gold chains: one plain, the other with three joined hearts.

Sexual assault was not likely, as evidenced by a tampon string dangling from her vagina.

Cold weather had slowed decomposition of the corpse. It would be difficult to identify the young woman. Her head and neck had been severed near the collarbone by some sort of serrated blade. It was not with the body.

As a police officer, Jones understood the need to preserve the crime scene. No one in his group touched the body or removed anything lying on or near it.

Officer Jones called for his friend Mr. Whitis "to run to my house and to notify the state police and to tell them what I had there and also there is an officer at the scene." He said, "It was probably a good hundred yards across the field to my house."

The call went out just after three p.m., but afternoon shadows had already begun to wisp through the lonely woods when Indiana state police investigators arrived. They lined up their vehicles along the dirt path and hiked about eighty feet through the woods to the crime scene.

An immediate search of the area turned up neither the victim's head nor a murder weapon. Soil samples were taken, but by five p.m., winter darkness blanketed any attempts to search further. A more thorough investigation would have to wait until the following day. Investigators hoped to identify the woman through the shriveled remnants of her fingerprints.

The leaves covering the body were collected, and then she was wrapped in a sheet and placed inside a body bag. Newton County Coroner Gerald A. Burman took the body to the Tippecanoe County Morgue in West Lafayette for autopsy.

The only potential evidence found was a piece of Styrofoam lying in the dirt beneath the corpse. A red rag hugged the ground fifty feet southeast of the site, and a piece of cloth lay seventy-five feet east. Investigators marked off the area with crime scene tape as darkness smothered the lonely saplings.

Investigators converged on the area the next morning to reexamine the slip of ground where the body had lain and to scour the surrounding area for clues. Indiana State Police Detective Sergeant William F. Krueger met with Detective Sergeant Richard Ludlow. Technicians called to the scene included Sergeant Rick Griswell, Sergeant Dave Kintzele, Gary Ekart, and Ken Buehrle.

The officers examined the area in a four hundred foot radius from the body's dumpsite. They combed an adjacent area containing items of trash for the missing head. The team also searched the sides of the field road and Jasper/Newton County Line Road. They found nothing but a silver and black PPG jacket in a ditch on the west side of County Line Road, about two hundred-fifty feet south of the dirt lane. The jacket did not appear to be evidence, but they collected it.

The young woman was no longer abandoned to the weather and the rats. Was she just another druggie, homeless and friendless? Surely she was someone's daughter, girlfriend, cousin, friend. The missing head could keep her nameless for years.

She would be easier to identify if anyone was actually looking for her.

Chapter 2

THE SHOCK OF the drive-by broke the peace of a perfect spring evening in Speedway, Indiana. The softball players stood on the field, open and defenseless. After a grueling and intense day at the Indianapolis Motor Speedway, members of the Marlboro-Penske team had escaped to a local park and challenged some other teams to a pickup game. Eager to unwind, drivers and mechanics were soon involved in the game, whooping and cheering the daring moves of team members and competitors alike.

A rented white cargo van swooped into the tidy small town park. The victims knew their attackers. The aggressors were three women who had tantalized them with a hot meal just hours before. Cynthia Albrecht, the thirty-one-year-old executive chef for Penske's Race Team, grinned with anticipation. Pretty and vivacious with blonde curls that bounced to her shoulders, Cindy exuded energy.

Cindy was joined by her best friends and partners in crime, Sandra Fink and Rebecca Miller. Cindy was the Penske Team's heartbeat, the personification of an enduring folk song. Sandi Fink, blonde and svelte, was their Barbie doll. Playful and stylish, she moved like soft rock. Jazzy little Becky Miller, the bright-eyed brunette, was quick and impromptu, always eager to swing into the next adventure.

As cooks for Penske, the three were acquainted with all the drivers, but they aimed their van toward Penske drivers Rick Mears and Emerson Fittipladi. Their crew chiefs Richard Buck and Rick Rinaman were also targeted. The assault came as a shock and everyone on the field began ducking and running — and laughing, as the three women pelted them with grapes, orange slices, kiwi, and strawberries.

"They loved it," Becky remembers. "We cleaned out the fruit basket that we stocked every day." Before any player could react, much less throw anything back, the three women sped away, cheering themselves for a successful drive-by fruiting.

"Did you see their faces?"

"We totally shocked them."

"Bet they can't make those moves in a race car."

Cindy, Sandi, and Becky were all married women whispering into their thirties but "acted like teenagers," Sandi says. "We were silly and goofy and bought each other underwear… it was a great time." And they danced with the thrill of being a part of IndyCar racing.

The race circuit was pure adrenaline. It had everything three young women could want: fast cars, excitement, travel. But most of all, the respect of their peers. Among Penske's IndyCar tribe, there was no pecking order. The hospitality team was held in no less esteem than drivers were. "We were family, all of us," Sandi says.

In the IndyCar community, team lines were fluid. If the women needed some tall guys with muscle to upright a tent, they only needed to ask. If Mary-Lin Murphy of Newman/Haas needed to borrow an ingredient, someone would gladly lend it.

Guests to the Penske hospitality tent included the cast of *90210* and George Harrison of Beatles fame. George made his way to the kitchen with his beautiful wife Olivia. Coffee was the hot beverage beneath the tent that day and the charming couple approached the cooks to ask for a cup of tea. Other VIPs included Donald Trump, General Norman Schwarzkopf, and Colonel Oliver North.

Food from the hospitality tent fueled much of the event, as no one had time to exit the track for a meal. No one wanted to leave anyway. The hospitality food could top the fare offered at any restaurant and it was plentiful enough to keep a hungry man hustling—no bologna sandwiches or limp noodle soup for these guys!

The parade of hot meals included Lobster Newburg, grilled blackened salmon with dill sauce, and southwest chicken with Mexican rice. Breakfast could include lox, caviar, omelets, and heart-shaped waffles with fresh fruit.

The Food Network channel had not yet been launched. If it had, Cindy could have starred on the channel as a gourmet chef. Her specialty was leg of lamb with fresh rosemary and mint. She had the talent to create her own sauces and dressings. The stylish Brazilian driver Emerson Fittipaldi liked to eat turkey on whole wheat with olive oil and red onion just before qualifying or racing. Cindy always made it just for him.

The three Penske hostesses were all married to IndyCar mechanics and met each other through their husbands. They traveled to all the races and made friends all over the country, but none of the events could top their hometown race, the Indianapolis 500, which is still the single biggest one-day sporting event in the world.

In 1992, Penske ran a three-car team, about fifty crewmembers. Another two hundred-fifty people, including sponsors, media, and special guests, were served at each meal. The hospitality tent buzzed like a school cafeteria. The service had to be fast, almost choreographed. Guests applauded the food as fabulous. Even on a budget, Cindy could dream up artistic meals which satisfied everyone from executives to famished mechanics.

The entire team embraced the Penske Way. In everything they did, their performance was to be exemplary. They were to be professional at all times. Presentation of the food first class. Most importantly, they were never, ever to run out of food.

Meals were cooked in a fourteen-foot trailer, its appliances and counters wedged in place with mathematical precision. Efficiency demanded the trailer carry all the cookware and service utensils needed to feed a variety of food to hundreds of people.

Penske hospitality was a team of five persons, the three hostesses and two men, working under the direction of Pete Twiddy. A born leader, Pete was the Marlboro side of Marlboro-Penske. In his trademark jeans and flip-flops, he was a bright-eyed and fluid guy on the beach, unhindered by his 6'8" height.

Canadian Glen Smith, tall and rugged, was Pete's right-hand man. He was humorous and ended his sentences with "eh." He was very protective of the women.

Smith and Bob Lawes, a British Adonis in short shorts, shared duties of transportation, setting up, and overseeing hospitality. Pete represented Marlboro while Lawes made sure the interests of the Penske family were respected. Working in sync, the five set up the awning, tables, chairs, and the buffet. "If we were on grass instead of concrete, we might lay down artificial grass to keep mud from guests' shoes," Lawes recalls.

All through the race they cooked, cleaned, and served and delivered food. Then they tore it all down and moved on to the next city on the race circuit. "Sometimes," Lawes recalls, "we'd be cleaning up a Sunday race and hurrying to get to the next race."

Each cook had assigned duties and a designated work area. Cindy created main courses, Sandi usually prepared desserts, while Becky was a sous chef, meaning she chopped tons of vegetables and juggled a myriad of other tasks.

From their trailer, the cooks could not see the race but they were very much a part of the excitement. The energy vibrated all over the Indianapolis Motor Speedway, and it was contagious.

Roger's rule was no alcohol would be served before the checkered flag, but once the race ended, Pete would say, "Make cocktails, girls. Make cocktails." They were also to keep champagne chilled and ready to pour in case a Penske driver won the race.

Becky says, "It was like Christmas every day, but very tiring." Although the race season only runs from April to October, the hospitality people who worked all the races were considered full time because the long hours over those frantic months equaled the hours a normal worker would log during a calendar year.

Bob Lawes says the schedule was nonstop. Sometimes they set out snacks for after the race and started tearing down to be off to the next race site by Tuesday. He recalls one weary morning when they were traveling to the track at five-thirty a.m.; Cindy was riding shotgun, singing cheerily with the radio. Bob, sitting in the back seat, asked who the song artist was. She told him and he said, "Well, why don't you let them sing it?"

Cindy turned, fuming, and smacked at him playfully. Bob says he can remember nothing but good times with Cindy, even though they were chronically exhausted and frequently under pressure.

Of course, they weren't the only team members racing the clock. Sometimes, Becky says, some driver or crewmember, due to car issues or other problems, would have no time to eat. They'd stand across the fence in Gasoline Alley and yell out, "Throw me a banana!" The women responded, flinging the fruit to their starving comrade or passing over a sandwich. The food was delivered with good wishes and the promise of more substantial fare later.

The trailer had no storage space and the women launched into the weekend running a grocery shopping marathon. "We'd trailer carts through the store," Sandi recalls, "and the bill would be, like, two thousand dollars."

Sandi's well-honed organizational skills enabled her to memorize the layout of all the grocery stores they used, from Pennsylvania to California. Cindy would hand the grocery list over to Sandi and have her organize it in the order of the aisles to save time.

Grocery shopping became an adventure in itself. First of all, the hospitality team was given thousands of dollars in cash to buy food at the beginning of the season. Becky says, "In May, that could be thirty thousand dollars, so we'd hide it in our pants, carry it inside our jackets, just stuff it all over the place, and act all innocent."

Cindy prowled the perishable departments, seeking ideas for tantalizing meals. She selected spices to blend into her own salad dressings. She bought packages of edible flowers and exotic vegetables that looked like they were fighting their way through puberty. Sandi describes Thumbelina baby carrots as "squirrelly-looking, stubby carrots with long strings on them." Cindy was horrified when Becky, while cleaning this alien produce, cut the strings off, but the women claim no one ever ate those carrots anyway.

Becky recalls that Cindy would eat anything, or at least try it. That would have been fine, except Cindy insisted her friends also try calamari, and cheese that smelled like an outhouse, and unpronounceable foods probably designed as torture by the CIA. Becky laughs, remembering, "If I wouldn't try something, she'd shove it in my mouth or just smear it on my face."

The cucumber game was Cindy's invention. When they shopped, she awarded the vegetable to whoever guessed closest to the register total. Becky claims Sandi always won, and usually guessed within ten dollars. "And she'd never guess an ordinary round number. She'd come up with some weird figure, like, $2,071.42, and she'd be maybe just a few dollars off."

The money was never really a game to Cindy. She kept careful watch over Penske's money. It was a matter of honor to her that the receipts and money matched to the penny. Between shopping trips, all the cash, including the loose change, stayed in a separate compartment in her travel bag.

On the way through the store, Sandi and Becky made a game of slipping items into Cindy's cart: adult diapers, feminine hygiene, dog treats, nasal spray… just any unexpected item that might startle her at the register. Now the women claim that when they're shopping, an odd item will simply fall off the shelf in front of them. They say it happens a lot. "And we'll be like, hi, Cindy!"

Whether shopping, working, or just being together, the trio had spontaneous fun. But not everyone was laughing with them.

Chapter 3

SANDI FINK'S LIFE revolved around racing. She worked with several IndyCar teams as a timer/scorer using the new Data Speed computer technology, one of the only positions open to women in racing. Then, in 1991, her job became obsolete. She says, "Basically, the timing and scoring technology overtook it. They started doing the timing with devices inside the car."

Cindy and Sandi's husbands, Michael Albrecht and Mike Fink, were IndyCar mechanics. Sandi and Mike were an easygoing couple, comfortable socializing together. The Albrechts seemed less in tandem.

If Cindy was sunshine, Michael was thunder. Dark and brooding, he stood ten inches taller than his wife and tried to keep her in his shadow. He had a reputation as a bully. Co-workers dubbed him "Crabby." Mike Fink was also big and powerfully built, but sociable with a quick smile.

Both worked for Dick Simon Racing. Cindy loved racing as much as Sandi did and the women quickly became fast friends, each couple dining at the other's home on occasion. Both were dazzling cooks.

Cindy's cooking skills had earned her a place in IndyCar hospitality, which was becoming the latest cutting edge for teams to showcase hot race cars and even hotter drivers. This was a rare opportunity. Women had only recently been allowed into Gasoline Alley at the Indianapolis Motor Speedway.

Cindy and Sandi were as good a team as Ben & Jerry. Cindy had mastered entrees and spices; Sandi was queen of pastries and desserts. The popularity of the Marlboro-Penske hospitality increased exponentially. Soon, a third person was needed.

When Sandi's good friend Becky Miller came on board, the bond was instant and unbreakable. All three had great culinary skills. They could have been sisters. Becky's husband Kirk also worked for Dick Simon Racing. Dark haired and tan, Kirk lived in work boots but moved as if he wore roller blades.

Sandi and Becky say Cindy was sort of a tomboy when they met her. She had a great personality, but she wore shapeless clothing and her hair looked like it had fallen asleep. They gathered Cindy under their wings. They took her to get her prematurely gray hair highlighted. They encouraged her to wear makeup and they bought her cute clothes to wear instead of her habitual men's t-shirts and jeans.

Along with these confidence builders, Cindy lost weight, about twenty-five pounds. Her newfound attractiveness bothered her husband, but Becky and Sandi cheered Cindy for leaving her shell.

The trio loved buying each other gag gifts, but honed in on Cindy's granny panties. They could not believe she would wear such non-fashionable undergarments and they introduced her to Victoria's Secret. They bought her beautiful lingerie. Becky and Sandi, happy in their own marriages, did not realize Cindy did not wish to entice her husband. They found out later that she saved the lingerie and wore it for Pete Twiddy, who was handsome, enthusiastic, highly motivated, and successful. He also made Cindy feel pretty.

Among the race circuit, Cindy's nickname became Ellie Mae. With her blonde curls flashing in the sunlight, she reminded people of the Clampett daughter from *The Beverly Hillbillies*. She was also like the Ellie Mae actress, Donna Douglas, in the way she greeted everyone with a dazzling smile. And she loved animals, all animals. She contributed money to wildlife groups.

Don't be late was Roger Penske's primary rule for all employees and Cindy would never risk tardiness unless she had a dire emergency, like she needed to stop and help an injured squirrel. Becky tried to point out that they had hundreds of squirrels but just one job—and a great one at that. Cindy might have listened to Becky if she'd had fur, a tail, and twitching ears.

But Cindy's greatest passion was for people. A couple of scruffy, motorcycle gang types the women referred to as Hutch and Wayne came around at the Toronto race. "They looked like ZZ Topp," Sandi says. In 1991, the women were working and heard a scuffle outside their kitchen window. Hutch and Wayne were hurt and Cindy immediately invited them to come inside the trailer.

Alarmed, Sandi pleaded, "Don't let them in here!"

But Cindy was already bringing out bandages and saying, "You're a human being. You are bleeding. Come here. Here's some water. Let me tape you up."

It turned out the scuffle was a takedown and Hutch and Wayne were undercover cops. "Deep, deep undercover," Sandi says. "No one would have ever known." Because of Cindy's compassion, Hutch and Wayne took all three women out for a meal that night and they all became great friends. Becky and Sandi are still in cahoots with their favorite constables. Hutch and Wayne are now both retired from the Toronto Police Department but still keep in touch.

Marlboro sponsorship had its benefits. "Back in the day, we were allowed to give away cigarettes," Sandi recalls. Cigarettes were on all the tables. The team had cases and cases of free product and could give them away by the carton. The free cigarettes lured a twenty-eight-year-old woman named Susie Harmon.

Tiny, dark haired Susie was sometimes stoned but was a decent girl with many problems. Her boyfriend Lee Kunzman was an older racer. She stayed with him and he looked after her. They all felt sorry for her, but Becky and Sandi cringed when she came around, fearing her presence would dull the shine on the Penske reputation.

"But Cindy was always so nice to her and she'd always give her cigarettes and a plate of food," Sandi says. The pair tried to warn Cindy it wasn't good for the team's image to have Susie seen around their hospitality area, but Cindy always defended her, saying, "Oh, she's a nice girl. She won't stay long after she gets her cigarettes." And she was right!

The Reverend Phil DeRea, a mirthful, barrel-chested, Washington, DC Catholic priest, served as chaplain to the IndyCar circuit. Each Sunday before Mass, Cindy greeted him with a big smile as she served him breakfast. "Say a prayer for me, Father," she would say. "You know I can't be there."

The women worked long hours, often from predawn until after a late cocktail hour. Their work was not completed until every person was served and everything was cleaned up. They also had to prep for the next day and go over the menu to make sure they had everything. Many nights on their way to the hotel, they stopped to pick up more groceries.

Sometimes Cindy would get an after-hours call at home. More people were coming. Add meals. A CEO required a specialty dish. The women had to be flexible to allow for these sudden changes.

The workload could be daunting, but Cindy, Sandi, and Becky were having the time of their lives. Working together in the food trailer, the trio developed a dance routine to Aretha Franklin's song, "Respect." They gyrated in unison, shouting out, "R-E-S-P-E-C-T!" and high-fived each other. Cindy belted out the song in a voice Sandi says sounded like Karen Carpenter's. It seemed like the more fun they had, the more people wanted to join the crowd at their tent.

One day they were practicing the routine, swishing around each other with oven mitts on their hands. Penske team coordinator Tim Lombardi caught them in the act. Laughter shook him to his toes.

Pete Twiddy often insisted they perform another routine for everyone. They had adapted an old classic, "King of the Road," to poke fun at a media writer who complained they lacked chopped onions for his hot dog. "Hot dogs for sale or rent!" they'd sing. "Buns are just fifty cents. No onions, no pickles today. Go to the concession stand if you want it that way!" The song continued, earning the trio a reputation for sass.

Garth Brooks, who was a rising country singer at the time, recorded Cindy's favorite music. Brooks first gained national recognition at Fan Fair in 1989 as a new artist for Capitol Records. Two years later, in 1991, he was named the Country Music Association's Entertainer of the Year. Cindy adored Brooks' music, but not for its popularity. The young singer performed with an authentic, navel-deep emotion that embraced her. His intensity and air of confidence matched Cindy's.

Brooks sang about rodeo riding, the transforming power of love, and the need for people to cherish each other. Cindy's favorite Brooks' song was "The Dance," a wistful ballad about death and loss and knowing there was nothing that could replace the time you had together with the one you lost.

Cindy attended Brooks' "Shameless" tour and prized the white t-shirt she bought with his face and cowboy hat. "Shameless" was Brooks' hit about loving without reservation and Cindy used to say, "I'd pay five hundred dollars to hear him sing that song." Cindy was so tiny the t-shirt fit her as a sleep shirt.

Brooks' singing career mirrored the blossoming of Cindy's own life. Like him, Cindy found her culinary career surging ahead due to her hard work, persistence, and ability to touch those around her in a meaningful way. For Cindy, hospitality went far beyond food on a plate; it was her best way to connect with people.

"She was one of those people who could light up a room," remembers friend and sometimes co-worker Kim Graham. "Cindy was a delight. She had that ability to make you feel special." Perhaps that was why Cindy felt so connected to the humanity that emanated from Garth Brooks' songs.

The happiness that permeated Cindy's life was not a prize package from heaven. Her habitual smile had not always come easily. She had temporomandibular joint disorder, commonly referred to as TMJ, a misalignment of her jaw. TMJ sufferers endure savage headaches, earaches, and pain in their face, neck, and shoulders. Cindy's parents, who divorced when she was young, could do nothing about it.

On November 1, 1989, Cindy had a Le Fort osteotomy to correct upper and lower jaw deformities. The surgery involves sectioning or repositioning the upper jaw to correct its abnormal position. Her husband Michael claimed he paid thirty to forty thousand dollars for Cindy's facial reconstructive surgery, which utilized titanium and a cadaver jawbone.

Cindy grew up in Hialeah, which is Miami, Florida's version of south Chicago, Harlem, or Watts. It was an impoverished, high-crime area of mostly Cuban residents. Hialeah was the kind of place where people hid their money in the bags of old vacuum cleaners because they expected to be robbed. It was the kind of place where people prayed the explosive noises in the night were just cars backfiring. It was the kind of place where Cindy's alcoholic and dysfunctional parents were nothing unusual.

Housing was crowded and cheap. In Hialeah homes, bugs darted from every crevice. At night, rodents scratched between the too-thin walls, hidden, but leaving evidence of ruin like the dark family secrets which drove Cindy from the house and into an early marriage at seventeen.

The escape was temporary. The marriage lasted barely two years. While Cindy was sleeping one night, her husband came home drunk, attacked her, beating her brutally. The wounds were so savage she had to be hospitalized. Cindy's mother came to the hospital, saw the trauma done to her daughter's body, and said, "Cindy, what did you do to him to make him do this to you?"

"Like it was her fault," Sandi grumbles, "but she was asleep." Cindy never learned what triggered the attack. Possibly the man was just drunk, but Cindy did not stay for round two.

Cindy also disconnected herself from the mother who could not nurture her, and began building her own life. She went to work for Publix Super Markets and rapidly earned a position as a deli manager.

Life in Hialeah diminished multitudes of young women. A tragic number would find themselves trapped between the walls, choiceless, and destined to be beaten down repeatedly.

But the hardship of her early years only made Cindy more feisty. It gave her courage and spunk. Water sports became her passion. Nothing was too challenging for her to try. The faster, the more daring, the more she loved it. It was as if her life craved the world's most thrilling roller coaster. She was determined to find herself a ticket and ride.

Working at the Miami Grand Prix for Provimi Veal, Cindy met Michael Albrecht, a mechanic for the Indy Lights team. He was a handsome man, six feet-five inches tall, with a roguish mustache and a crown of boyish brown curls. They started dating. As a race car mechanic, Michael was powerfully built, with the strength to lift a tire as easily as a basketball. He was also at home on the water.

Cindy had found her prince. He was from Milwaukee but she did not care. She would go anywhere with him. It did not pain her to leave behind the nightmare that was Hialeah.

Chapter 4

CINDY MOVED TO Wisconsin and, for a while, worked as Arie Luyendyke Jr.'s nanny. Then she found out Michael was already married. He had a wife named Kathleen and three daughters. But it was too late; Cindy was in love and had moved her entire life to Milwaukee.

Still, she was willing to walk away. Her heart might break, but she would not destroy his marriage. Michael begged her to give him a chance. His marriage was over except for some paperwork, he said. He insisted he loved Cindy and only her. He said it would be all right. She believed him.

Michael divorced his wife and married Cindy. The wedding was at the Mitchell Park Historical Conservatory in Milwaukee, where they made their home. Later, they moved to Indiana to be nearer to the Indianapolis Motor Speedway.

Friends describe a glowing relationship between the two during their first five years of marriage. They seemed to be constantly going places, doing things, always together. When another member of the racing team got married, Michael and Cindy hosted the wedding reception at their home. They invited all their friends to a spectacular dinner party to celebrate Christmas in 1991.

Michael had a broken relationship with his eldest daughter, Noel. "The girl can't even send her dad a birthday card," Cindy fumed. The younger two girls, Missy and Dawn, would come to visit.

When the girls arrived, Cindy dropped everything to do things with them. Michael continued with his work and his life. Nothing took precedence over his career, but the girls were in good hands with Cindy. She made a sincere effort to see they had a good time.

Cindy made a caring connection with everyone she met. One of Roger's rules was *Never run out of food* so the Penske team frequently had food left over. The women packed up the uneaten food and delivered hot meals to workers on other teams, buzzing up to garages on a golf cart with full, steaming trays.

Bob Lawes still chuckles about a day when Cindy neatly aligned metal pans of leftovers on the deck of the golf cart and drove off to serve starving crewmembers. But she misjudged a turn "and all that food slid off onto the ground," Bob says. "She was embarrassed, of course, and just fuming about the wasted food."

On May 15, 1992, during rookie orientation and practice for the Indy 500, Jovy Marcelo came out for warmups. Marcelo had never won an IndyCar race, although he had won races the previous year at Lime Rock Park and Nazareth Speedway, but the twenty-seven-year-old Filipino driver was still little known. At warmup speed, his car snapped around and crashed at the entrance to Turn 1. The young man was killed instantly.

Marcelo was the first driver killed at Indy in ten years. Cindy bought a wreath of flowers to hang on his garage and mourned the racer who had shown so much promise.

In a couple of years on the race circuit, Cindy's career had taken some winning laps. She'd gone from part-time hostess to sous chef to executive chef of a prosperous and winning team. She was well liked and respected. Her job offered her opportunities to meet important people and attend some grand functions.

She was dazzled when the team boarded Roger Penske's private yacht. She loved meeting the crew. Her social life had sped miles past any dreams a Hialeah girl could conjure.

The only thing that put a damper on Cindy's spirit was when her husband Michael stopped attending functions with her. While Cindy's career continued to escalate, his was sinking. He stayed away from the fun, claiming since he was working for a competing team, he could not be associating with Penske team members. Cindy was expected to attend team functions, so she usually went alone, sometimes riding with Mike and Sandi Fink.

If Michael's behavior disappointed Cindy, she did not complain about it. She continued to be the fun and spontaneous young woman who reigned as Miss Popularity among the racing community.

Fruiting became a fun tradition which was endearing to other team members. Sandi recalls the guys yelling, "Here come the girls! Duck!"

One night they had a team dinner, serving steak and lobster in the hospitality area. Roger Penske was there, along with some executives. The celebration morphed into a food fight when some crew guys began throwing cake. Then a banana flew and someone counter-launched a carrot. Roger stepped out of the tent. A couple of the higher-up people wanted Roger to stop the chaos, but he didn't. He knew his people had put in some long, brutal days and needed to blow off steam.

Bob Lawes said Roger was a businessperson to his core, but very fair minded toward his employees. The food fight was acceptable recreation to Roger because the danger of racing magnified the fun times. During the race, the entire team tensed with the knowledge their driver or crewmembers could die suddenly and fiercely.

Cindy, Sandi, and Becky all had husbands working on the other side of the pit wall, where they were often in more danger than the drivers. Fire, a spinning car, or a thrown tire could mangle or kill a man.

The food fight was their joyful sigh of relief that all had gone well for one more day. They took a picture afterward.

Then Becky and Sandi helped clean Cindy up. Seeing herself in such a mess, Cindy's laugh was the joy of heaven. Becky and Sandi plucked banana out of her hair, sprayed her curls, and found her a clean t-shirt. They cleaned her up, literally wiping the smile from her face before she went home. Michael would have a fit if he saw she'd been having so much fun.

No. Michael Albrecht wouldn't like it at all.

http://wbp.bz/rtja

In 2012, the Canadian Press ignited a firestorm of criticism by naming killer Luka Magnotta as its "Newsmaker Of The Year." But while the recognition was questionable for its sensitivity, there's no doubt that few people had captured the public's attention like the young murderer and internet sensation.

A male escort and sometimes model, Magnotta had earned his notoriety by videotaping himself stabbing Chinese student Lin Jun to death with an ice pick and dismembering the body, before posting the video online. After mailing

Jun's hands and feet to elementary schools, he then led Interpol on a manhunt that ended when he was arrested at an Internet café in Berlin where he was reading news stories about himself.

An international celebrity in a macabre sort of way, with a legion of fans, Magnotta was brought back to Canada, convicted of first-degree murder and sentenced to prison. During this time, Anna Yourkin, his estranged mother, troubled by Magnotta's abused childhood and her role in that, reconnected with her killer son.

Despite his internet fame, Magnotta never agreed to any in-depth interviews. Now Magnotta has given award-winning journalist and author, Brian Whitney (RAW DEAL, THE SHAWCROSS LETTERS) an exclusive look inside the mind of this "social media" killer. Joining Whitney to tell this unique true crime story is Anna Yourkin. The book also contains exclusive photos provided by Yourkin.

http://wbp.bz/mstka

More True Crime You'll Love From WildBlue Press

A MURDER IN MY HOMETOWN by Rebecca Morris
Nearly 50 years after the murder of seventeen year old Dick Kitchel, Rebecca Morris returned to her hometown to write about how the murder changed a town, a school, and the lives of his friends.

wbp.bz/hometowna

BETRAYAL IN BLUE by Burl Barer & Frank C. Girardot Jr.
Adapted from Ken Eurell's shocking personal memoir, plus hundreds of hours of exclusive interviews with the major players, including former international drug lord, Adam Diaz, and Dori Eurell, revealing the truth behind what you won't see in the hit documentary THE SEVEN FIVE.

wbp.bz/biba

SIDETRACKED by Richard Cahill
A murder investigation is complicated by the entrance of the Reverend Al Sharpton who insists that a racist killer is responsible. Amid a growing media circus, investigators must overcome the outside forces that repeatedly sidetrack their best efforts.

wbp.bz/sidetrackeda

BETTER OFF DEAD by Michael Fleeman
A frustrated, unhappy wife. Her much younger, attentive lover. A husband who degrades and ignores her. The stage is set for a love-triangle murder that shatters family illusions and lays bare a quiet family community's secret world of sex, sin and swinging.

wbp.bz/boda